YOUTH, POLICING AND DEMOC

Also by Ian Loader

CAUTIONARY TALES: Young People, Crime and Policing in Edinburgh
(*with Simon Anderson, Richard Kinsey and Connie Smith*)

Youth, Policing and Democracy

Ian Loader

Lecturer, Department of Criminology
Keele University
Staffordshire

First published 1996 by
MACMILLAN PRESS LTD
Houndmills, Basingstoke, Hampshire RG21 6XS
and London
Companies and representatives
throughout the world

ISBN 0–333–63660–0 hardcover
ISBN 0–333–63661–9 paperback

A catalogue record for this book is available
from the British Library.

10 9   8   7   6   5   4   3   2   1
05 04 03 02 01 00 99 98 97 96

Printed and bound in Great Britain by
Antony Rowe Ltd
Chippenham, Wiltshire

For Mum and Greg

The power of judgement rests on a potential agreement with others, and the thinking process which is active in judging something is not, like the thought process of pure reasoning, a dialogue between me and myself, but finds itself always and primarily, even if I am quite alone in making up my mind, in an anticipated communication with others with whom I know I must finally come to some agreement. And this enlarged way of thinking, which as judgement knows how to transcend its individual limitations, cannot function in strict isolation or solitude; it needs the presence of others 'in whose place' it must think, whose perspective it must take into consideration, and without whom it never has the opportunity to operate at all.

Hannah Arendt, Between Past and Future

Contents

Preface

The task I attempt in this book often seems a rather daunting one. Drawing inspiration from recent social and political theory, I strive to bring together within a single account normative theorising and critique, and sociological investigation and interpretation. In particular, I try to develop an understanding of police accountability that is informed by both the recent work of Jürgen Habermas on communicative action, and interview-based research with young people and police officers. My hope is that our theoretical appreciation of democratic communication and its prospects will be enhanced by its encounter with a particular set of social issues – namely, policing and police–youth relations; and that our understanding of those issues can be enriched by looking at them through the lens of democracy.

This book started life as a doctoral thesis (something one hesitates to mention lest one invites the stock refrain 'this reads like a PhD'). In revising it for publication I have been preoccupied with two overarching concerns. I have endeavoured, first of all, to make sense of the managerialism that has recently become such a predominant feature of the policing scene in Britain. Using Habermas's theory of communicative action, I have tried to develop both a principled critique of managerialism and an alternative, more democratic way of thinking about police accountability, one I then use to inform the empirical enquiry. In so doing, I hope to have made some some small – and accessible – contribution to the important theoretical task of combining normative reflection and social research.

In dealing with the research material I have tried, in so far as is possible, to allow young people and police officers to speak for themselves about the issues which confront them. But I have also interpreted their accounts in the light of my concern with democratic communication, something which inevitably entails pursuing certain lines of enquiry while at the same time neglecting others. I have in this respect – and this has not always been easy – taken care to keep the interpretation within certain bounds. Carrying out and reflecting upon this research has thrown up a host of puzzles, problems and ideas, some theoretical, others substantive. These, concerning such matters as place, crime and insecurity, crime and collective memory, and the social meanings of policing, I am now pursuing elsewhere. It is very tempting, however, to somehow 'write these in' to one's interpretation of the problem that first gave rise to them;

a problem which suddenly appears to demand an analysis couched in these revised theoretical terms. This temptation I have resisted. Thus, to take but one example, while the research was conducted in and around Edinburgh, the account that follows is not primarily about crime and policing in Edinburgh (cf. Anderson *et al.*, 1994). I do not describe the areas in which the young people and police officers interviewed live or work in any detail; nor does the history, culture, or spatial and social structure of the city figure prominently in the analysis. For although these questions are both interesting and important they do not immediately pertain to the theoretical and political concerns which animate this text.

What follows then is a book about democratic policing, its prospects and the consequences of its absence for police–youth relations. First and foremost, I would like it to be judged in those terms.

Since this project began back in 1989, I – and it – have benefited from the encouragement and support of a great many people. I would like therefore to take this opportunity, if not to repay the debts accrued over the last few years, then at least to acknowledge what is owed and to whom. Thanks are due, first of all, to Richard Kinsey and Neil Walker, who supervised the original PhD, and whose enthusiasm, support and criticism have been invaluable. My appreciation also goes to all the young people and police officers who gave of their time to answer my questions; as well as to the teachers, youth workers, youth training supervisors and senior police officers who helped arrange the interviews. Special thanks in this regard are due to David Garbett, (then) Assistant Chief Constable of Lothian and Borders Police, who did much to facilitate the research with the police. Thanks also to Jean Goldring and Margaret Penman for transcribing the interviews.

Intellectually, I have benefited much from friends and colleagues who have at various times read draft chapters, made suggestions or generally engaged me in discussion of the book's themes. I owe a debt to them all. Particular mentions are due here to Pat Carlen for her help in the final stages of the thesis, to Robert Reiner and Peter Young for so constructively examining it, and, more recently, to Penny Fraser, Richard Sparks and Neil Walker (again) whose comments and suggestions have done much to improve the end product. It goes without saying that the remaining faults are all my doing.

Finally, I would like to thank all those friends who have over the last few years shared with me the joys and frustrations of life. For their support, countless good times and a whole lot else besides, an especially big thank you to Simon Anderson, Rachel Early, Connie Smith and, above all, Penny Fraser.

The author and publisher would like to thank Sage Publications Ltd for permission to reproduce in Chapter 7 material which appeared in an earlier form in *Social and Legal Studies* (1994, vol. 3, no. 4).

Keele   *Ian Loader*

Introduction

It is seven o'clock on a Friday evening in June. A group of teenagers – mainly though not exclusively boys – are hanging around outside the shops on a usually quiet residential street. Local residents, fed up with the noise and anxious about levels of street crime in the area, call the police. Some 20 minutes later two officers arrive at the scene; they talk to the youths, a few muffled complaints are heard and the young people are moved on. The residents, for the moment at least, are placated.

This sequence of events – one enacted time and again, day and night, across many of Britain's towns and cities – represents one of the principal means by which young people come into contact with the police (teenagers rarely call the police as victims of crime). It is also one of the few occasions in which young people and police officers 'communicate' with one another. These encounters thus contribute much to the tensions that bedevil police–youth relations, causing frustrations and resentment among both parties, and generating a sense that nothing much of value is to be gained from talking to the 'other side':

> You're probably saying 'why don't the police go in and speak to the sixteen to twenty-one-year-olds?' The thing is, do the sixteen to twenty-one-year-olds want to speak to the police? You'll probably find they don't unless they are in a church fellowship group. (*Male area officer*)

> The police can do what they want as long as they don't worry me. And they do what they want anyway. So all your opinion polls and your charts and that'll not make any difference to them. (*20-year-old male, Niddrie*)

These mutual suspicions suggest that all is not well in relations between young people and the police. And the experiences from which they stem remind us that, in practice, the doctrine of policing by consent means the police responding to the claims of some social groups rather than others. So what can be done? Can forms of policing be developed which take account of the experiences, concerns and aspirations of young people?

In the present political situation this possibility seems far-fetched, even utopian. Although senior police officers now talk about 'opening up the service to the public' and 'responding to consumer demand', young people appear not to be included within the operative definition of the consumer. In the aftermath of the murder of Jamie Bulger in February 1993 (and the

frenzied public debate about juvenile crime that followed) the enduring
image of youth as 'trouble' has been reinforced. In official and popular
discourse alike young people are a problem – for teachers, social workers,
police officers and local residents. Seldom do we pause to consider that
young people may have experiences of crime (as victims, for example)
which mean that they too have demands to make of the police.

My aim in this book is to think anew about the relationship between
young people and policing and suggest an alternative way of approaching
the problems that currently afflict police–youth relations. Drawing upon
the resources of social and political theory, and interview-based research
with young people (aged fifteen to twenty-three) and police officers conducted in and around Edinburgh, I argue that democracy – or, more specifically, democratic communication – is central to understanding relations
between young people and the police. I contend that the absence of opportunities for communication outside of contexts marked by mutual postur-
ing and defensiveness – what Muir (1977) calls the 'paradox of face' –
contributes a great deal to prevailing suspicions, such as those evidenced
above. And I suggest that the construction of institutional spaces in which
open and inclusive dialogue about policing issues can take place might
do much to alleviate existing tensions.

This approach has a number of corollaries. It entails, first of all, re-
establishing the connections between policing and democracy that have been
largely lost sight of since the controversies of the 1980s (cf. Jones *et al.*,
1994). This, in turn, requires a critical engagement with the managerialism
that structures so much political and professional discourse about policing
in Britain at present (McLaughlin and Muncie, 1994). Current managerialist preoccupations with economy, efficiency and effectiveness are – in as
much as they disconnect police practice from deliberation about the ends
and values of policing – antithetical to the realisation of a democratic
police service. Cognate attempts to construct the public as consumers of
policing services are similarly inimical to such a project, in so far as they
are unconcerned with questions of power and inequality, and unaware that
routinely policed social groups – such as young people – lack the resources that might enable their claims as consumers of policing to count.

Approaching the question of youth and policing from the standpoint
of democracy further requires that juvenile delinquency is moved from
centre stage. For far too long now the youth question has served as a eu-
phemism for the criminal question. Popular and political discourse about
young people remains fixated with adolescent offending, its meanings and
motives. Yet recent research suggests that young people face daily – and
often more serious – risks as victims of crime. As regular users of public

space, they also witness lots of crime happening around them (Anderson *et al.*, 1994; Aye Maung, 1995; Hartless *et al.*, 1995). My ensuing concern is thus with the multiplicity of ways in which crime impacts upon the everyday lives of young people, and with how they make sense of, and negotiate, issues of crime and personal safety. I shall also be attentive to young people's adversarial experiences of policing, as well as to the ways in which they understand and make use of the police as a service.

An investigation of the potential of democracy for enhancing police–youth relations also requires an explicit engagement with social and political theory. As Tony Bottoms (1987, p. 262) has noted, criminological research has for the most part been inattentive towards 'the revivals of social and political philosophy that have taken place since about 1970'. Perhaps nowhere has this neglect been more keenly felt than in debates about police accountability. With few exceptions (Jefferson and Grimshaw, 1984), the academic conversation about policing and its governance has proceeded without any explicit conceptual engagement with questions of democracy, legitimacy and social justice; an odd omission, and one which has severely delimited the scope of enquiry. Thus, in order to infuse sociological investigation with an 'enlarged way of thinking' (Arendt, 1961, p. 220) about policing, I shall in what follows seek to demonstrate how the insights of contemporary social and political theory (and especially the work of German social theorist Jürgen Habermas) can be employed to illuminate the vexed question of police accountability.

THE STRUCTURE OF THE ARGUMENT

The book begins by setting out the institutional contours within which relations between young people and the police are currently enacted. In Chapter 1, I outline and evaluate the present arrangements for governing the police and develop a critique of the managerialist turn taken by the public conversation about policing in recent years. This approach to policing is criticised both for its impoverished, technocratic conception of democracy, and in terms of its likely adverse consequences for police–youth relations. I argue that young people provide a crucial 'litmus test' for any system of police governance that claims to rest upon the doctrine of policing by consent, a test managerialism abjectly fails.

In contrast to the strand of contemporary social theory which emphasises the irrelevance of ideas of justice and legitimacy to the late-modern world, I contend, in Chapter 2, that the residual attachment of managerialism to the idea of policing by consent affords a space for immanent critique.

Drawing upon Habermas's theory of communicative action, I set out a theoretical framework which is capable of making good the claims of managerialism. I argue that this approach – which stresses the intimate connection between police legitimacy and the democratic participation of all those affected by police practice – provides a cogent basis for both thinking about alternative forms of police governance, and for understanding the dynamics of police–youth relations. The chapter concludes by setting out a methodology of interpretation that can advance such an understanding.

Drawing upon interview-based research, the next four chapters explore how young people and police officers communicate their experiences and perceptions of crime and policing. In Chapter 3, I consider the ways in which young people use, and ascribe meaning to, public space. Focusing upon the idea of belonging, the interpretation examines the consequences for identity and safety of the loyalty that both male and female teenagers attach to peer group and place, and explores the practices young people develop to manage their security while out in public. Against this backdrop, young people's reluctance to communicate their experiences of crime to the police is analysed and discussed.

Drawing upon interviews with the police, Chapter 4 explores the ambivalence officers feel towards the policing of young people's use of public space, an ambivalence that encompasses orientations to both regulation and non-intervention. I argue that prevailing organisational pressures enable the former to win out over the latter, and that young people's use of public places is as a consequence over-controlled. In stark contrast, I demonstrate that officers' paucity of experience of young people as victims means that youth victimisation impacts minimally upon the police, with the result that young people remain under-protected as users of public space. Nevertheless, it is shown that a police-centred view of these issues generates considerable frustration among officers about young people's reluctance to report crime.

Chapter 5 explores the effect various post-sixteen transitions have upon young people's experiences and understandings of crime and policing. I argue that the fragmentation of young people's use of public space is accompanied by what are termed – for analytical purposes – inclusive and marginalising transitions. I suggest that inclusive transitions (those providing access to employment and independent financial resources) tend to concentrate in time and space young people's experiences of crime, and that the decline in their adversary contact with the police means young people more readily accept the police as service providers. By contrast, teenagers experiencing marginalising transitions (those associated with long-term unemployment) tend to encounter a continuing reliance upon the locality, and (for some) an intensification of their contact with the police and criminal justice system. The overall effect of this, I argue, is to render enhanced dialogue between the police and dispossessed young people a distant prospect.

Chapter 6 focuses more specifically on the prospects for, and obstacles to, communication between young people and the police. I consider young people's practical philosophies of policing, and their understanding of good and bad policing, and good and bad police officers. I argue that, while narratives of both kinds circulate among young people, they have a very different character and force; accounts of bad policing occupying a far more prominent place in young people's overall 'picture' of the police. I conclude by exploring the aspirations for dialogue that exist among police officers and young people alike, and considering how such aspirations are confined to the realm of the unthinkable by current patterns of experience.

Finally, in Chapter 7, I outline and defend a principle of 'discursive policing' and, through an examination of its limits, institutions, boundaries and practice, explore how it might improve police-youth relations and make the police more democratically accountable.

1 Policing and the Youth Question: Against Managerialism

Policing in Britain is currently in a state of considerable flux. Over the last few years, the questions of democracy that dominated public discourse about policing in the 1980s have evaporated. The Conservative government's 'public sector revolution' – launched by the Thatcher administration back in 1979 – has finally caught up with the police. The issue of 'who controls the police?' has been superseded by concerns about effectiveness, quality of service and even privatisation. The debate on the futures of British policing has, in short, taken a managerialist turn.

The evidence of this lies all around us. Political and professional talk about policing is now preoccupied with how to make the police more 'business-like'. A host of government initiatives – including the Citizen's Charter, the Sheehy Report and the Police and Magistrates' Courts Act 1994 – have set in motion potentially far-reaching changes in police organisation, policy and practice. Her Majesty's Inspectorate of Constabulary and the accountants of the Audit Commission have become the chief regulators of police performance. The spectre of privatisation (at least of those tasks deemed 'ancillary' to the 'core' police function) and the further proliferation of private security also hang uneasily in the air. The police themselves have responded to these challenges by endeavouring – through initiatives such as the 'Statement of Our Common Purpose and Values' and the 'Plus' programme – to 'professionalise' the organisation. The public has been constructed as consumers of policing, entitled to expect a prompt, courteous and efficient service. A whole panoply of training courses, performance targets and consumer satisfaction surveys have followed, all geared to creating a 'culture which insists that all officers . . . measure up to the requirements of the customer' (Woodcock, 1991, p. 182).

How are we to assess these developments? Are they a short lived fad destined to pass leaving little trace? Do they augur some significant transformation in the delivery of public (and private) policing services? Might they even be part of some more fundamental reconfiguration of relations between the state and the citizen? At present, while the precise contours and implications of these shifts remain unclear, it is difficult to formulate adequate answers to these questions (Clarke et al., 1994), a task that would, anyway, lie beyond the scope of this book. My purpose is a more specific one. I shall in this chapter critically assess the presuppositions and claims of managerialism, paying particular attention to its likely impact on both police accountability and the relationship between the police and young people. However, it is first necessary to set out in more general terms the factors that currently shape policing and its governance.

SITUATING POLICE ACCOUNTABILITY: LAW, DEMOCRACY AND WORK

The institutional practice of policing involves dimensions of both force and service, and in structurally divided societies these functions will be experienced differentially by individuals and social groups (Stephens and Becker, 1994). Some groups – such as young people – encounter the police most frequently on occasions signifying 'trouble', while others – the inhabitants of a residential suburb for example – are unlikely to come across the police unless they report a crime or require some policing service. In this respect, policing has both general and specific functions, being concerned with enforcing the conditions of organised existence overall, as well as with protecting the interests of particular social groups and classes (Marenin, 1982).

The social distribution of these functions is, however, neither predetermined nor unchanging. The balance between force and service experienced by different groups within the population varies over time and from place to place. Their precise mix depends on asymmetries of power pertaining within the wider social realm and the institutional arrangements in place to govern police policy and practice. It is thus of great importance to understand both these relations and their substantive effects.

Grimshaw and Jefferson (1987) outline an analytical framework that is particularly useful in this regard. They argue that police work is a product of the relationship between three 'structures of control'; namely, law, democracy and work. This approach – instead of positing a single dimension of control, such as police culture, as uniformly dominant (cf. Punch, 1979) – focuses attention on both the actual and potential determinants of policing practice. It posits 'control' as a 'social relation whose character varies in different contexts' (Johnston, 1988, p. 67), and emphasises that in any specific field of policing, the substance of police work will depend on the relative strength of a range of institutional regulators. Determining the relationship between these structures thus becomes a task for investigation within particular spheres of policing.

Let us examine the law first. How effective is law – traditionally, the principal means of bringing police work in Britain to account – as a mechanism of control? The legal structure has to be considered in respect of both chief constables and officers on the ground. Its efficacy as a mode of regulation depends upon such matters as the constitutional position of chief constables and the provisions governing their accountability; the substantive powers of police officers and the legal safeguards determining their use, and the powers of judicial and supervisory bodies such as the courts and the Police Complaints Authority (Grimshaw and Jefferson, 1987, pp. 15–18).

The most significant of all these is the constitutional position of the office of constable. The legislation governing police policy in both Scotland and England and Wales apportions responsibility for policing between a tripartite structure made up of chief constables, local police authorities and the Home Secretary (in England) or Secretary of State (in Scotland).[1] While the legislation somewhat fudges the boundaries of responsibility between these different bodies, and has been the subject of much interpretive dispute, it is generally agreed that it situates operational decision-making in the hands of chief constables (Lustgarten, 1986). In this respect, the law enshrines the principles of 'legal accountability' and 'constabulary independence'. The former stipulates that police officers – at the level of chief constable, as well as officers on the ground – are required to undertake their tasks within the confines of the law. The latter holds that a police officer's duty to enforce the law is an independent (rather than delegated) one, and that in pursuing it, officers are precluded from taking direction from any external authority.[2]

This understanding of the office of constable rests on the belief that the role of the police within a liberal democratic polity is one of universal and impartial law enforcement. Proponents of such a position – including the body of chief constables (Reiner, 1991, ch. 11) – contend that the strictures of legal accountability and the prohibition on external direction are essential to secure both the political neutrality of policing from government (whether central or local), and the non-partisan and even-handed enforcement of law against all offenders. Sir Robert Mark – a former Metropolitan Police Commissioner – encapsulates this view perfectly when he states:

> The fact that the British police are accountable to the law, that we act on behalf of the community as a whole and not under the mantle of government, makes us the least powerful, the most accountable and therefore the most acceptable in the world. (Mark, 1977, p. 56)

This conventional justification of policing has a number of flaws. Chief among these is its failure to grasp the practical impossibility of realising the ideal of universal law enforcement, whether at the level of chief constable or officers on the ground. In terms of the former, a formal legal conception of accountability forgets that chief officers lack the time, knowledge or resources to organise their force for such a task. It takes no account of the fact that policing is a necessarily *partial* and *selective* practice; one that requires chief officers to exercise considerable discretionary judgement over such matters as which offence categories to prioritise, what styles of policing to adopt and how to allocate limited resources. Chief constables are, in other words, engaged in the enterprise of formulating 'public policies for upholding the law' (Jefferson and Grimshaw, 1984, p. 148), a task for which the principal mechanism of control – the law – provides little guidance.

By contrast, there are occasions in which the law can enact some controlling force over the actions of constables on the ground. Grimshaw and Jefferson (1987, pp. 15–18) argue that the legal structure is capable of regulating police work in circumstances where there is both a complainant and a clear legal provision to be enforced; situations where the police officer's task can accurately be described as 'the objective and honest application of a rule or standard of conduct' (Lustgarten, 1986, p. 164). Such circumstances rarely obtain, however. Police officers are far more frequently required to deal with situations requiring the exercise of discretion – deciding, for example, between competing accounts of an incident (such as a pub fight or 'domestic' dispute), and determining what if any course of action to pursue (such as whether to warn, caution or arrest any of the disputants). Similarly, in many public order settings, police officers are granted considerable discretionary space in which to define proactively the legality of particular behaviours (Jefferson, 1990).

This raises the question of whether – and if so to what extent – legal rules are capable of controlling the exercise of such discretion. Some 'interactionist' police commentators argue that the invisibility of police work, coupled with the attendant difficulties of direct supervision, enable police officers to subvert any attempt to place legal controls on their activities (Smith and Gray, 1983). Against this, the 'structuralist' perspective of Grimshaw and Jefferson (1987) holds that it is possible to identify circumstances in which the legal structure is able to have an impact. This can be achieved by closing down – through the enactment of tighter legislation – the discretionary space in which police officers operate, thereby providing a framework of rules which can negatively exclude certain modes of police operation (Dixon, 1992).

However, while legal regulation may in some contexts be able to cir-
cumscribe the discretionary leeway within which police officers operate,
the 'open-texture' of rules, and the requirements for justice to accommodate the exigencies of specific incidents, make street-level discretion
an inherent and even desirable aspect of police work (Kinsey *et al.*, 1986,
pp. 165–8). This places some obvious limits on the capacity of legal
rules alone to regulate police practice. In exercising their discretionary
judgement in particular encounters, constables are placed in a position
akin to that of chief officers. They become in effect 'street-corners politicians' (Muir, 1977); called upon to resolve disputes in situations where
the law can provide little positive guidance about how to proceed. This,
as we shall see, is of some consequence for the policing of young people's
use of public space.

What, then, of democratic accountability, the other means by which the
police can be externally brought to account? What kinds of democratic
influences on police work currently exist and how effective are they? The
democratic structure pertains to these questions. It refers to the sites –
or 'access points' (Giddens, 1990) – through which various public constituencies are able to have an effect over police policy and practice
(Grimshaw and Jefferson, 1987, pp. 20–2). It encompasses both the
formal institutional means through which the police are rendered democratically accountable for their actions, as well as the informal channels
through which particular social groups may influence police decision-
making. The democratic structure is thus concerned with some fundamental questions regarding public participation in policy formation.

The democratic components of the present institutional arrangements
for police governance comprise the Home Secretary (or, in Scotland, the
Secretary of State); local police authorities and, in England and Wales,
police-community consultative committees. At present, none of these bodies
has any explicit legal entitlement to direct chief or operational constables
in the conduct of their responsibilities; the *raison d'etre* of constabulary
independence is precisely to preclude this kind of democratic control (Oliver,
1987).[3] Rather, the democratic element of current institutional arrangements revolves around chief officers 'retrospectively accounting' (Brogden
et al., 1988, p. 152) for their actions to the democratically constituted bodies
within the tripartite structure (through, for example, the provision of annual
reports). It is a model of 'explanation and cooperation' rather than 'subordination and control' (Marshall, 1978).

However, this formal equality of impotence effaces the fact that the
parties to the tripartite arrangements vary greatly in the influence they can
muster over policing matters. In recent years, the Home Secretary and
Secretary of State for Scotland have come to assume a powerful place in

the formulation of police policy. Central government, for example, controls the bulk of police funding, providing 51 per cent of police resources directly, plus a further proportion by way of grants to local authorities. Under the Police and Magistrates' Courts Act 1994, the Home Secretary can also cash limit the central contribution to local police budgets. Secondly, the Home Secretary and Secretary of State arbitrate in disputes between chief constables and police authorities – a power of final decision recently given judicial backing by the English Court of Appeal in *R v. Secretary of State for the Home Department ex parte Northumbria Police Authority* ([1988] 2 WLR 590). Thirdly, the Home and Scottish Office have since the 1980s increasingly employed government circulars as a means of influencing police policy-making on a national basis (Reiner, 1991). And most recently, again under the auspices of the Police and Magistrates' Courts Act, the Home Secretary (though not the Secretary of State for Scotland) has acquired the power to establish national objectives and performance targets for the police.

In stark contrast, local police authorities have seen their influence over policing wane markedly in recent years. Though always the weakest party in the tripartite structure, they did for a time in the early 1980s acquire some prominence, when a number of Labour-controlled councils (such as those in London, Manchester and Sheffield) became active in trying to influence policing policy (on the Manchester case, see McLaughlin, 1994). For the most part, however, police authorities have had neither the powers nor the inclination required to exercise any meaningful control over policing, something confirmed by the recent research of the Policy Studies Institute (Jones *et al.*, 1994).

In some respects, the Police and Magistrates' Courts Act 1994 has strengthened the role of local police authorities. Within the context of a revised statutory obligation to maintain an 'effective and efficient' force, these authorities are now required – after consulting the 'community' – to draw up local policing plans for their area. These changes are unlikely to enhance local democracy, however. Not only must these local plans be consistent with national police objectives laid down by the Home Secretary, but the Act has also diminished further the role of elected representatives. On the new (usually) seventeen member authorities, nine elected councillors are joined by eight unelected members of what Stewart (1992) calls the 'new magistracy'; in this case, three justices of the peace, and five 'independent members' in whose appointment the Home Secretary has a central role.[4] Local democratic influence over policing seems set to recede to the point of insignificance, with police authorities operating under both the direct control and indirect influence of the Home Secretary.[5]

The final democratic component of current institutional arrangements in England and Wales (though not Scotland) is provided by police-community consultative committees, set up in the aftermath of the 1981 Brixton uprisings (Scarman, 1982). The official aim of such committees is to facilitate public discussion between the police and community representatives about local crime and policing issues. The available research suggests, however, that these arrangements have neither made the police more locally responsive, nor served as forums for critical public deliberation about policing issues (Morgan, 1989; 1992). Their agendas tend to be constructed by the police and they are most often attended by police middle management, rather than by officers with experiential knowledge of the locality. In terms of public involvement, they have served largely as a vehicle for the concerns of the local 'good and the great', rather than eliciting the views of those – such as young people – who constitute the 'routinely policed' (Jefferson, 1990).

There exist, then, few institutional channels through which different 'publics' – young people included – can exercise a meaningful influence over police policy and practice. This does not mean, however, that different police constituencies are entirely unable to affect police work on the ground. The democratic structure – as Grimshaw and Jefferson (1987, pp. 21–2) point out – also operates at an informal level. Individuals and social groups encounter the police through a whole range of 'contacting roles'; they may do so as victims, suspects and witnesses, or as representatives of community groups or state institutions. And these contacts occasion – depending on their circumstances and subject matter – varying levels of conflict or reciprocity, and differing degrees of influence over police behaviour. Social groups also enter such encounters with contrasting amounts of what French sociologist Pierre Bourdieu (1986) calls 'cultural capital'; that is, with a varying capacity to articulate their claims with the appropriate language and disposition, and varying degrees of social prestige and recognition. This confluence of situational roles and unequal distribution of cultural capital is significant because it shapes the informal 'democratic' processes through which different constituencies influence police practice, enabling some social groups to obtain a greater share of available policing resources. This, as we shall see, is particularly pertinent in terms of young people's experience of the police.

A third set of mechanisms capable of regulating police practice is to be found within the police organisation itself. Police sociology has often represented the police as an organisation comprising two (conflicting) occupational cultures; a 'management culture' concerned with police legitimacy on a system-wide basis, and a more pragmatic and parochial 'street culture' geared to getting the job done with the minimum degree of fuss (Ianni and Ianni, 1983). Grimshaw and Jefferson (1987, pp. 18–20) contend, however, that this opposition rests upon a number of weakly supported assertions about the dispositions and practices of senior police management. Drawing on their research in an English metropolitan force, they outline a more holistic view of the work structure consisting of two constituent parts:

> an 'organisational' one – referring to the vertical dimension of rules, policies, approved procedures, command and control – and an 'occupational' one, referring to the horizontal dimension of the norms and practices of colleague groups. (Grimshaw and Jefferson, 1987, p. 19)

So what modes of regulation exist along each of these dimensions, and what influence do they exercise over a police officer's decision-making? Along the 'organisational' dimension, such controls include disciplinary offences and procedures (such as those under the Codes of Practice governing the operation of the Police and Criminal Evidence Act 1984), as well as managerial controls over staff recruitment, transfers and promotion. They also encompass, more broadly, the use of internal policy directives to implement a government circular or change some other aspect of force policy.

There are undoubtedly occasions – not least, as we shall see, in respect of regulating how young people's use of public space is policed – when these internal managerial controls have a significant impact over police behaviour. For the most part however, the available evidence suggests a weak or non-existent mode of control, especially in respect of internal policy. Grimshaw and Jefferson's research (to date one of the few systematic accounts of police policy-making in Britain) found that formal policy – in the sense of 'an authoritative statement signifying a settled practice' (Grimshaw and Jefferson, 1987, p. 204) – was either absent or so ambiguous as to be effectively so. This confirms earlier research on the Metropolitan Police which found that the vacuum generated by the lack of policy guidance is 'filled by the preoccupations, perceptions and prejudices that develop among groups of constables and sergeants in response to the people and the problems they have to deal with' (Smith and Gray, 1983, p. 336).[6]

The 'preoccupations, perceptions and prejudices' of rank and file officers have – in contrast to those of police management – been the subject of repeated investigation within police sociology (Reiner, 1992a, ch. 3). A rich vein of research and reflection has documented how police officers construct – and figuratively reproduce (Shearing and Ericson, 1991) – a series of informal resources that enable them to cope with shared and routinely occuring problems, such as the threat of unpredictable violence, the need to maintain authority and the pressure to get results (Skolnick, 1975). Such research has also unearthed an occupational culture in which 'deviance, the cover-up, secrecy, colleague loyalty, mistrust of outsiders, cynicism and violence recur as characteristics – to which are opposed 'due-process', senior officers and the public' (Grimshaw and Jefferson 1987, p. 8).

The importance of these characteristics – according to 'interactionist' interpretations of police work – is that they exercise a determining influence over policing practice as it happens on the ground, often to the detriment of certain minority groups within the population, such as black youths (Holdaway, 1983). It has also been suggested that the autonomy of an officer's working environment means that legal, democratic and managerial controls are of limited utility as modes of regulation; and that the creation of a more responsive police force requires – not enhanced democratic or legal accountability – but the engendering of respect within police culture for the rights of all citizens, unpopular minorities included (Reiner, 1992a, p. 216).

While there is much of merit in these arguments, it is important not to overstate the case. In striving to make sense of the influence of police occupational culture in particular spheres of police work, one must take care to avoid the reification that presents this culture as some kind of monolith – invariant across time and space, always and everywhere opposed to due-process and suspects' rights, and an obstacle to any enlightened police reform. What is called for instead is a sensitivity to the variances in rank and file cultures both within and between different geographical locations, as well as to changes in police cultural norms and practices over time (Dixon, 1992). It is also necessary, and this is of some significance to the present study, to avoid positing the influence of police culture as unimpeachable. Rather, we must remain cognisant of how the impact of the occupational culture over different domains of police operation – such as the policing of young people in public space – always also depends on the presence or absence of other modes of regulation.

ECLIPSING DEMOCRACY: THE MANAGERIALIST TURN IN BRITISH POLICING

Public services in Britain are currently experiencing – and have been for some time – a period of radical change. Since 1979 successive Conservative administrations have pursued a programme of reform which has endeavoured to transform the organisation, culture and delivery of public provision across a range of social services. For the Conservative – or more accurately neo-liberal – new right, the bureaucracies of the welfare state that developed in the post-war period had become inefficient monopoly suppliers: exempt from the rigours of the market, unresponsive to public demand, riddled with vested interests and a burgeoning drain on government expenditure. They were deemed in need of fundamental overhaul.

Managerialism has been the principal instrument of this overhaul. Managerialist ideology holds that better management provides a rational, objective and scientific solution to economic and social problems; a solution that can overcome the sectional, irrational and hence uncertain business of democratic politics. For believers of the new right, managerialism represents the best way to deliver responsive and efficient public services. It serves, in particular, as a means by which:

> Private-sector disciplines can be introduced to the public services, political control can be strengthened, budgets trimmed, professional autonomy reduced, public service unions weakened and a quasi-competitive framework erected to flush out the 'natural' inefficiencies of bureaucracy. (Pollitt, 1993, p. 49)

Throughout the 1980s these various strands of managerialist ideology were employed in a radical restructuring of the public sector (Clarke *et al.*, 1994). Though the substance and impact of government reforms (not to mention the resistance they encountered) varied across different social services, organisations ranging from universities and the civil service, to schools and hospitals, underwent considerable change (Pollitt, 1993). Public services were subjected to an increasing concern with financial stringency and cost effectiveness; an emphasis on injecting competition from the private sector (as in compulsory competitive tendering); an array of new managerial controls over staff (such as performance-related pay, appraisal and short-term contracts), and a great rhetorical emphasis on responding to consumer demand.

Since the demise of Margaret Thatcher in 1990 this 'public sector revolution' has undergone a subtle yet significant change of direction. The virulent anti-statist tone that marked government policy during the eighties has been tempered, and in its place, a 'new wave' of public sector reform has been initiated in which the provision of quality services to individual customers is the guiding principle. The Citizen's Charter – launched by Prime Minister John Major in 1991 – has become the principal vehicle for a series of reforms which endeavour to achieve 'quality' public provision by means of further market (or where no 'natural' market exists, quasi-market) competition, and the setting and enforcing of national performance targets (Home Office, 1991).[7]

For much of the 1980s policing largely escaped this managerialist assault upon public bureaucracies. In the early part of the decade especially, the police enjoyed a prolonged honeymoon with the Conservative administration. As well as being required to quell the urban disorders of 1980/1 and assist in the defeat of the miners in 1984/5, the police were, more generally, accorded a prominent place in government 'law and order' strategies. Not only were the police spared the cuts experienced in other parts of the public sector, but they actually found their role and prestige enhanced. The recommendations of the Lord Edmund-Davies pay review body were implemented in full, police numbers rose sharply (by some 17 per cent between the late 1970s and 1990), and legislative changes (such as the Criminal Justice (Scotland) Act 1981, the Police and Criminal Evidence Act 1984 and the Public Order Act 1986) accorded them greater powers.

However, by the early 1990s a combination of rising crime rates and escalating police budgets forced the government to take a long hard look at the police service. And what they saw was yet another inefficient and poorly managed public bureaucracy in urgent need of reform (McLaughlin and Muncie, 1994). There ensued a host of government initiatives – such as the Sheehy Report on Police Responsibilities and Rewards (1993), the Police and Magistrates' Courts Act 1994 and an internal Home Office review of 'core' and 'ancillary' police functions – that ushered in (often in the face of considerable opposition from the police themselves) a potentially radical departure in ways of thinking about, and acting upon, problems of policing. So what does the new managerialism mean for the future of policing in Britain? What are its implications for police accountability and police–youth relations? The rest of the chapter is concerned with these questions.

Three prominent managerialist themes can be identified, some of which have been touched upon already. We have witnessed, first of all, a burgeoning preoccupation with questions of financial accountability and value for money. This in fact began back in 1983 when Home Office Circular 114 made extra police resources conditional upon evidence of increased economy, efficiency and effectiveness. Since then the police have come under progressively greater control from a range of outside accounting agencies. The most prominent and influential of these have been the Audit Commission (which, as of 1992, had produced no less than eleven reports on various aspects of policing), and Her Majesty's Inspectorate of Constabulary, which under a new and more dynamic staff, has produced (and since 1990 published) a series of focused reports on individual forces. The police, as a result, have been made far more attentive to questions of efficiency and cost effectiveness (Weatheritt, 1993).

The government has, secondly, adopted a distinctive approach to the perennial problem of bringing about reform in a large public bureaucracy such as the police. There is little doubt here that there is a genuine problem to be addressed. The police – as left-liberal commentators have consistently pointed out (Reiner, 1992a) – are notoriously difficult to reform in such a way as to impact upon policing on the ground. The existence of entrenched and conservative occupational cultures within the organisation represent a serious challenge to anyone – from whatever quarter – concerned with effecting change in the police. The Home Office and the Audit Commission have thus correctly identified police culture as a serious impediment to the success of managerialist reform strategies:

> Perhaps the single greatest handicap to securing improved value for money . . . is what might be termed management style or the prevailing culture of the organisation. Time and again possibilities are blocked – or slowed down – by cultural constraints. (Audit Commission, 1984, p. 6)

The government's chosen solution to this problem – one termed by Reiner and Spencer (1993, p. 177) as 'calculative and contractual' – involves imposing reform on a reluctant and recalcitrant workforce by means of nationally established performance targets and fixed-term contracts for senior police personnel.[8] It is a mix clearly designed to impel police managers – on pain of losing their jobs – to take seriously the task of ensuring that reforms are implemented on the ground and force objectives met. As such, it is a development that threatens to drive a coach and horses through the received traditions of constabulary independence, not in the name of enhanced democratic accountability, but for the purpose of greater managerial efficiency and control.

There has, finally, been a significant transformation in the vocabularies that are used to talk about and evaluate policing in Britain. Official discourse about policing has in recent years constructed the public as consumers of policing services. On the one hand, this has been a consequence of The Citizen's Charter which has impressed upon the police a concern with quality of service and customer responsiveness (Butler, 1992). But it is also the product of a shift in the professional ideology of senior police officers themselves. In recent years senior officers have – through initiatives such as the Metropolitan Police's 'Statement of Our Common Purpose and Values', the ensuing 'Plus' programme, and a host of other force 'mission statements' – made great efforts to 'professionalise' the service by providing it with a coherent ethical rationale. Senior officers have also begun to talk with some frequency about 'opening up the service to the public' and 'listening to the customer' in a manner that would have been almost inconceivable only a decade ago (Hirst, 1991). Customer satisfaction surveys of all kinds have ensued.

While these managerialist developments are not without virtue, they have, I believe, a number of fundamental shortcomings. Perhaps the most significant of these is the technocratic understanding of policing which underpins them. Managerialism takes policing to be an unproblematic and clearly defined product, and posits policing problems as a series of technical dilemmas capable of resolution by means of more professional and efficient administration. Policing decisions are not, however, matters of technical judgement requiring merely a managerial or practical competence (Ericson and Shearing, 1986). They are, rather, political decisions, both in the sense that they set priorities for the distribution of a particular public good, and in so far as they impact upon both the ordering of social relations and the quality of people's lives in significant ways. Policing, in short, is about the regulation of social conflict and in societies that wish to claim the mantle 'democratic' the formulation of police policy is properly a matter of politics not administration.

Managerialism also purports to be a discourse concerned solely with means and uncommitted to any normative or political ends. This claim – one pivotal to the belief that managerialism stands above politics – fails to withstand much scrutiny, however. The theory and practice of managerialism is saturated with a particular substantive vision of how policing is to be understood and evaluated, one that privileges 'Economy, Efficiency and Effectiveness' over and above the other values associated with policing (such as justice or fairness). Internal incoherence aside, the principal problem here concerns the way in which managerialism promotes such values as ones to be pursued for their own sake; something which fails to appreciate that the meaning of the 'three E's' depends entirely on the purposes to which they are connected. While an efficient and effective police force may be a desirable objective, the pursuit of this objective must, if it is to amount to anything other than a technicist triumph of means over ends, go hand in hand with reflection on the question 'what is policing for?' (Reiner, 1992b).

Managerialism has also served to focus contemporary political and professional debate almost exclusively on policing as a service. This again is by no means unwelcome. The public conversation about policing in the 1980s was often unduly restricted by its predominant concern with the issue of 'who controls the police?' and recent developments have usefully raised some hitherto neglected questions concerning the quality of policing provision. However, in privileging the dimension of service, managerialism has forgotten not only that policing necessarily involves considerations of force, but also that the care and control dimensions of police work cannot be separated, either analytically or in practice (the service provided for one person frequently entailing the use of force against another). More importantly perhaps, it has effaced almost entirely some crucial issues pertaining to the justification and legitimacy of the state's monopoly of coercive regulation (Jefferson *et al.*, 1992).

The government's attempt to bring about successful reform by means of enhanced managerial control is also replete with difficulties. At the level of principle, its chief problem is that it rests on a limited and impoverished conception of the role of both senior and rank and file police officers. In an approach redolent of its handling of other public sector unions and professional organisations (such as teachers), the government has constructed police officers (and their staff associations) as little more than an obstacle to be surmounted, rather than as active participants with something valuable to offer the debate on the futures of British policing. Hence its neo-Taylorist preoccupation with using performance measurement, appraisal and short-term contracts as a means of organisational control.

This way of proceeding is also likely to be counterproductive. The history of attempts to impose reform on the police from the outside is a sorry one, and the evidence thus far suggests that, far from combating the defensive proclivities of senior and rank and file cultures, current developments are producing further demoralisation and alienation among officers, and reinforcing the fortress mentality that so often pervades the service. (The police's reaction to the Sheehy Report – chief constables threatening to resign if the recommendations were implemented in full and police officers demonstrating at Wembley Arena – is telling in this respect). This is not to suggest that the police be granted a veto over police reform. Far from it. It is merely to point out that such reform – for both principled and prudential reasons – must take seriously the concerns and experience of police officers themselves, and suggest ways in which their role can be productively enhanced by the reform process.

A third set of problems surrounds the way in which the 'public' is constructed within managerialism. On the one hand, official discourse on this question imagines the 'public' as an undifferentiated mass who require a policing service. Much of the talk about the police 'responding to the community' and 'listening to the public' (not least, that of police officers themselves) proceeds as if the 'public' and the 'community' were coherent entities existing without conflict and capable of expressing a single voice. This is quite simply not the case. Recent criminological research has shown that individuals and social groups differ markedly in both their experiences of crime and policing, and in the demands they have to make of the police (Crawford *et al.*, 1990). To imagine therefore that there is a 'community' to be listened to is woefully mistaken. It is also dangerously anti-democratic, especially when – as so often happens in practice – the claims of the most noisy, powerful or sympathetic to the police outlook (such as those who turn up at police-community consultative committee meetings) are taken to be representative of the 'community' as a whole.

On the other hand, an important – and perhaps dominant – strand of the new managerialism (one most evident in The Citizen's Charter) constructs the public as individual consumers of policing services. The consumer is a figure drawn from the world of economic liberalism, where he or she is understood as a bundle of preferences waiting to be satisfied. It follows that producers are required to engage in market research so as to discover whether existing products are meeting consumer requirements, as well as to test new products and stimulate new demand (a lesson not lost on private security firms). In these respects, the construction of the public as consumers of policing may well be positive in its effects, requiring the police to elicit and take note of public demand, and helping to break down an insular occupational philosophy which has hitherto insisted that 'we know best'.

Despite this, the figure of the consumer remains – in my view – fatally flawed as a way of conceiving of police–public relations. There are simply too many aspects of police work which render the analogy of market exchange of dubious worth. Policing is, first of all, one of a range of public services whose delivery is at times compulsory, supplied to its recipients against their will. There are also occasions when individuals or groups who wish to consume the service are denied an effective opportunity to do so, such as when an offence is 'no-crimed', or if the police refuse to take seriously an incident of racial harassment. And in these cases the problem is not solved – as it might be in the private sector – by increasing supply to meet public demand. Nor is the hallowed doctrine of consumer sovereignty of much help here; the police remain (for the moment at least) the monopoly supplier of many aspects of the service they provide and disenchanted consumers have nowhere else to go. Considerable violence has to be done to the meaning of the word 'consumer' for it to fit the realities of police work.

Problems also arise from the 'market model' of accountability upon which consumerist discourse rests (Black, 1980). Managerialism posits a formal equality between consumers in terms of the demands they can make of the police and the service they are entitled to receive; and it presumes an accountable police force to be one that responds promptly, courteously and efficiently to articulated individual demand for its services. But are individuals and groups who make explicit demands on police time the only relevant consumers? Surely not. In constructing express demand as the primary arbiter of police performance, managerialism forgets that policing is a public good whose costs and benefits are experienced throughout society, and which all citizens (not just current users) have a stake in (Pollitt, 1988). It also fails to realise that responding to the overt demand of some individuals and groups may in effect mean ignoring the unarticulated and therefore hidden demands of those sections of the population who remain alienated from the police. Behind the veil of formal equality, managerialism risks silencing the collective demands of those – such as young people – whose experiences, lack of resources and acquired predispositions render them unable or unlikely to press their claims as consumers of policing.

A market model of accountability is also insufficiently alive to the fact that demand for policing always tends to outstrip supply, and that choices consequently have to be made between the claims of competing constituencies. It is noteworthy in this respect that managerialist utterances say precious little about how exactly public demand is to be elicited (other than through the somewhat thin 'democratic' mechanisms of police-community consultative committees and consumer satisfaction surveys) or, more importantly, about how the conflicting demands of different constituencies (and the police) are to be resolved. There is next to nothing in The Citizen's Charter, or in any of the other recent reports and legislative provisions, that has provided consumers with increased formal opportunities to influence police policy formation, or with any legal right to be consulted about matters of policing. Neither has much public deliberation gone into formulating the performance indicators according to which the police are now assessed. It seems that the police themselves (though now hemmed in by a range of government controls) will – as providers – continue to determine what kind of service the 'public' are to receive.

These developments in the sphere of policing must, finally, be considered in a broader context. When set alongside cognate transformations in other fields of social policy such as education and health, these changes may be viewed as being of potentially far-reaching significance (Clarke *et al.*, 1994). Managerialism can be understood as part of an attempt to reconfigure the relationship between the state and the citizen in a quite fundamental way. Increasingly, this relationship is being couched, not in terms of a universal entitlement to public services premised upon membership of a shared political community, but in terms of a contractual nexus. The central and local state (and the agencies to whom they delegate their responsibilities) are seen as contracting to administer – as efficiently as possible – a range of services to a public viewed as individual consumers (Cooper, 1993).

We are witnessing the transformation of the universal political citizen of social democracy into the fragmented economic consumer of free market liberalism (Barron and Scott, 1992). The citizen is being reduced to an economic actor, imagined as if he or she is a consumer in a market place – a process likely to reverse a long historical struggle to disconnect citizenship from market generated discrepancies of wealth and power. In this respect, the attraction of managerialism for free market liberals is its claim to be politically neutral and value-free, concerned only with means and agnostic about substantive ends (Jones, 1993). It is of course nothing of the sort. The managerialist turn – in policing as elsewhere – is part of a process in which the values associated with democratic citizenship such as justice, equality, representation and participation are marginalised, and public services are restructured and relegitimated according to administrative criteria of economy, efficiency and effectiveness.[9]

In terms of policing, these developments signal an eclipse of democracy, not just in the sense of restricting the opportunities available for different 'publics' to influence police policy within a political public sphere, but more fundamentally, in terms of denying that the very category of democracy has any relevance to policing. The likely outcome of all this is that the idea of public consent which has long been so central to the legitimation of British policing will be emptied still further of substantive content; a consequence with profound implications both for the democratic character of policing as a whole, and for those social groups excluded from the few formal and informal channels for influencing police practice that currently exist. Prominent among such groups stand young people.

YOUTH AS POLICE PROPERTY: THE SILENCES OF MANAGERIALISM

The police often take a dim view of the public they serve. Much sociological research on police culture has found among officers a pronounced 'them and us' disposition towards the outside world (Holdaway, 1983). The police, it seems, posit themselves as the 'thin blue line', engaged in the isolated and thankless task of keeping social chaos at bay; while the public are deemed insufficiently appreciative of the police officer's lot and impervious to the moral decay that officers confront on a daily basis.

The metaphor of 'public as enemy' should not be taken too far, however. For while it captures the insular solidarity so often found among officers, it fails adequately to account for other significant aspects of police work. It tends, first of all, to view police culture as autonomous from any external public influence, thereby disconnecting the professional ideologies and practices of the police from wider asymmetries of power and inequality. What is more, it draws attention away from some of the important distinctions officers make between different public constituencies. Perhaps the most important of these is that forged between 'respectables' and 'roughs'. As Shearing (1981, p. 285) puts it:

> A fundamental distinction is made by the police between the people they serve, and the troublemakers they control in the course of providing their service – that is, between the people they do for things for and those they do things to.

These classifications – together with the more particular subdivisions that officers generate (Reiner, 1992a, pp. 115–21) – are drawn from a broader register of social divisions and mediated through the occupational problems, dilemmas and experiences of police officers. They equip the police with a series of working predispositions towards the individuals and groups they encounter on a daily basis, enabling officers to situate various 'publics' according to the values they are deemed to hold and the trouble they are likely to cause.

In this regard, 'respectables' – the social groups the police 'do things for' – consist of those sections of the middle and working-classes who are deemed supportive of the police and the social order they uphold. 'Roughs' by contrast denote those social groups who the police 'do things to'. Commonly found among economically and socially excluded populations, they are understood as hostile towards the police, and as a challenge to established values and prevailing conceptions of order. In respect of these groups – evocatively referred to by Lee (1981) as 'police property' – the police perform a largely order maintenance function, freely mobilising a range of resources (including, as a last resort, the law) as a means of securing social control on a routine basis.

So does the notion of 'police property' adequately describe the policing predicament of young people? In important respects the answer to this question must be no. The vast majority of contemporary youth are embedded in – and regulated by – such institutions as the family, formal schooling, youth training and employment. The police do not therefore figure as a primary agency of social control. There are, nevertheless, a number of ways in which the metaphor of 'property' might usefully be employed to describe the ways in which young people are conceived of, and acted upon, in the realm of policing. It is these I propose briefly to elaborate upon, for they provide an important indication as to why it is that young people are both unable and unwilling to press their claims as consumers of policing.

Let us consider first official and popular discourse about crime. What images of youth prevail within these discourses? And what effects do they have?[10] At the most general level, young people figure in public discourse as both a signifier and harbinger of – often unwelcome – social change. Since the discovery of 'adolescence' in the late nineteenth century, young people have been a repeated source of political and public disquiet, and routinely subjected to the official regulatory gaze. Whether in respect of crime, sexuality or schooling, young people have been – and continue to be – mobilised as an object of 'respectable fears' (Pearson, 1983). The values and practices of successive generations of youth become a way of focusing upon and talking about an otherwise diffuse set of social anxieties and aspirations. As Davis (1990, p. 18) puts it:

> The youth question – since at least the turn of the century but especially in the post-war period – has served as a kind of 'screen' upon which social commentators and analysts of all ideological and political persuasions have 'projected' far more general hopes and fears concerning the condition and future of our society as a whole.

In this regard, the youth question is all too easily (and often) collapsed into the criminal question. Official and popular discourse propounds a conception of crime and its causes in which young people (and especially teenage boys) appear prominently and in particular kinds of ways. Within the received traditions of criminology and social policy, as in the public imagination more generally, the intimate connection between youthfulness and crime is well established, even taken-for-granted. Indeed, the youth–crime connection has become such a 'firmly embedded aspect of cultural self-understanding in the modern era' as to perhaps be immune from any evidence that might refute it (Pearson, 1994, p. 1195).

The figure of the 'juvenile delinquent' continues to shape public debate and understanding about crime in Britain (especially in the aftermath of the murder of toddler Jamie Bulger by two 10-year-old boys in February 1993). The predominant way of talking about (and acting upon) young people is in terms of 'trouble'; a tendency most evident in relation to black youth – the 'black mugger' being a consistent object of right wing 'law and order' mobilisations and 'respectable' fears alike (Hall *et al.*, 1978) – but which can also be said to apply to the category of youth more generally. Young people are understood first and foremost in terms of the problems they cause for others, whether they be local residents, teachers or the police themselves. They are the unproductive and unsocialised generation, untrammelled by the burdens of 'adult' responsibility and marked by a manifest, if temporary, hostility towards received tradition and authority.

A second – ultimately complementary – conception of youth constructs young people as 'vulnerable'. Here the dominant category is one of risk. Young people are conceived of as at risk, not from victimisation as such (this being one aspect of 'growing up' that – the important exception of child abuse aside – eludes professional and popular understanding), but from the constant and varied possibilities of 'getting up to no good' – possibilities that can encompass anything from 'falling in with bad company' to drug experimentation and sexual promiscuity (the latter concern usually being reserved for teenage girls). The central focus here is on adolescence as a time of impulsiveness and immaturity, as well as one in which learning and moral development can – with appropriate supervision and instruction – occur.

But what are the effects of images such as these? What impact do they have on the manner in which young people are policed? The first and perhaps most significant feature of official and popular discourse is that it speaks *about* youth. It embodies (if only implicitly) a claim to 'know' and 'own' the experiences, concerns and aspirations of young people. Young people themselves – as we have seen in relation to policing – play little or no part in constructing the discourse within which such claims are made, and it in this respect that the metaphor of 'property' is so pertinent. For it signifies perfectly the ways in which young people are constructed as objects of social policy – police policy included; an objectification in which they become a 'problem' to be analysed and solved, rather than citizens with demands of their own to voice (cf. Said, 1978).

Prevailing public discourse about youth serves, secondly, as a climate within which the routine policing of young people takes place, a climate that structures such policing in certain kinds of ways. These constructions, articulated day after day in the local and national media, provide a subtle, powerful and enduring message to the effect that young people require a mode of regulation in which they are subject to constant if varying degrees of control and care, whether it be from parents, teachers or the police. In the realm of policing, they provide a broad ideological licence for a set of practices that are concerned both with the routine supervision of young people's use of public space, and with a paternalistic pedagogy geared to the production of 'respectable' citizens.

With this in mind, let us turn to young people's actual contact with the police in public places. What combination of the force and service aspects of policing do young people experience? In respect of the former, the extent and pattern of police–youth contact is well-documented. Criminological research has suggested time and again that the weight of adversarial policing falls disproportionately on the young, especially black, male and working-class youth (Smith and Gray, 1983). This applies both to the sixteen to twenty-five-year-old section of the population (Crawford *et al.*, 1990), and, to an even greater extent, to those aged between eleven and fifteen (Anderson *et al.*, 1994; Aye Maung, 1995). It is a contact that focuses both on the questioning and apprehension of young people on suspicion of technical delinquency and, more generally, on the routine supervision of their use of public space.

With respect to young people's experience of a police service evidence is less readily available. Criminological research in Britain has – echoing an 'extraordinary blindspot' in the culture in general (Pearson, 1994) – been preoccupied for most of its history with questions of juvenile delinquency, and has consequently had little to say about young people as victims of crime or as recipients of a police service (cf. Morgan and Zedner, 1992).[11] The little evidence to hand indicates, however, that young people rarely report crimes they have witnessed to the police, and infrequently call upon the police to do things for them as victims of crime (Anderson *et al.*, 1994; Aye Maung, 1995; Hartless *et al.*, 1995). Despite the strides made by the police in recent years to improve police–youth relations (through schools-liaison schemes and the like), young people still rarely encounter the police outside of situations marked by conflict and mutual distrust.

One reason for this pattern of police–youth contact is that young people – working-class youth especially – lack the rights and protections conferred by the social institution of privacy. Avoiding police attention is heavily bound up with being able to shield one's activities from the public sphere (Stinchcombe, 1969), and the majority of young people simply lack the resources to do this. More than any other social group, young people are dependant on a range of public places, especially in relation to the pursuit of leisure. Denied access (initially, at least, by reason of age) from a whole host of cultural amenities, young people come to rely on local streets, city centres, shopping malls and the like as a means to build cultural identities away from the direct supervision of adult authority. Their social practices – both legal and illegal – are thus rendered public and visible.

But why should this usage provoke such suspicion? Perhaps most significantly because young people's unstructured reliance of the streets and other public places lays claim to occupy public space in a fashion that is incongruous with what Sacks (1972) calls the 'normal ecology' of local social ordering. Routine social existence in late-modern societies is increasingly organised around either the domestic sphere, or the purely functional and consumption-related use of public places (Worpole, 1992). Against this backdrop, the unstructured and expressive use of the streets is all too often deemed illegitimate in and of itself, irrespective of what activities are actually being engaged in. This is even more likely to be the case if such usage involves young people, a group tinged with a prior construction as a symbol of trouble.

There is, secondly, and more mundanely, little doubt that young people's collective use of public places can be a source of considerable nuisance and anxiety, both for other users of public space and for local residents more generally. A number of recent studies have suggested that groups of youths (especially boys) hanging around the streets comes high on people's list of local social problems (Anderson *et al.*, 1990; Campbell, 1993). There is similarly little doubt that the streets provide young people with a site in which to engage in delinquent activity of various kinds. Petty offending in public places is a predominantly youthful enterprise, the peak age of officially-recorded offending currently standing at eighteen for males and fifteen for females (Prison Reform Trust, 1993).

Police attention then is directed towards young people's use of public space by a whole series of concerns and anxieties. This attention is the product, first of all, of the fact that young people's occupancy of public space presents a potential, and at times all too real, challenge to the police officer's ability to command and maintain control over his or her 'patch'. It arises, secondly, from local residents' requests for the police to 'do something' about the latest groups of boisterous youths to have descended on their doorsteps (a process likely to be exacerbated by managerialist exhortations that the police respond quickly and efficiently to the demands of their customers). And finally, it is the product of the fact that, when faced with situations in which the claims of young people and local residents collide, occupational expediency demands that it is the residents who are satisfied; lacking the required cultural capital, young people are the least likely of the respective parties to bring a formal complaint.

But does the pattern of relations that follows from this – in which young people and the police continually appear and reappear in situations of conflict – reflect the ways in which young people actually use and experience public places? The answer, it seems, must be no. A rich vein

of criminological research and reflection has, for example, suggested that
youthful offending is for the most part trivial, ephemeral in nature and
ultimately something that young people 'grow out of' (Matza, 1964;
Rutherford, 1992; Anderson *et al.*, 1994, ch. 4). Moreover, much of the
time young people spend on the street involves simply 'doing nothing'
(Corrigan, 1976), or at least not doing anything which contravenes the
terms of the criminal law. The amount of police resources currently given
over to the routine regulation of young people appears both unjustified
and counterproductive.

By contrast, recent research has suggested that young people experience
relatively more serious problems as victims of crime while out in public.
For example, Anderson *et al.* (1994) report that – irrespective of class,
place or gender – eleven to fifteen year-olds in Edinburgh experience
levels of victimisation that greatly exceed those of older populations (see
also, Aye Maung, 1995; Hartless *et al.*, 1995). Similarly, the British and
Scottish crime surveys have both repeatedly shown that victimisation from
personal crime falls most heavily on the sixteen to twenty-five year-old
age group (see, for example, Kinsey and Anderson, 1992). Few of these
experiences are reported to the police, however, and youth victimisation
consequently tends to occupy a small proportion of available police time
and resources. Among most forces it fails to register on the list of police
priorities at all.

It seems that young people experience a marked imbalance in the
dimensions of police force and service that they receive. As users of public space, they encounter levels of routine police supervision that for the
most part bear little relation to the problems they actually occasion. Young
people are in this respect over-controlled. In stark contrast, young people
remain under-protected by the police in relation to the degree of victimisation they encounter while out in public. This disproportionate balance
of force and service signifies, perhaps above all else, that young people in
public spaces are the effective property of the police; acted upon at the
bequest of others, yet unable to articulate their own concerns and demands.

With this in mind, let us return to managerialism. What are the implications of these reflections on police–youth relations for its central presuppositions and claims? Managerialist discourse rests, as we have seen, on
the proposition that the consumers of policing services are formally equal
– all entitled to a responsive service, and all able to demand that the police
meet their requirements. However, this understanding of the position of
police consumers fails – like all ideologies of formal equality – to recognise
that the different constituencies the police serve are, in substantive terms,
far from equal. They in fact differ profoundly in terms of how they are

understood within official (including police) and popular discourse; the types of policing they experience, and the cultural capital available to them to make their claims as consumers of policing count. Managerialism has no working conception of the ways in which inequalities of power within the wider social realm impact upon policing, and as a result, it seems set to maintain some marked and unjustifiable imbalances in the social distribution of policing benefits and burdens.

As a group constituted as 'police property', both within the political and popular mind, and in terms of their use of public space, young people are among the least able of all social groups to press their claims as consumers of policing. Yet young people, as we have seen, are an important police constituency, and police actions (and inaction) play a significant part in determining the quality of young people's lives. It is therefore of some significance that there exist so few formal or informal opportunities for young people to articulate their concerns *vis-à-vis* policing, and that their experiences remain almost entirely absent from the agendas of police policy and practice. This, in turn, is of some consequence for managerialism and its claim to be able to effect quality policing services for all. Young people represent an important 'litmus test' for any system of police governance which professes to rest upon the doctrine of policing by consent – a test managerialism abjectly fails.

2 Communicative Action, Democracy and Social Research

Can a democratic, inclusive and viable alternative to managerialism be developed? An important strand of contemporary social theory would suggest not. It would situate the emergence of managerialism within a more far-reaching set of social changes that has seen questions of democracy rendered increasingly irrelevant to institutional and societal reproduction in the late-modern world. Bauman (1987), for example, argues that issues of democratic legitimacy have been made redundant in societies where the majority are seduced by the material benefits of consumer capitalism, while the marginalised (such as young unemployed men) are increasingly subjected to coercive social regulation (cf. Galbraith, 1992).

While it is possible to concur that the values and practices of a critical public sphere have been rendered increasingly remote and abstract by processes of rationalisation and state intervention (Habermas, 1987), one must not jump too readily to the conclusion that the resources of democracy have been exhausted. Rather, one must ask why it is that formal democracy is retained at all in late-modern liberal societies? Or, as Cohen (1985, p. 93) puts it: 'What precludes the acceptance of the gradual abolition of these civil and political rights by a populace to whom their relevance is no longer evident? What prevents the administrative system from justifying the abolition of these forms in the name of technical rationality?'

One reason is that democratic values have been embedded – however selectively – in the political culture of modern societies such as Britain; something that requires even managerialism – which seeks the triumph of administration over politics – to press its claims with some reference to themes drawn from the register of democracy. It is significant, for example, that in the debate on the future of public services in Britain the Conservative administration continually feels impelled to speak the language of citizenship, albeit one couched in terms of individuated consumers. It is similarly pertinent that senior police officers now feel obliged to talk about 'listening to the customer' and 'opening up the service to the public', and that the debate over the Police and Magistrates' Courts Act generated an opposition moved by the language of democratic accountability.

Far from effecting a technicist closure, managerialism has in fact opened up a new and contested terrain in relation to British policing and its futures, its supposedly neutral language affording both a political and theoretical space (Clarke *et al.*, 1994). Politically, talk of consumer responsiveness and quality of service enables currently excluded 'users' to insist on their inclusion. Theoretically, the residual attachment of managerialism to the idea of public consent creates the opportunity for an immanent critique of how such consent is currently conceived of and obtained. A space exists in which to explicate the failure of managerialist discourse to make good its claims, and suggest alternative, more adequate and more democratic means of doing so.

My purpose in this chapter is to prise open that space. In so doing, I draw upon the resources of contemporary political and social theory (and especially the work of Jürgen Habermas) in order, first, to explore the connection between policing and democratic legitimacy; and second, to set out a methodological framework within which to unravel the consequences for prevailing police-youth relations of a system of police governance in which questions of democracy have been marginalised. Before proceeding further however, it is necessary to outline briefly the theoretical standpoint which informs these endeavours and establish its relevance.[1]

BEYOND MANAGERIALISM: CRITICAL THEORY AND COMMUNICATIVE ACTION

German social theorist Jürgen Habermas is currently the foremost exponent of what has become known as the Frankfurt school of critical theory (Held, 1980). In reformulating the legacy bequeathed by this tradition of social enquiry, Habermas has over the last three decades pursued two related concerns. He has endeavoured, first of all, to understand the historical and theoretical promise of the 'public sphere', a term he uses to describe that 'realm of our social life in which something approaching a public opinion can be formed' (Habermas, 1974, p. 49). In particular, Habermas has traced what he views as the degeneration of the bourgeois public sphere that emerged in early modern Europe (and in which the principle of inclusive, rational and critical public debate was first acknowledged) to the mass-mediated public spheres that mark late-modern societies (Habermas, 1989).

More recently, he has introduced and developed the concept of 'communicative action' in order to steer a path between the instrumental rationality that has come to dominate contemporary public life, and those post-modern critics whose response has been a deep scepticism towards the prospect of employing rationality in the service of human freedom (Lyotard, 1984). In pursuing this path, Habermas has viewed communicative action as a means to deliver modernity from processes of bureaucratic rationalisation that have severely restricted the possibility of institutionalised democratic communication among citizens (Habermas, 1984; 1987).

The political goal that has guided the various threads of Habermas's critical theory has been the realisation of a future in which people are capable of collectively and individually developing their potential free of illegitimate social constraints; a future in which social integration is secured through public discourse rather than strategic persuasion or coercion. This objective has been taken to require the embedding of undistorted communication within the institutions of a democratic public sphere. As such, the theory of communicative action anticipates:

> A new principle of social organisation, according to which action-orienting norms and principles would be generated in processes of public and unlimited discussion. The new principle of social organisation would be that of discursive will formation through communication freed from domination. (Benhabib, 1986, p. 229)

The theory of communicative action is important here because it enables us to situate, deepen and move beyond the critique of managerialism outlined in the previous chapter. Two aspects, in particular, are of relevance. In an explanatory vein, Habermas's work allows us to understand managerialism in terms of a broader process of social rationalisation; one which has seen the institutionalisation of instrumental reason and the decline of a critical public sphere. Secondly, and in a normative vein, it can help us formulate an alternative way of thinking about the question of police accountability. I want in this section to deal briefly with each of these issues.

Habermas's critical theory rests upon a distinction between several types of social action, the most important of which is that between communicative and instrumental action (Habermas, 1969, pp. 81–121; 1984, pp. 8–42). Communicative action is that oriented towards reaching a mutual understanding about an unclear situation, with the goal of consensually coordinating objectives through 'the unforced force of the better argument'. The rationality associated with it refers to the competence of social actors to raise validity claims and criticise the claims of others. Through a process of rational deliberation these claims can be challenged, evaluated and revised; something that requires relations of reciprocity and symmetry to obtain between the parties involved.

By contrast, instrumental action is oriented towards controlling the social world in such a way as to bring about a desired state of affairs. It involves deploying existing knowledge, resources and persuasive techniques in ways that make others act in accordance with an agent's purposes. The associated rationality here is one that attempts to calculate the best means to achieve certain specified ends, something which envisages an active subject prevailing upon, and doing things to, a passive object. Historically, instrumental rationality has been connected with the claim that the ends of social life lie beyond the reach of reasoned argument.

The distinction between these two types of rationality – both of which Habermas views as part of the promise of modernity – serves as a framework within which processes of social rationalisation can be reinterpreted. Rationalisation was seen by both Max Weber and the first generation of critical theorists to have entailed the increasing domination of the modern world by instrumental reason, and its orientation towards mastery and control. Employing a broader concept of rationality, Habermas is able to concur with the overall contours of this thesis while avoiding its fatalistic conclusions. His central claim is that the 'paradoxes of rationalisation' have occasioned an institutionalisation of instrumental reason accomplished at the expense of communicative reason.

The dominance of institutional and everyday life by instrumental reason has, Habermas (1987) contends, severely diminished the democratic quality of public life. It has created a political culture in which decision-making about practical affairs becomes largely the province of professionalised, expert cultures; one where public policy is reduced to a series of technical questions, formulated and determined on the basis of expert knowledge. Within the institutions of the modern economy and administrative state, public participation, and the untutored, practical knowledge it introduces, is viewed as merely a hindrance to efficient and effective decision-making; it gets in the way, complicates matters, slow things down, disrupts the rhythms of bureaucratic life. In such circumstances, a public sphere in which people can deliberate about matters of common concern, and exercise an ongoing influence over the institutions which dominate their lives is unable to flourish. Citizens are made passive spectators of a decision-making process whose outcomes affect them, but whose intricacies they are deemed not to understand (Fischer, 1990).

Managerialism, I believe, needs to be located and understood in this context. In policing as elsewhere, managerialist ideology is permeated through and through by instrumental reason. It is concerned, as we have seen, with calculating the best means to bring about an efficient and effective police service. In so doing, it takes the ends of policing as given and disconnects policing issues from a whole complex of democratic values. In these respects, managerialism is both a feature of, and contributor towards, a thinly democratic public sphere characterised by privatism, the mass-mediated construction of 'public' opinion and consent, and unaccountable expertise.

But can alternative, more democratic ways of approaching the question of police accountability be found? And upon what basis might they proceed? Here, the normative dimensions of the theory of communicative action offer a potentially valuable resource. One of Habermas's long-standing preoccupations has been to think through how one might distinguish between different types of 'consensus'. He has sought to establish what public consent undistorted by asymmetries of power entails, and explored whether – and if so how – such consent may be realised in late-modern societies. The procedures for differentiating between a communicatively achieved consensus and other forms of empirical agreement Habermas calls 'discourse ethics'.

Discourse ethics rests upon two main propositions. Habermas seeks to establish, first, that communication oriented to reaching mutual understanding is an immanent possibility rather than a utopian dream conjured from thin air. The theory of 'universal pragmatics' attempts to do this by articulating the presuppositions that speakers anticipate every time language is used (Habermas, 1979, pp. 1–69). Habermas contends that, when engaging in speech, actors implicitly raise four validity claims and presuppose that they can be justified if challenged – a claim to be comprehensible, to speak the truth, to speak legitimately in context and to speak sincerely. These claims constitute a subtle common sense that speakers always already assume in the course of ordinary language use. If they are absent, the shared experience upon which communication depends collapses and has to be (consensually) rebuilt through argumentation.

Discourse ethics rests, secondly, upon the claim that it is possible to distinguish between a 'rationally motivated consensus' and what Habermas calls 'mere agreement' (Habermas, 1990, pp. 43–115). The purpose of the 'ideal speech situation' – or better, the criteria of 'ideal speech' – is to provide the procedural tools required for this evaluative task.[2] The criteria of 'ideal speech' are that (1) each participant has an equal chance to initiate and continue discussion; (2) each must have an equal chance to assert, recommend and explain their claims and to challenge the claims of others; (3) all must have an equal chance to express their feelings, wishes and intentions, and (4) there must be an equal distribution of chances for speakers to order and resist orders, to promise and refuse, and to be accountable to, and demand accountability from, others.

Taken together, these criteria anticipate communicative processes from which untruthfulness and duplicity, and inequality and subordination have been removed (Benhabib, 1986, pp. 284–6). They constitute a set of procedural rules and social relations that must obtain in order for it to be said that a consensus over disputed claims is based upon 'the unforced force of the better argument'. In this sense, discourse ethics provides the normative basis on which the theory of communicative action rests. The critical standards it evokes enable prevailing public discourse and agreement to be called into question and evaluated. They function as a 'hermeneutics of suspicion' (Ricoeur, 1976), drawing attention to the ways in which 'public' opinion and consent are manufactured in late-modern societies, and endeavouring to uncover spurious claims to universality and legitimacy.

But if the critique launched under this banner is to have any historically situated purchase on current institutional practices, discourse ethics cannot be immanent merely in the sense of its presupposition in language. To be genuinely immanent in late-modern societies the criteria of ideal speech must also be anticipated in some way or other in the institutions and cultural traditions of those societies; for, as Paul Ricoeur (1981, p. 99) points out, 'upon what will you concretely support the reawakening of communicative action, if not upon the creative renewal of cultural heritage?'. On this matter however, Habermas has become increasingly ambivalent of late. His recent – rather formal – emphasis on locating the possibility of communicative action in the universal presuppositions of language (Habermas, 1990) bespeaks a pessimism about the prospect of redeeming the emancipatory promise of liberal democratic institutions by means of immanent critique. But is this pessimism justified? Can discourse ethics claim no practical point of connection with prevailing social practices? Or, alternatively, do the resources for democratic transformation continue to inhere within the very claims that democratic institutions mobilise for the purposes of legitimation (Cohen, 1985)?

It is this latter possibility that I want, theoretically and substantively, to pursue in respect of the police. Such an enterprise is likely to meet with a certain amount of scepticism, however. It is hard to imagine a more difficult arena of social life in which to explore Habermas's ideas than that of policing, and especially police–youth relations. The police, sceptics will point out, are only ever mobilised when communication breaks down. Relations between the police and young people, they will say, appear to have more to do with force than dialogue. In either case, they undoubtedly have a point.

Yet, at the same time, policing in Britain is supposed to proceed with the consent of the policed. This is the basis of the police's claim to democratic legitimacy. Rarely, however, is this long established doctrine reflected upon or taken seriously. Policing by consent is, for the most part, taken-for-granted, presumed in the absence of large scale complaint and disorder to exist. But in a society which claims for itself the mantle 'democratic' is this sufficient? Do we not need to think more deeply about what it means for the public to consent to policing in a democracy? Might discourse ethics provide us with a useful resource for this task?

DISCOURSE ETHICS, DEMOCRATIC LEGITIMACY AND POLICING BY CONSENT

While the theory of communicative action is not in and of itself a substantive theory of democracy, discourse ethics can plausibly be argued to have an intimate connection to questions of democratic legitimacy (Cohen and Arato, 1992, ch. 8). In a negative vein, discourse ethics provides a means of establishing whether or not institutional legitimation claims that purport to universality in fact rest upon the systematic exclusion of various social groups. More constructively, it serves as a basis for developing alternative ways of thinking about the democratisation of public institutions. In either case, discourse ethics is concerned 'not with the realisation of the ideal speech situation, but with specific problems of power and powerlessness, with ideology, legitimation and democratic politics' (Forester, 1985b, p. xvi).

But upon what basis are these tasks to proceed? Does discourse ethics employ a series of external (and otherworldly) criteria by which existing institutions are almost sure to be found wanting, or do the claims it makes have some foothold in the present? Cohen and Arato (1992) suggest that, in so far as we have witnessed a 'selective institutionalisation of the emancipatory potentials of modernity' (1992, p. 405), the latter is in fact the case. They argue that contemporary liberal democracies have embedded in their political institutions and traditions the principles of basic rights and public discourse. These societies acknowledge both a body of substantive political rights (such as those relating to freedom of assembly and expression) as well as the more general idea of 'the right to have rights'.[3] Yet, at the same time, these rights are the subject of both ongoing struggle and possible reversal (as in the Criminal Justice and Public Order Act 1994), as well as being circumscribed in a whole number of ways – they tend, for example, to be conferred on individuals rather than social groups. This partial recognition of principles drawn from the register of democracy is important nonetheless:

[For] even if the normative development that represents the positive side of modernity is only selectively established in stable institutions, such partial achievements create the space for social movements to renew and re-establish the relevant principles in less selective ways. (Cohen and Arato, 1992, p. 405)

The establishment of at least a minimal conception of liberal democracy is important in so far as it allows discourse ethics to press its claims in contexts where the principles of democratic legitimacy are already partially recognised and embedded. This means that it can proceed – initially at least – by way of immanent critique. Immanent critique involves turning the standards an institution professes to hold back on the institution itself and bringing it to account for a failure to make good its own legitimation claims. Its efficacy lies in the fact that, instead of mobilising standards from the outside, proposing them as alternatives and criticising an institution for failing to meet them, it employs the very principles that the institution concerned claims to hold dear.

But what significance do these issues have to the police? Why, if at all, is it important that policing is democratically legitimated, and of what value is discourse ethics in thinking through the relevant questions? There are three principal reasons why policing might be said to require democratic legitimation. Policing, first of all, is fundamentally about the exercise of power over others. The police are the institutional locus of the state's monopoly of coercive force and their actions can have serious detrimental effects on the lives and liberties of citizens (as the Guildford Four, Birmingham Six and other officially recognised miscarriages of justice have recently testified). In a democratic polity, the possession and wielding of such power is quite properly viewed with some suspicion, and deemed always to require justification (Beetham, 1991, ch. 2). So too must redress be available for those subjected to its illegitimate exercise.

But the democratic legitimation of police power cannot be confined to the prevention of, and redress for, the abuse of its exercise, important though that is.[4] For as well as being the locus of coercive regulation, the police also play a crucial and potentially enabling role in the mediation of social conflict. They have a significant effect on the ordering of social relations and the capacity to impact considerably (for better as well as worse) on the quality of people's lives. Policing decisions are, in short, political ones concerned with the allocation of a significant public good. It is thus of prime importance to the democratic legitimacy of the police that all the social groups whose lives are touched by policing can have some more proactive say in how its benefits and burdens are distributed.

The democratic legitimacy of policing has, thirdly, a close connection with its effectiveness. Beetham (1991) has noted that the exercise of power is more likely to be stable and effective if it is able to appeal to moral grounds for compliance among citizens. Democracy is important, in other words, not only for principled reasons, but also because a legitimate institution holds out greater hope of achieving its purposes. And this we have seen demonstrated quite starkly in the realm of policing. The withdrawal of cooperation from the police by sections of the community in Britain's inner cites has contributed much to the decline of police effectiveness in these locales, prompting, in turn, the kinds of proactive policing that was to spark the urban disorders of the 1980s (Kinsey *et al.*, 1986).

It can be established theoretically then that the democratic legitimacy of the police is of vital importance. But according to what general principles is such legitimacy presently judged? And do resources exist within the established conventions of police governance that might provide discourse ethics with some initial purchase? One can, I think, find reason enough to answer this latter question with a 'no'. It was argued in Chapter 1 that both the mechanisms and relevance of democracy are being increasingly eclipsed in relation to the police, and that the new managerialism has set out to relegitimate policing according to predominantly administrative criteria. Nonetheless, I believe that the resources of democracy are not so easily disposed of, and that a foothold for immanent critique can still be located.

The central democratic principle that has historically been mobilised to legitimate the police in Britain is that of policing by consent. The police – from the time of Peel onwards – have been officially represented as 'citizens in uniform' operating within, and circumscribed by, the contours of public approval. In many respects, of course, this doctrine has amounted to little more than ideology – affording policing a social meaning that bears little relation to the experiences of groups such as black youth. Yet it is has also found partial embodiment in the legal regulations and democratic arrangements that currently govern police practice, whether they be the safeguards provided by the Police and Criminal Evidence Act 1984, the Police Complaints Authority or local police-community consultative committees.

The received traditions of public consent also infuse the claims of managerialism. Though mainly concerned to forge a set of depoliticised, administrative criteria with which to reconstruct and relegitimate policing, one finds within managerialist discourse a residual attachment to terms drawn from the register of democracy. Official talk about 'opening up the service to customers' and 'listening to the public' has proliferated in recent years. Public opinion surveys have begun to play a major role in ascertaining consumer demand and satisfaction with policing services. And the concept of 'community' – however ill-defined – continues to crop up in police discourse. In a liberal democracy such as Britain, the connections between policing and democracy are perhaps not so easily elided.

The significance of this selective embodiment of democratic values and principles is that it provides a space for an immanent critique of the ways in which they are currently understood and enacted. Discourse ethics engages a shared if contested terrain. The attachment of official discourse to notions of 'policing by consent', 'listening to the community' and the like permits some critical questions to be posed in respect of how they actually operate in practice. By what means is such public approval elicited? How genuine and universal is the consent upon which policing depends? Upon what exclusions do the resulting policies rely?

Discourse ethics seeks to contest the boundaries of actually existing democracy on the basis of two conditions which it takes to be central to the production of genuine, uncoerced consent – those of communication and inclusion. The significance of communication is that it enables participants to raise their claims, defend them with reasons and judge – in the context of actual deliberation – the extent to which they are valid. In this respect, discourse ethics encourages mutual recognition of the claims of the Other, renders existing interests contingent, and facilitates the emergence of more informed perspectives on relevant issues (Bohman, 1990). It holds further that only those claims which survive the test of public communication can form the basis of reflexive and unforced agreement and, as such, it serves as a means of reaching a rational, democratic consensus – or, if the issues so demand, compromise – over disputed issues. In short:

> Discourse ethics provides a way of discovering or reaffirming what, if anything, we who come into contact with one another and who are affected by the same political decisions and laws have in common. (Cohen and Arato, 1992, p. 368)

So how do existing arrangements for generating public consent for policing measure up in this respect? Not very well. We saw in Chapter 1 that there presently exist few formal opportunities for public deliberation about matters of policing to occur. Those that do – such as police-community consultative committees – tend to be structured around police agendas and are marked by a substantial imbalance of information as between the police and the individuals and groups who attend. Nor is the proliferation of customer satisfaction surveys likely to improve matters. For while such surveys might generate useful information about public experiences and demands they provide no opportunity for the claims that are raised to be discussed; they tend, that is, to generate 'the automatic opinion of each and the considered opinion of none' (Keane, 1984, p. 148).

Inclusiveness – the second principal tenet of discourse ethics – is concerned with two further conditions of rational agreement. It requires, first, that the whole gamut of substantive issues at stake are susceptible to discussion, and second, that all interests, needs and aspirations are accorded an equal place in the deliberative process. In these respects, discourse ethics is an ethics of citizenship, concerned to facilitate the universal participation of individuals and social groups on the basis of their membership of a shared political culture. It anticipates public discourse in which 'collective decisions [are] reached through procedures that are radically open and fair to all' (Benhabib, 1992, p. 9), and views such discourse as central to the production of democratically legitimate power. In the absence of these conditions, the consent generated by processes of public deliberation is rendered ideological, distorted by the very relations of domination that it helps to reproduce (Beetham, 1991, ch. 4).

The prevailing institutional arrangements for the governance of the police are some way from satisfying these criteria. In the first place, as we have seen, current arrangements remove decisions about policing policy from forums of democratic decision-making altogether, thereby preventing a host of substantive policing issues from becoming the subject of effective public deliberation. Moreover, those communicative mechanisms that do exist – such as police-community consultative committees – serve largely as a vehicle for limited and unrepresentative sections of the population to voice their concerns. Current arrangements for the production of public consent rely, in other words, on the systematic exclusion of a whole range of affected social groups. Those – young people for example – whose experiences and acquired predispositions mean that they are rarely minded to call the police, turn up at consultative committee meetings, or fill in customer satisfaction surveys, simply do not contribute to whatever consent can meaningfully be said to be accorded to police policy and practice. Indeed, public consent all too often means merely the agreement of certain sections of the population for the police to 'do things' to those constituted as 'police property'.

Few would claim that policing by consent should be interpreted as the agreement of everyone for everything the police do – offenders, it is often trivially remarked, seldom consent to their own arrest and detention. But in liberal democratic societies, legitimate policing must be able to command broad levels of public agreement for its policies and practices among both dominant *and* subordinate groups. It is in this respect that current arrangements are found wanting. The 'consent' that currently underpins policing in Britain is simply too assumed and prereflexive, too empty of substantive content, and the product of too many exclusions, to be able to make good its own legitimation claims.

RESEARCHING POLICE–YOUTH RELATIONS: TOWARDS A DEPTH HERMENEUTICS

Are the claims of critical theory limited to the realm of normative critique, or can it also be used in the service of empirical social research? This question, much debated of late by critical theorists (Forester, 1985a), is pivotal to the concerns of this book. I want to suggest that, as well as facilitating a critique of actual existing democracy, discourse ethics can provide a methodological framework for substantive sociological investigation, one which focuses attention both on the empirical consequences of current democratic forms, and on the opportunities that might exist for pushing these forms in the direction of greater democracy. I want, in particular, to employ the theory of communicative action as a basis from which to develop a theoretical case study of police–youth relations. Taking as its point of departure the presence of institutional arrangements which severely delimit the opportunities for public deliberation about policing matters, such an enquiry endeavours to unravel the practical consequences of such arrangements for aspects of police–youth relations, and examine the possibilities for enhanced democratic communication that obtain within the present.

The case study has three related purposes. It seeks, first of all, to explore the substantive issues that figure most prominently in shaping relations between youth, crime and policing. Most apparent in this respect are the questions of juvenile offending and disorder that so dominate public representations of the youth question. But we must not confine ourselves – in the manner of politicians and pundits – to these questions alone. We must instead encompass within our focus the multiplicity of ways in which young people come into contact with crime, and perhaps most importantly, pay attention to the much neglected issues of youth safety and victimisation. Similar considerations apply to policing, where a hitherto predominant focus on adversarial police–youth encounters and their effects needs to be coupled with an exploration of how young people think about and use policing as a service. The case study will attend to all these aspects of police–youth relations. It will explore how young people and police officers talk about their respective concerns and experiences, paying

particular attention to how the relevant issues affect young people during
the crucial few years that follow the end of compulsory schooling.

The research endeavours, secondly, to prefigure (in so far as this is
possible) institutional arrangements for police governance that are more
inclusive and democratic in character. In this respect, the case study functions as a means of giving a voice to the respective claims of young people
and police officers, groups who – in different ways and with different
effects – are largely precluded from participating in current arrangements
for police policy-making. And it seeks to bring those claims into an 'imaginary dialogue' with each other, enabling one to envisage the kinds of
issues and disputes that might surface within forums of democratic decision-
making. This primarily involves reflection on the substance of young
people's and police officers' accounts of the world – the claims that are
being made, what is being said about what, the reciprocities and antagonisms
that exist. But it demands also that some consideration be given to how these
accounts are generated; for the (methodological) problems and pitfalls
associated with the research process can provide some pointers – and no
more – as to how democratic processes might operate if embedded in
institutional forms of various kinds.[5]

The case study serves, finally, as a means of making concrete the abstract conceptions of communication outlined earlier in this chapter. In
particular, democratic communication provides a standpoint from which to
make some meaningful sense of prevailing police–youth relations. On the
one hand, this entails an exploration of the view that the fissures which so
often bedevil such relations are a product of a system of accountability
that precludes communication other than that which takes place during
brief (and often fractious) encounters in public places. And it means considering how and in what respects these situational encounters contribute
to current tensions. On the other hand, it entails an analysis of whether –
and if so in what ways – the accounts of young people and police officers
can be said to hold, in however inchoate and contextualised a form, the
possibilities of enhanced democratic communication.

The research comprised interviews undertaken with young people and
serving police officers in and around Edinburgh. Thirty-three interviews
(thirteen individual and twenty group interviews) were carried out with a
total of 99 young people, 61 young men and 38 young women. They were
aged between fifteen and twenty-three and interviewed between July 1990
and June 1991. Thirteen young people were selected by following up the
sample drawn for the Edinburgh crime survey, and interviewed individually (Anderson *et al.*, 1990). Twenty groups of young people were selected
from further education colleges, youth clubs, unemployed clubs and youth

training schemes. They were chosen from different areas of Edinburgh and Lothian region and encompassed a range of post-school educational and vocational trajectories.

The resulting sample were differentiated along the following lines. All but one of those interviewed were white. In terms of age, five of the sample were fifteen, 43 were sixteen and nineteen were seventeen. Of the rest, 24 were aged between eighteen and twenty and a further eight between twenty-one and twenty-three. Within Edinburgh, the majority of the sample lived in the mixed (though predominantly working) class areas of Broughton, Leith and Portobello in the north of the city; the peripheral housing schemes of Wester Hailes and Craigmillar/Niddrie, and the mainly working-class areas of Mayfield and Gracemount in the south. Outside Edinburgh, the bulk of those interviewed lived in small towns in East and Midlothian, such as Bonnyrigg, Dalkeith, Gorebridge, North Berwick and Penicuik. Forty-one of the interviewees were in full-time education; three of these were still at school, 31 were pursuing vocational qualifications at college, with a further six studying for 'Highers' and one at university. Of those who had left education, seven were in full-time employment, 31 were on youth training schemes and seventeen unemployed. A further two were female single parents, and another was undergoing a community service order.

Forty-nine serving police officers were interviewed individually in two separate phases. Twenty-seven officers were talked to as part of research carried out for the Safer Edinburgh Project on multi-agency policing (Kinsey, 1992). They were drawn from three stations in central Edinburgh and interviewed in May and June 1990. The sample consisted of eighteen beat officers, six area officers, and three community involvement officers (including one juvenile liaison officer). A second series of interviews with twenty-two officers was undertaken in September 1991. They were conducted at six police stations in Edinburgh chosen to dovetail with those areas of the city in which the interviews with young people had been carried out. Of the twenty-two officers selected, thirteen were beat officers, seven area constables, and two juvenile liaison officers.

This leaves us with the question of how the accounts generated by the interviews are to be interpreted. What kind of approach does the stand-point of communication require? The first thing to note here is that the practice of interpretation requires the taking up of some standpoint or other. The option of presuppositionless interpretation is not open to us. There is no God's-eye view to be had, no place of hiding far above the discursive fray, no *tabula rasa* waiting to be filled. Interview material does not speak for itself, presenting to its readers a clear, unambiguous, objective meaning. Meaning is always multiple and shifting (although not – as deconstruction would have it – infinite) and it has to be constructed, interpreted, recreated.[6] The process of reconstructing meaning is always also dependent upon the particular concerns and starting points of the reader – a text produced by a police officer, for example, would 'mean' different things to a sociologist trying to understand police work, than it would to a lawyer assessing it as evidence in a criminal trial, or a police manager deciding upon the officer's promotion prospects.

It is therefore incumbent upon interpreters to be open and reflexive about the frame of reference that enables the interpretation of meaning to proceed. For the theoretical standpoint we adopt has all sorts of consequences for the kinds of claims that are capable of being generated. As Thomas McCarthy puts it:

> Our hermeneutic starting point ineluctably figures in our selection of key phenomena, the angle of vision we adopt on them, the categorial frame in which we articulate them, the judgements of significance we make about them, the connections we draw among them and so on. (McCarthy, 1994, p. 231)

The procedures followed in this study are best summed up by the term 'depth hermeneutics'. This refers to a set of interpretive techniques that endeavour to situate the practical, taken-for-granted knowledge of everyday life within the context of existing institutional and social relations, so as to generate a critical reinterpretation of the meanings of such knowledge. Depth hermeneutics is the nearest that contemporary critical theory has come to formulating a set of procedures that can be fruitfully employed in the course of empirical social research (Giddens, 1984, ch. 6; Thompson, 1990, ch. 6). However, the development of a depth hermeneutic approach has to date been largely confined to the level of theoretical specification; its application to the actual practice of social research has been rare (cf. Pile, 1990; see also Forester, 1992). I want therefore to set out briefly its central tenets as a prelude to its mobilisation in the substantive enquiry that follows.

Depth hermeneutics endeavours to steer a path between two established forms of interpretation which it takes to be misconceived in some important respects. It rejects, first of all, the notion that interpretation can be conducted in accordance with a series of methodological rules which – if rigidly followed – guarantee the production of valid knowledge. For no elaboration and application of rules – however detailed and precise – can accomplish such certainty, the indeterminacy of language rendering all social interpretations conjectural and open to question. On the other hand, depth hermeneutics departs from the idea that interpretation is an imaginative, creative process which is not susceptible of methodological elaboration at all. This approach is rejected because it renders the interpretive enterprise opaque and unaccountable, and on the grounds that it fails adequately to grasp the fact that interpretation is always germane to, and shaped by, particular theoretical starting points.

Depth hermeneutics holds that a minimal explication of the process by which interpretations are generated, and of the relationship between that process and one's theoretical standpoint, is vital in enabling the validity of interpretive claims to be judged. Such explication should make explicit the 'angle of vision' on the social world that is being adopted and the kinds of questions that it generates; for only on that basis can it be made clear why some meanings are emphasised over others and why certain kinds of conclusions have been arrived at.

In the present context, a theoretical concern with democratic communication gives rise to three related interpretive tasks. These are (1) an appreciation of the propositional content of young people's and police officers' accounts; (2) a contextualised exploration of the relationship between these accounts and the institutional arrangements and social relations about which they make sense, and (3) a critical reinterpretation of the (possible) meanings of these accounts viewed from the standpoint of communication. Let us take each of these in turn.

The initial concern of depth hermeneutics – one it shares with interpretive sociology and cultural anthropology alike (Schutz, 1967; Geertz, 1975) – is with grasping from the inside the meanings that people ascribe to aspects of the social world. This task – one of developing an appreciative understanding of the world as others see it (Matza, 1969) – cannot be adequately accomplished from the position of a detached and dispassionate 'third person' gazing down from on high. It requires instead the adoption of what Habermas calls a 'performative attitude' to the social world, a cast of mind which recognises that meanings are only amenable to interpreters who participate in the world of which they are a part:

> Understanding a symbolic expression fundamentally requires participation in a process of reaching understanding. Meanings – whether embodied in actions, institutions, products of labour, words, networks of cooperation, or documents – can only be made accessible *from the inside*. Symbolically pre-structured reality forms a universe that is hermetically sealed from observers incapable of communicating . . . The lifeworld is only open to members who make use of their competence to speak and act. (Habermas, 1984, p. 112; emphasis in original)

This follows from the fact that social science confronts a domain which has always already been interpreted by its members (Giddens, 1993). The social world is not made up of 'cultural dopes' entirely at the mercy of structural forces about which they are, at best, dimly aware. It consists rather of people who in the course of their everyday lives 'are constantly involved in understanding themselves and others, and in interpreting the actions, utterances and events which take place around them' (Thompson, 1990, p. 275). Everyday life, in other words, is a skilled accomplishment, produced and reproduced by the actions of reflexive agents, who acquire and monitor a practical knowledge which helps them both 'go on' in routine activities and retain a sense of 'ontological security' (Giddens, 1991, ch. 2).

This knowledgeability of agents – what Giddens (1984, pp. 41–5) calls their practical consciousness – is a vital component in the reproduction of social life and a constituent part of the 'structures' that simultaneously enable and constrain social action. It is for this reason that an appreciative understanding of practical knowledge is a crucial aspect of – and unavoidable starting point for – social research. Practical knowledge, moreover, is something that people think with rather than about. It has a situated, taken-for-granted quality that is not easily articulated to others. The skills and knowledge that comprise it are embedded in practical activities, or carried in highly contextualised forms – such as in the stories, symbols and vocabularies of everyday life. The appreciative understanding of such knowledge thus requires a reconstruction of meanings and claims that are couched in concrete and often narrative terms.

But how is such an appreciation to be constructed? Must it involve – as interpretive sociology believes – a process of 'empathetic understanding' during which the interpreter transposes her or himself into the mental states of another subject? Or does it mean – as Clifford and Marcus (1986) propose – positing the subjects of research as partners in a collaborative hermeneutic enterprise? Critical theory rejects both these (relativistic) ways of proceeding, which it sees as privileging 'first order' accounts of the world, and of failing to articulate clearly a position from which the understanding of meaning is to proceed. Instead, depth hermeneutics views appreciative understanding as a dialogue between a range of competing perspectives, one in which the practical knowledge of situated subjects is entered into a conversation with the standpoint of the interpreter.

This dialogical conception of interpretation has two aspects to it. It entails, first of all, that interpreters bring to mind the reasons that people might introduce if called upon to defend, and make good, the validity claims embedded within their contextualised utterances. These claims can then be brought into a dialogue with the *weltanschauung* of interpreters, during which interpreters come to some kind of assessment as to the validity of the claims that are being made (Habermas, 1984, pp. 115–16). However, the discursive character of the process requires also that the horizons of the interpreter are sufficiently contingent to enable them to be shifted by the practical knowledge of research subjects. Interpreters must always keep open the possibility that they will learn something from the perspectives that are subject to interpretation (what, otherwise, is the point of doing social research?). Conceived of in this way, appreciative understanding amounts to a process of mutual critique and education.

Depth hermeneutics then contains within it an anthropological moment (Giddens, 1987, ch. 1). It sets out to appreciate – by means of a critical dialogue – the meanings that people ascribe to the social world. To this extent it shares with interpretive sociology and cultural anthropology an aspiration, even if it differs in how this purpose is to be accomplished. At this point, however, depth hermeneutics parts company quite fundamentally from all interpretive approaches to understanding social life. For while interpretive social science views the production of a phenomenological 'account of accounts' as exhaustive of the hermeneutic enterprise, depth hermeneutics views it as but an initial stage in the formulation of a more ambitious explanatory account.

The next step in the construction of such an account involves the contextualisation of people's practical knowledge. Practical consciousness always consists of grounded and routinised assessments of particular configurations of institutional arrangements and social relations. These arrangements and relations make possible certain kinds of experience and knowledge while confining alternative ways of doing things to the realm of the unthinkable. Depth hermeneutics thus seeks to couple an appreciative understanding of practical knowledge with an exploration of the relationship between the situated knowledgeability of agents and the social conditions within which it arises. This involves the interpreter drawing upon a social scientific knowledge of relevant contexts so as to explore the 'conditions of possibility' of different kinds of experience and consciousness (Bourdieu, 1977, ch. 1) – a task which necessitates a shift towards a 'third person' perspective.

In the field of police–youth relations, three sets of questions are relevant in this respect. In the first place, one needs to connect the dispositions and claims of young people and police officers with the patterns of interaction within which they are embroiled; for their respective outlooks are always in some measure a product of relatively enduring relations of contact and non-contact. Thus, as we saw in Chapter 1, police–youth encounters – to the extent that they occur at all – revolve principally around adversarial meetings in public places. Only rarely do they involve young people as victims in need of a police service. Here, the interpretive objective is to analyse how young people and police officers generate ways of making sense of these routine contacts, as well as to explore the meanings, understandings and possibilities which get marginalised by extant patterns of interaction.

These patterns of interaction only ever occur, however, within the contours of particular institutional arrangements. We have seen in Chapter 1 that these arrangements – or, more precisely, 'structures of control' (Grimshaw and Jefferson, 1987) – currently enable police resources to be directed towards young people in particular ways, while at the same time denying young people the possibility of either individually or collectively voicing their claims *vis-à-vis* policing. Against this backdrop, the objective of the ensuing analysis is to explore the effects of these arrangements, focusing on how young people and police officers make sense of such exclusion, and considering what issues might possibly arise were their respective voices to be included within any – as yet unrealised – mechanisms of deliberative policy-making.

It is, thirdly, necessary to pay attention to the relationship between existing institutional arrangements and patterns of experience, and the character of social relations within late-modern liberal democracies such as Britain. These relations are currently marked by asymmetrical distributions of wealth and power as between different social groups; the principal axes of division being class, gender, ethnicity, sexuality and age. These remind us that 'youth' is not a natural but a socially-constructed category, and that the crime and policing experiences of young people are always also shaped by a number of other structural determinants. Experiences and understandings of risk and safety, for example, may vary markedly between teenage men and women. Police perceptions of 'youth' may similarly be structured by gender – with boys more likely to be constructed in terms of 'trouble' and girls in terms of 'moral danger' (Gelsthorpe, 1986). The experiences, understandings and cultural capital of young people *vis-à-vis* policing may also depend greatly upon matters of class and place. The consequences of these divisions and the ways in which they shape the experiences and dispositions of different strata of young people must therefore be central to the enquiry.[7]

The final dimension of depth hermeneutics is concerned with formulating a critical reinterpretation of existing social phenomena. This moment of the interpretive enterprise endeavours to draw together the threads of appreciation and contextualisation in a reconstruction of the possible meanings of people's accounts. This future-oriented – even utopian – aspect of depth hermeneutics provides it with its radical, transformative edge. It engages with the present from the standpoint of an immanent yet unrealised future; an engagement which proceeds by 'positing "possible worlds" of what might become the case via programmes of social reform' (Giddens, 1987, p. 48).

This, in the present context, demands that young people's and police officers' accounts are approached with a view to examining both the possibilities for democratic communication, and the obstacles that might stand in its way. This involves the explication of meanings that may be embedded – in inchoate and contextualised forms – within people's concrete understandings of the present. It means constructing from such understandings a set of possible futures which may (at best) be only dimly grasped by agents themselves. It is this reconfiguration of meaning that gives depth hermeneutics its critical (not to say political) purchase on the social world; for by projecting an alternative way of seeing familiar, taken-for-granted states of affairs, it invites people to view themselves and the world differently and act on this basis:

> Criticizing a belief means (logically) criticizing whatever activity or practice is carried on in terms of that belief, and has compelling force (motivationally) in so far as it is a reason for action . . . Now social beliefs, unlike those to do with nature, are constitutive elements of what it is they are about. From this it follows that criticism of false belief is a *practical intervention* in society, a political phenomenon in a broad sense of that term. (Giddens, 1984, p. 340; emphasis in original)

The critical reconstructions of meaning generated by depth hermeneutics are likely to diverge both from interpretations offered by subjects themselves, and from those of analysts employing different standpoints and approaches. In this respect, depth hermeneutic interpretations are – like *any* interpretation of social life – fallible and open to dispute, and their validity can only ever be established by means of a dialogue with those who hold competing perspectives on, and assessments of, the issues at hand. The task of social research informed by critical theory is to construct interpretations which challenge established, taken-for-granted ways of seeing, and to defend these interpretations in any ensuing disputation. In so doing, critical theory aims to keep alive the possibility of a world in which ongoing, reflexive and democratic learning can take place.

3 The Uses and Meanings of Public Space: Belonging, Identity and Safety

Public space looms large in the lives of many young people. Teenagers, perhaps more than any other social group, make routine use of a whole host of local public locations; and they are certainly one of the few groups whose use of public space is not merely fleeting, instrumental and organised around consumption. Yet young people's routine use of such space is not altogether a product of meaningful choice. Rather, it is one consequence of an age-based exclusion from both autonomous private spaces and cultural resources of various kinds; an exclusion often articulated by young people themselves in terms of a lack of any choice – of having nowhere to go, nothing to do, no money to spend:

IL: Why do young people spend so much time hanging around on the streets?

A: There's nothing else to do in Niddrie, except go round somebody else's house. (*21-year-old female, Niddrie*)

IL: Why did you spend so much time on the streets?

A: Nowhere else to go. No money to go anywhere. (*18-year-old female, Craigmillar*)

My aim in this chapter is to make some sense of how young people understand and deal with these exclusions, focusing in particular on how they use – and ascribe meaning to – public space. I examine how the sense of belonging that both male and female teenagers feel towards peer group and place contributes to their identity. I discuss the ways in which the practices of some young people – most notably that of hanging around in groups – can have a detrimental impact upon the safety and well-being of others, and consider how young people seek to maintain their safety while out in public. The strengths and limitations of these security generating practices are also examined and, against this backdrop, young people's reluctance to communicate their experience of crime to the police is analysed and discussed.

In respect of these issues, this chapter consists largely of the reflections of older teenagers on their recent past. This in and of itself may be significant, however. For although the vast majority of the young people interviewed no longer use public space expressively on any kind of routine basis, their memories of such usage and its meanings remain an important constituent of their identities. It will also become apparent during the next four chapters that young people (and, for that matter, police officers) talk about the relevant issues in a largely narrative form; their accounts comprising stories of concrete experiences and events. What follows, therefore, is a reconstruction of the (possible) meanings embedded within these situated narratives, one that focuses, in particular, on their implications for democratic communication.

PLACE, BELONGING AND IDENTITY: THE USES AND MEANINGS OF PUBLIC SPACE

> Because they are so restricted to their neighbourhood or its immediate vicinity, [young people] may be the major producers and carriers of neighbourhood life: its local stereotypes, its named boundaries, its known hangouts, its assumed dangers and its informal groupings. (Suttles, 1967, p. 38)

One of the principal means by which young people use public space is by hanging around in groups; whether on street corners, in local parks, outside local shops, or in city centres and shopping malls. Of course, hanging around is by no means the only way in which young people come to terms with their predicament. Some social practices – such as watching television or playing computer games – are conducted, individually and collectively, in the private sphere (Willis, 1990). Access to public space also depends on the amount of domestic labour that teenagers are called upon to perform, as well as on parental restrictions upon going out – both things which tend to fall most heavily upon girls (Griffin, 1985; Hollands, 1990). Yet the collective appropriation of local public places is an important feature of many young people's lives. It is also a source of much conflict between young people, local residents and the police, as well as figuring prominently in public discourse about the youth question. It is consequently worth exploring its meanings and dynamics in more depth.

One important attraction of public space is that it provides a series of sites in which young people can pass the time free of direct adult supervision. Young people develop male, female and mixed informal groups that enable them to explore public places in a mundane and unstructured manner. As one sixteen-year-old female put it discussing Edinburgh's Leith Walk: 'That's where everybody goes . . . to sit and talk, smoke ourselves to death, that's all we do.'[1] In this regard, collectively hanging around the streets often involves long periods of 'doing nothing' punctuated by outbreaks of sporadic and unpredictable excitement (Corrigan, 1976):

IL: When you say you hang around, whereabouts do you go?

A: Just go about in gangs walking about the main streets, Chinese takeaways and that. Chippies.

IL: Is it boring?

All: Yes.

IL: Why do you do it then?

A: Nothing else to do. (*16/17-year-old males, Gorebridge*)

We used to stand along at the bridge. It was all right we used to get a laugh. Used to be stupid, carrying on, smoking, occasional weekend carry-out, that was really it. Annoying the neighbours. (*20-year-old male, Craigmillar*)

Young people's dependence upon often narrowly circumscribed areas of public space means they develop a detailed practical knowledge of the locality that escapes many other social groups; though, of course, such knowledge is as much constituted by absences, local folklore and stereotypes as by routine experience (Smith, 1986; Anderson *et al.*, 1994). These 'cognitive maps' enable young people to embellish the physical structure of the city with a 'working' interpretation of its divisions and boundaries, and their place – spatially and socially – within it (Suttles, 1967). In this sense, hanging around the streets in groups is strongly associated with defining a sense of place, an integral feature of which is the development of a shared informal understanding of what constitutes 'our area':

A: The Leith area is the bottom of Leith Walk, to ken where Balfour Street is.

B: Pilrig isnae in Leith. It goes right down to ken Bonnington and it stops at the Anfield along at the harbour. And it'll go up to Trinity School.

IL: Who decides where the boundaries are?

C: It's just like they'll not walk into our boundary because we could be walking about there.

A: We ken where Leith is, it goes away along past the docks.

B: This side of the Links is the rough side. (*16/18-year-old females, Leith*)

This attachment to a locality has both an existential and strategic significance for young people, according meaning to particular public places and
enabling them to regulate their routine spatial movement. The existential
identity provided by the collective appropriation of parts of the locality is
built upon both the material use of the streets and a series of symbolic
meanings denoting the importance of different areas: in Unger's (1987)
terms, the city for young people is 'made and imagined'. The significance
of these practices is that they sustain a purposeful identity premised upon
a sense of 'belonging' to an area and its informal youth groupings:

A: Number one is the YLT. Young Leith Team, number one. They
could take anybody.
IL: Do you know any of them?
All: Aye.
A: We're in the YLT.
B: Have you not heard of the YLT?
IL: No.
B: Have you not seen YLT written about? Give us a pen and I'll
show you it. That's the Y, goes along there, and that's the L and
the T. Young Leith Team.
IL: How do you know if someone's in the YLT or not?
B: Because we ken their faces.
IL: What do you have to do to get in?
B: It depends where you stay.
A: YLT is for Leith, YLS is for Lochend; YNT is for Niddrie; YCT
is for Craigentinny. (*15/16-year-old females, Leith*)

It is within this interpretive context that the 'rivalries' which so often
surface between youths from different parts of the city can best be located
and understood. The identities some young people (mainly, though by no
means exclusively, teenage boys) build around an attachment to place is
sustained largely through demonstrating the verbal (and when required,
physical) capacity to 'defend' their area. In terms of the identities such
loyalty occasions, these two endeavours are of connected significance, in
that a central facet of any inter-area conflict concerns the story-telling
which surrounds it:

IL: What problems do you think the police face round here?
A: They face a few problems. Like there's an annual event – about
four months ago – at the Niddrie tunnel, happens exact same day
every year.
IL: What's that about?

A:　All of Niddrie fight all of Bingham, ken at the tunnel. We all have an annual fight, nothing better to do? We enjoy it, it's good.

IL:　How many people?

A:　Sometimes twenty a side sort of thing. If everybody's into the swing of things there's a good 50 of us, 50 or 60. All battering each others' brains out.

IL:　Do people get hurt?

A:　Aye folk get hurt, broken noses, broken legs and everything.

B:　I've seen a few people get a couple of bricks over the head. (*17/ 18-year-old males, Niddrie*)

Much of the available supporting testimony suggests that incidents of violence such of these are relatively rare, if occasionally deleterious in their consequences. For example, during the course of the research a local head-teacher described how the railway tunnel between Niddrie and Bingham served as a protective barrier over which insults could be exchanged and missiles *safely* thrown (cf. Marsh *et al.*, 1978). The police also believe that such 'fights' generate few serious problems:

I've never been to one yet where there's ever been any serious bother. Generally speaking, they're either well gone or it's been blown out of proportion by whoever has phoned in ... The ones I have been to it's usually been a verbal fight more than a physical one and I have never seen anybody who has been seriously injured. (*Male beat officer*)[2]

IL:　Are there any serious fights, or is it just messing around?

A:　Oh, they'll square up to each other from a distance with sticks or golf clubs, but very rarely do you see them attacking each other, somebody's always phoned before then, or if one lot approaches the other will run away. That's all it is. There's never anybody hurt or anything. But cars get damaged, they climb over cars, smash windows of cars, but they dinnae hurt each other. (*Male beat officer*)

My concern is not with 'what actually happens' on these occasions. It lies, rather, in the part these tales of violence play in the construction of young people's identities. It is, of course, difficult to assess the extent to which these stories circulate among young people outside of an interview context. However, the frequency with which violent inter-area confrontations were recalled, coupled with the ease (not to say relish) with which they were narrated, suggests that they play a significant part in young people's oral culture, helping to constitute the individual and collective identities of many teenagers. An identity organised around loyalty to place is not so much sustained by acts of physical violence as transmitted through informal networks of communication, and in this regard, the 'truth' of these narratives is of less significance than their incorporation within young people's daily practices and understandings. For a central aspect of belonging to a place is the capacity to demonstrate an often intricate practical knowledge of the relationship between different locales, and the (usually prominent) position of the local area within the prevailing hierarchy:

> The just dinnae like the folk from Bonnyrigg or something like that. It's nothing to do with Penicuik, because Penicuik is basically a dump . . . Gorebridge, Newtongrange and Mayfield sort of really fight between each other, but if Newtongrange is fighting against Mayfield and Ormiston is also fighting against Mayfield then Newtongrange and Ormiston join up, ken. Then the next again week you can see Ormiston and Mayfield joining up and fighting against Newtongrange. You beat folk up and the next again week you join up with them to batter the folk you joined up with the week before . . . Easthouses, well they're just really pretty small. They just go about with the folk from Whitburn and that. (*16/17-year-old males, Gorebridge*)

Perhaps the most significant feature of identities focused around loyalties such as these is the extent to which they are constituted by narratives of opposition and exclusion. Young people's collective understandings of the local area manifest the characteristics of what Sennett (1970) calls a 'purified community', one defined in a largely negative fashion and based upon distrust of other people and places. This, as we shall see, has a number of far-reaching consequences. For the moment, it is merely necessary to note that such practices are sustained by an aggressive masculinity oriented to asserting superiority over other parts of the city:

> And once you beat Bingham, obviously Portobello have to step in. Then you got Broomhouse, Wester Hailes. Wester Hailes are the biggest in Edinburgh. Niddrie dinnae really fight Wester Hailes. Niddrie fight Craigmillar, Bingham, Porty, the Inch. If you stayed up Broomhouse, it would be Broomhouse fighting Lochend. (*17/18-year-old males, Niddrie*)

BELONGING AND BRAVADO: THE CASE OF 'FOOTBALL CASUALS'

Some of the young people who routinely hang around in public places reinforce this culture of exclusion with the sense of belonging that comes from being identified as a 'member' of the 'football casuals'. In recent years, the 'problem' of 'casuals' has come to assume great prominence within public discourse about the youth question in Scotland. Stories of 'casuals' also figured prominently in the accounts of the young people interviewed, encompassing both those who identified themselves as present or erstwhile 'members', and, more commonly, those who talked of the threat posed by groups of 'casuals' in various parts of the city.

The signifier 'casual' has come to denote two related phenomena of late. In the first place, it refers to a particular youth style consisting of baggy jeans, big trainers and a variety of expensive designer tops. 'Casuals', however, are unusual among post-war British 'subcultures' in that they do not primarily define themselves around a consciously created 'style' (cf. Clarke, 1976). 'Casual' style has over recent years been incorporated into high street fashion in such a way as to lose its connection with any particular youth grouping. Unlike 'subcultural' codes containing moments of genuine invention and spontaneity (Hebdige, 1979), 'casuals' have to a great extent been both literally and metaphorically manufactured by the commercial fashion industry:

> It's people who, like, wear really expensive clothes. There's loads round here. (*21-year-old female, Craigmillar*)

> The 'casuals' are all smart gear and that, ken. A hundred quid for a jumper. (*17-year-old male, Leith*)

A second dimension of 'casual' identity concerns its association with football. In Edinburgh, this takes the form of an attachment to one of the city's two Premier League football clubs, Hearts and (more especially) Hibernian. While this identity can additionally be connected to the areas in which the clubs are located, the 'casuals' are generally perceived to be centred around football:

IL: Is it all to do with football or does it matter where you come from?

A: Certain areas matter, like Leith is a Hib's area and Gorgie's a Hearts area. They're the two main areas. All the areas in between like the Southside, I think it doesnae really matter as a long as you stick with your own group. These two main areas are Hibs and Hearts. (*18-year-old female, Niddrie*)

IL: What do you think the 'casuals' thing is about then?

A: Football, that's all it is. Football and nothing to do. They've got nothing to do but fight. It's a war you can't win. There's so many groups about. They may be cowards, I don't know, but they've got each other. (*16-year-old male, Broughton*)

Many youth accounts made a clear demarcation between practices and understandings oriented towards loyalty to place and those centred around particular football clubs. One even distinguished between the long-standing traditions (and folklore) surrounding inter-area rivalry, and what was taken to be the more recent and transitory phenomenon of football related violence:

IL: What's the difference between say, groups from Wester Hailes fighting Muirhouse or Leith fighting Trinity, and groups of Hib's 'casuals'?

A: Hib's 'casuals' are the ones. They fight for a name.

B: Leith fight for their part of the town. Hib's fight for, I mean like CCS [Capital City Service] and that fight for Hib's, but Hib's only . . .

A: To get a reputation.

B: Leith and all the other groups fight for an area. (*16/18-year-old males, Leith*)

IL: Is all this 'casuals' stuff the same as the football 'casuals'?

A: No, I wouldnae say that because that was going on a long time before football actually got out of hand. Football's only got out of hand the last decade or something like that, whereas that sort of carry on has been going on for years. The old knuckle dusters in the sixties and that, that's what all that's about, between different territories and that.

IL: So do you think that's always gone on round here?

A: Oh yeah, it's gone on for years. I don't think you'll ever stop them. No matter what you do. (*21-year-old male, Bonnyrigg*)

In recent years, 'football casuals' have come to be associated in the popular imagination with organised public violence, both at football matches and in urban public places more generally. They have also attracted a considerable amount of attention from both the media and the police (at the time of the research, for example, Lothian and Borders Police kept a 'casuals' register, and had assigned an officer full-time to monitor their activities). In this context, 'football casuals' are frequently seen to fit the sociological stereotype of the tight-knit subculture; orchestrated by a small clique of older professional criminals who run protection rackets, arrange fights at football matches and raids on pubs, as well as paying any fines accrued by their 'members'. The majority of police officers interviewed apprehended the 'casuals' in this way:

They've got their leaders and they know who's boss and we've seen them getting cars hired and running around in cars. You don't know who owns the car and it'll be false names they've hired the cars under. They drop them off at the pub, they'll do the pub then they're away in these cars. They're well organised, they know what they're about. (*Female area officer*)

They are organised in that you have a core of twenty to twenty-five-year-olds telling fifteen and sixteen-year-olds what to do. They have a gang of eleven and twelve-year-olds running around after them, and they introduce the eight and nine-year-olds to it. But it's not as sinister as people make out. (*Male beat officer*)

Many of the young people interviewed shared this view of 'football casuals' as an organised practice replete with hierarchical structures of decision-making. Such perceptions are, moreover, central to the distinctions young people make between different youth groupings:

A: There's a monthly thing in the CCS. Everybody puts money in a kitty and it goes towards fines, bail an that. The thing is the top men don't do anything at all, they just basically run the place. They get all the others to do the stuff.

IL: But how do you go about organising all these young people all over the place?

A: Well, likes of football, just basically everybody who's a CCS member just meets at the football, newsletters are sent out to each other. They've got campaigns, they had a campaign to get members. And they had something saying to younger members, 'do not carry any weapons' like knives and that. That's quite sensible, but these guys are carrying baseball bats and the top man carries a shotgun. (. . .) I know that the top men in the CCS are all wealthy guys, have jobs with banks and things like that.

IL: What do they get out of it then?

A: Money. It's money, but they dinnae get involved. The run the place, but if there's something they want done they get somebody else to do it for them. (*17-year-old male, Gorebridge*)

A: I know the 'casuals' is an organised gang, it's not just hearsay.

IL: In what way is it?

A: It's like 30 people get together and say we're going to Motherwell this week. So that 30 people will tell their pals and they'll tell their pals. It's all organised. Then they'll all meet up at the end of the week and go to Motherwell and start a bit of chaos and all come back and say, 'did you see what I done to so and so?' That's only impressing. I bet he's got sixteen stitches, and all that shite. It is an organised thing.

IL: What about some of the police saying that they put money together to pay their own fines, videoing their fights and showing them?

A: Of course it's true man, if you dinnae believe that you've not lived man. You have a word with the 'casuals' . . . Just go to any Hib's match, man. You can fucking spot them . . . there's buses and everything, it's all organised. The police are right, I'll give them their due. But the reason they're right is because they've got inside information. And I bet you anything you want that they've got plain clothes policemen amongst the 'casuals' acting, fighting, battering. (*23-year-old male, Niddrie*)

There is little in these various accounts, however, to warrant the conclusion that 'football casuals' are some kind of pernicious Weberian bureaucracy. Rather, they suggest an 'organisation' operating on the basis of a loose pattern of informal networks ('people will tell their pals and they'll tell their pals'). In this respect, perhaps the most significant aspect of the cascade of voices evoking 'football casuals' as a military style operation is that such official and popular imagery helps sustain the existential identity central to the appeal of the 'casuals' as a collective social practice. For it provides those who participate in the (often brutalising) activities of 'casuals' groupings with the sense of belonging and bravado that is an integral part of what group 'membership' means:

IL: You used to knock around with them, the CCS?

A: Aye, Capital City Service. The Hib's 'casuals', the worst in Scotland.

B: Yeah, the worst in Scotland.

IL: Why do you say they're the worst?

A: They've got about a thousand members, probably more, they're basically an organised group. They're like Nazis.

B: Aye, they're like the British Nationals, ken, they're a group but they're organised. They've got newsletters an that. Basically it's a family that runs it, or they used to have a family that run it from Portobello or Prestonpans, one of them, and they're just all mental.

IL: Older people like?

A: Aye, basically from about twenties onwards.

IL: How do you find out all this?

A: I'm a Hib's supporter. I used to go to all the games. (*16/17-year-old males, Gorebridge*)

Viewed from the standpoint of democratic communication and its prospects, these youthful identities have something of an ironic consequence.
The shared practices and understandings young people develop as a response to existent institutional arrangements that preclude the voicing of
their felt experiences and concerns, tend to occasion defensive dispositions
that render genuine mutual dialogue more difficult to accomplish. In the
absence of such arrangements, young people generate a worldview which
divides people into 'insiders' and 'outsiders', those who belong and those
who don't. Against this backdrop, communication with 'outsiders' often
amounts to little more than a symbolic display of the narratives of invulnerability and exclusion that young people develop as a way of making
sense of their marginalisation.

BEING OUT OF PLACE: THE CONSEQUENCES OF NOT BELONGING

The shared practices and understandings discussed in the preceding two
sections are by no means central to the identities and routines of the
majority of young people.[3] However, the interview accounts suggest that
the collective appropriation of public space by groups of young people
generates effects stretching beyond the lives of those who engage in it.
The narratives sustaining such practices come to assume a vicarious
place in the understandings of other young people, representing a constituent part of their interpretations of both the locality and the city as a
whole. Thus, a number of youth accounts demonstrate a practical – and
at times condescending – awareness of the collective activities of their
contemporaries:

IL: What do these groups fight over?
A: Just cos they think they're harder than them, because they're from
      a different area. Most of them are mindless idiots. (*16-year-old
      male, Penicuik*)

They think they're hard. It makes them feel big and important. (*18-year-
old female, North Berwick*)

The manner in which some young people appropriate public space may
also impact upon the lives of other young people in a more material sense,
significantly colouring their perception and consequent use of local public
places. Official and popular discourse – preoccupied as it is with youth
as 'trouble' – seldom registers this aspect of the issue. Yet many young
people's accounts testify to the ways in which groups of youths hanging

around are liable to undermine the safety and well-being of their peers. Such groups can, it seems, constitute a routine nuisance which other young people are required to come to terms with:

A lot of 'casuals' hang around that launderette there. A gang of them. They're really nasty. They pass you and just bump into you . . . I go out on a Saturday and all of them are in town. You get a lot of them hanging round Waverley Market [shopping centre]. Sometimes some of them are so stupid they just walk straight into you and that just fires it off. You've got to get out of there. (*16-year-old male, Broughton*)

It is intimidating for people. I mean that's the central street if you're coming down from town and it is intimidating. And you sometimes get people, you know if you're walking, well unless you walk in the road you have to walk through them, and you get a certain amount of antagonism. (*19-year-old male, Broughton*)

The impact of these collective social practices on other young people is an important consequence of the narratives of opposition and exclusion that constitute them. Such dispositions operate to position other youths either as 'insiders' or 'outsiders' – designations which depend on either their locality, or (relatedly) on whether they 'belong' to a particular youth grouping. This dimension of youth social practices can occasion hostility and violence for those young people apprehended in some practically significant way as Other:

IL: What did you think of the area when you were at school?
A: I thought it was okay. Being at the [private] school it was different though, because you had to wear a uniform, people round here tend to think of you as a snob. I got mugged once and that was definitely because I was wearing a school uniform. That was the reason. (*19-year-old male, Broughton*)

If I wear 'casual' clothes and they're 'casuals', they think I'm a 'casual' and they might think I'm from another team, like if they're Hearts they might think I'm Hib's. I wish you could wear what you want to. I can't without having to avoid trouble . . . They slash people. I got my jacket done. They just slashed it right round the back. Nothing happens because they never get caught. It's a stupid business in Edinburgh because when I was living in the States you never got this crap. You could wear what you wanted to. (*16-year-old male, Broughton*)

Many of the anxieties young people expressed *vis-à-vis* their personal safety revolved around groups of 'casuals' and, in particular, the threat of theft and violence they were taken to represent. In keeping with their more general disposition towards 'football casuals', this was the one aspect of youth victimisation towards which police officers evinced a marked sense of recognition. As one male area officer put it: 'They ['casuals'] pick on sort of teenagers, who have a nice jacket or basketball boots on and they'll steal them off their backs.' The following accounts provide pertinent illustrations of such dangers, the latter coming from a sixteen-year-old male who had experienced a persistent campaign of intimidation from local 'casuals':

> A: If you've got good clothes they'll try and steal them off you. If you're going about wearing an Armani t-shirt they'll beat you up and nick it.
>
> IL: Physically take it off you?
>
> A: They tried to do that to my wee brother and my cousin. My cousin's been beat up a few times because he wears all Armani clothes and everything. (*17-year-old female, Dalkeith*)

> It's not funny when it happens to you. There was a gang when I caught a No. 22 to Canonmills and I walked about and I phoned one of my friends from the phone box down there and two guys came up, three of them, sorry. I said 'Ally, I got to go a minute'. I said goodbye and crossed the road, three of them also crossed so I started walking faster and they walked faster. I was just coming round to the bend. They sprinted up, two of them chased me and one of them ran back. So I jumped into a hedge and I ran. I looked into a doorway and it was closed, and I didn't have a key. So I ran and I was just about to jump over the fence so I could run to the other side and the guy kicked me in the side. I didn't feel it until later I felt some kind of tingling, my whole hand was absolutely drenched in blood. They wanted my bomber jacket and I said 'no'. So two of them held on to it. I can't remember what happened. That's how serious they are. (*16-year-old male, Broughton*)

One particularly evident feature of young people's accounts concerned the problems caused by 'casuals' in Edinburgh's city centre. At one level, these anxieties are a product of the routine use young people make of the city centre and the consequent frequency of their encounters with groups of 'casuals'. Yet such concern is also connected with the fact that the centre of Edinburgh is a partially known space, where the informal networks and local knowledge that provide for ontological security closer to home are correspondingly 'thinner'. In this respect, groups of 'casuals' provide both a focus for more disparate concerns about the anonymity of public space, as well as a reason why it remains so unfamiliar:

> You've got the Hearts at one end you've got the Hib's at the other end, and you get people fighting in the middle all the time. Any time day or night you'd see them, you cannae miss them. It's like on Princes Street 90 per cent of people walking along are young 'casuals', and it's like that anywhere in the town, in the city centre. (*18-year-old female, Craigmillar*)

> A: I'd feel a lot better if the police just got big groups of 'casuals' off the streets, at least to places that arenae so popular. Cos if you're in the town or if you go for a drink and you see all these 'casuals' hanging outside a pub, you dinnae go into that pub. Things like that. It's not even just drinking, it's during the day as well. You see big groups of them hanging about, outside the Waverley Market. I wouldnae pass them. If there was three or four of them at the doors of Waverley Market, I wouldnae go in there. I'd be feared to go passed them.
>
> IL: Are there places in the town you avoid for that reason?
>
> A: There's certain shops I avoid. All the shops where the 'casuals' buy all their clothes. I dinnae like the look of the people. You hear about them. Some of them are people who just dress up like that. It's just the clothes they wear. But you dinnae think of that at the time. (*18-year-old female, Niddrie*)

One must note, finally, that the collective use of public space is a gendered process. While hanging around in groups is resorted to by both teenage boys and girls alike, the extent to which they do so, and the meanings it has for them, vary markedly. A number of the interviews suggest that young women tend to be marginalised within mixed groupings, especially if present with their male partners. As one twenty-one-year-old woman from Niddrie reflected: 'Well ken, I just used to sit at the church and watch them all mucking about; they were all mucking about and I was just sitting there.'

The appropriation of public places by young men can, moreover, have a significant adverse impact upon the lives and well-being of teenage women (Campbell, 1993). During the course of the interviews, young women evinced a particular series of concerns with regard to groups of young males hanging around. The following account, for example, details the problems occasioned for a young woman by groups of male teenagers while she was homeless and 'living' in Edinburgh Waverley railway station:

You get your usual people that'll come up and start acting wide in front of you and that, and start threatening you. Just young people, people my age start threatening you, or they'll call you names, cos you've not got anywhere to stay . . . they just sit there and they make you feel small. Now and again they'll look for a fight, they'll sit and threaten you or whatever, but oh, I dunno . . . Like they used to sit and call you prostitutes and all the rest of it, and I'd get dead angry for being called a name like that, and they'd get dead angry and try to fight you, just for stupid things like that . . . They think they're hard men and all the rest of it . . . I could usually rely on my mouth to get me out of trouble. But I've been hit a few times. Nothing serious, they used to just give you a slap across the face and walk away and leave you. They've got a certain respect, they would never . . . I don't think the people I ever met would ever really batter a lassie senseless. (*18-year-old female, Niddrie*)

Accounts such as this illustrate starkly that young people's access to public space – though formally free and unrestricted – is in reality determined by a whole series of social processes that have to be reflexively monitored and accommodated. For young women, the social practices of their male peers represent one of the most significant factors conditioning the understanding and consequent use of public places. The following account provides some sense of this:

IL:	Have you ever had hassle in a different area?
A:	Hassle from saying stuff, just like 'come here darling' stuff like that. Wolf whistles, I hate them. You get that.
IL:	Do you think it's any different for you being out than it is for young boys being out, boys of your age?
B:	Aye, we get hassled more . . . They're quite crude to us and everything, they just shout abuse and everything.
IL:	What about the rest of you, have you had hassle like that?
C:	You get a few clowns.
IL:	Does it bother you?
C:	Sometimes it does, it depends what they're saying. (*16/18-year-old females, North Berwick*)

Incidents of this kind cannot, however, be interpreted in isolation. For as Stanko (1990) has pointed out, what stands behind the mundane, everyday forms of harassment young women experience in public places is the ever-present threat of male sexual violence; a threat which serves as the framework within which these encounters are routinely interpreted:

I was coming home one night. I was in a taxi but I only had a certain amount of money and I couldn't get right home so I had to get him to drop me off and . . . I stay in Magdalene but it's Portobello district, and it was at Niddrie and I was walking past and there was a man at the bus stop . . . I kept walking and he was walking down the road just walking behind me sort of. He stopped someone else and I think he was just looking for a light. But he seemed to go everywhere I was going. Nothing happened but it really . . . (*17-year-old female, Portobello*)

MANAGING RISK: THE CONTRADICTORY DYNAMICS OF YOUNG PEOPLE'S SAFETY

The above accounts illustrate how the collective practices that provide some young people with a positive identity become part of the back-drop which others have to accommodate if they are to 'go on' safely in public space. It is against this backdrop – one pertaining to the risks of public space – that youth practices take on a more strategic significance as routines for the production of personal safety. As regular users of public places young people individually and collectively become practical 'experts' in managing risk; developing a set of understandings and prac-tices that position particular people and places according to their perceived danger, and regulate young people's everyday spatial movement.

Though much of the practical knowledge young people come to rely upon in this regard is shared, it is always also appropriated by individuals in particular ways. Young people forge a number of *individual* routines concerned to enhance both their material safety and their sense of personal well-being. One of the most prominent of these routines is avoiding sites of perceived danger altogether, through for example, treating certain places as personal 'no-go' areas, or simply keeping a distance from groups of youths believed to be 'trouble':

I never walk up Broughton Street any more. I've been chased up there twice. I always go round the back way to St. Andrews Square. It's not much safer. (*16-year-old male, Broughton*)

No, I've not had any hassle from these gangs. I just keep out of their way. (*16-year-old female, North Berwick*)

They dinnae really bother me, as I say I keep myself to myself. I dinnae open my mouth, I dinnae go about trying to be wide and all the rest of it, you get no problems. (*17-year-old male, Niddrie*)

Trouble, however, cannot always be avoided, and as a consequence, young people have to find ways of negotiating a way out of danger if and when they are confronted by it. One seventeen-year-old male, for example, used to employ the negative stereotype of one of Edinburgh's peripheral housing schemes to deter potential assailants: 'They think it's a rough place . . . you say you're from Niddrie and that and they dinnae bother.' Another describes how his female friend handled an attempt to intimidate her:

> She can handle the 'casuals' no bother . . . She was walking down Leith Walk and they were all standing, you know the corner, there's places where you can go and see them and look at these specimens. On Leith Walk, where the barber's shop is, by Tommy Younger's bar, just down there there's a road, that's where they used to hang about, and I'm not exaggerating, there was twenty 'casuals' at least, twenty of them and they were all staring at Jane and she turned around and she gave this big statement: 'Who the fuck do you all think you are looking at, have you seen enough, do you want to see more!' She pulled her skirt up: 'You sure you've seen enough now, cos you are staring at me that much!' I said 'you better shut you're mouth or they'll all set about you'. They never said nowt to me. They must have thought that this lassie's crazy. *(19-year-old male, Broughton)*[4]

By contrast, others manifest the somewhat resigned belief that carrying on as normal is the most appropriate way of coming to terms with both the risks of public space and their potential magnitude:

IL: Do you avoid 'casuals'?

A: No. I make a point of not avoiding them, because I've been mugged before by 'casuals' and to avoid being mugged I actually ran into a shop, and got wasted by three of them in a shop. So I figured if I'm gonna get wasted in a department store, when there's tons of people about to stop it, you're gonna get wasted anywhere. *(19-year-old male, Broughton)*

> I think women dinnae report it because if those that are shouting at them find out, they're going to do it even more, they ken they'll get a reaction. If you just leave it they think 'we'll get nothing out of her, we'll try somebody else'. *(18 year-old female, North Berwick)*

These various practices and understandings serve as routines for managing (though not transcending) the threats that mark everyday life. Such practices become part and parcel of the mundane process of 'going on' with social existence, serving to minimise the intrusiveness occasioned by the dangers of public space. In this respect though, these individual practices exist in a relation of some tension with one of the central ingredients of young people's safety; for it is being on your own and feeling out of place that most often undermines young people's feelings of personal security:

IL: Do you feel safe when you're out and about?

A: During the day I'm all right, but at night I dinnae, not if I'm on my own. I dinnae feel safe anywhere on my own.

IL: Does it matter where you are? Are there particular places you'd avoid or groups of people you'd avoid, things like that?

A: No. I feel all right even if I'm with one person. But if I'm by myself in the dark I dinnae really feel safe. (*16-year-old female, Leith*)

IL: Why do you think you get chased then?

A: I'm not sure why I got chased. I'm not sure why they chase you.

B: It's purely because you dinnae come from that area.

A: It's usually because you're on your own. See if I was in a group or a foot taller I wouldnae get any bother. (*16/17-year-old males, Bonnyrigg*)

Against this backdrop, the *collective* appropriation of public space by young people can be viewed as a means of establishing and sustaining personal security. It serves to effect both safety and a *sense* of safety for young people in two associated respects. In the first place, hanging around in groups provides young people with a material means of generating security – safety in numbers:

They was usually a lot of us during the day anyway that was down there, and people get . . . when you see a big group of people hanging about the twenty-four hour toilets you feel a wee bit apprehensive anyway. It's safety in numbers for us, and for them as well. There's always safety in numbers. I'd feel scared walking past them if I was by myself or if it was just me and somebody else, but I wouldnae feel scared if there was a big group of us. (*18-year-old female, Niddrie*)

By providing a loose informal network for transmitting experiences of relations in public, the collective use of public places also enables young people to generate a shared practical knowledge of the local landscape and its dangers. Such knowledge, though not shared equally and in the same way by all, enables a sense of collective security *vis-à-vis* public space to be maintained. In this respect, many youth accounts alluded to the connection between a detailed knowledge of the local area, its people and places, and feelings of personal safety:

IL: Are there any places round here that you won't go, places you avoid?

A: No. We just ken everybody.

IL: Is that a good thing or a bad thing?

B: Well it's good if you stay here. If you've stayed here for a long time you're all right. (*16/17-year-old females, Craigmillar*)

IL: Can you remember what you thought about the area when you were at school?

A: I liked it then aye. As long as you keep away from the junkies and that. But with being brought up in this area you ken all the bad folk and the good folk and they dinnae really bother you really, as long as you keep yourself to yourself. (*18-year-old female, Craigmillar*)

However, in terms of their security enhancing functions, these collective practices and understandings have a number of significant shortcomings. It is important to note, first of all, that they depend largely on the oral reproduction of narratives about dangerous events, people and places; stories that become integral to perceptions of public space and its attendant dangers. In circumstances where such narratives are the dominant constituents of young people's knowledge of particular places, such accounts can easily take the form of 'atrocity tales' – rendering places symbolically more dangerous than they are in any material sense, and exacerbating feelings of vulnerability and powerlessness:

IL: Do you find it safe walking about the streets here?

A: No, I hate walking about here, I dinnae walk about here.

IL: Why not?

A: Nothing's ever happened to me, it's just the things you hear about happening though, make you a bit feared to walk about anywhere in case something does happen to you. I mean it's not as bad as everybody makes out, but there is ... I've been warned by the staff in here as well that there is a lot of bad people. (*18-year-old female, Niddrie*)

A further limitation of the security provided by collective social practices arises from their strong association with a loyalty to particular areas and people, a process which operates by defining the boundaries of the locality and excluding others from it. In so far as these collective understandings cognitively divide the city up into 'safe' and 'dangerous' zones (as well as people deemed 'insiders' or 'outsiders'), well-being is achieved only by making certain places 'no-go' areas. Young people are rendered anxious and vulnerable by the very loyalty to people and place that is so important to their identity and security:

IL: Is it a safe place to live here?
A: It is if you ken everybody.
IL: What if you don't?
B: You've had it!
IL: Why have you had it, just if your face isn't known? Why is that?
B: Because we might not like them. They're walking about our streets and we dinnae ken them.
IL: If someone from Muirhouse walked through Leith would they be safe?
A: If we ken they were from Muirhouse they'd get battered. (*16/18-year-old females, Leith*)

IL: Do you get a lot of harassment from them ['casuals']?
A: If it's a different area. In my area I know practically everybody. But in a different area I would. (*16-year-old female, Portobello*)

Taken together, these dynamics generate a situation in which young people end up informally regulating each other's use of urban public spaces; the collective practices and dispositions young people forge serving to reproduce the very problems to which they are a response. The reflections of a twenty-one-year-old male encapsulate perfectly the processes involved:

I think it's backfired on the whole lot of them because they cannae go anywhere and enjoy themselves now because they've all got to stay in Bonnyrigg and what have you. They cannae go down to Dalkeith or anything because if they did they would have to take a baseball bat or something like that, whereas if they hadnae started that in the first place you could have went down and had a good laugh and that. It's totally backfired on them. (*21-year-old male, Bonnyrigg*)

IS CRIME A PROBLEM FOR THE POLICE?: THE REFRAIN AGAINST 'GRASSING'

I'm not going to the police, they make it worse. (*16-year-old female, Portobello*)

I have suggested thus far that the routines and practical knowledge constitutive of hanging around as a social practice serve two purposes. They provide those young people involved with an identity and assist, both materially and cognitively, in the production of personal security. These practices, as we have seen, have both brutalising dimensions and some significant limitations. Yet they enable young people to inject meaning into local public space and equip them with a means of minimising the place that crime occupies in their everyday lives. It is against this backdrop that it is necessary to locate young people's reluctance to communicate their experiences of crime to the police.

One of the most consistent findings of recent crime survey research – both national and local – is that a significant proportion of victimisation is not reported to the police (Anderson *et al.*, 1990; Payne, 1991); something which is even more pronounced in respect of teenage crime victims (Anderson *et al.*, 1994; Aye Maung, 1995). In thinking about youth victimisation it is thus important to avoid a 'police-centred' approach to the issue: one that privileges the police – either empirically or normatively – as the central agency for dealing with (youth) victimisation, and postulates increased levels of reporting as the most appropriate policy objective. Conversely, it is important to avoid a critique by inversion that merely celebrates the informal practices young people use to cope in the absence of the police – their attendant limitations preclude this option.

Any individual decision as to whether or not to report victimisation is of course inscribed with a whole vocabulary of motives. However, in seeking to reconstruct the meaning of youth accounts on this issue, it is possible to make an analytical distinction between, first, non-reporting that may be a *specific* consequence of prevailing police–youth relations and the resulting perception among young people that the police fail to take youth victimisation seriously; and, secondly, that which flows from a practical appreciation of the *generic* limitations of formal policing in securing young people's safety in public places. Let us deal with each in turn.

For the most part, young people associate the police with the routine supervision and control of their collective use of public space. Though it is recognised that the source of police activity is often a complaint from local residents, many young people object to what they believe is unwarranted police infringement of their territory and person:

> The thing that annoys me is that you cannae walk down Leith Walk without getting stopped by them. A persons check, or your pockets searched, or whatever. (*17-year-old male, Leith*)

IL: How did you feel about it when the police moved you on?
A: Aggressive. Because I live in the street, and I thought what right have they got because I live there. I just wanted to punch them. *(17-year-old female, Gorebridge)*

IL: Why do they move you on if you're just standing around?
A: Because they think you're going to cause trouble.
B: They're just being awkward.
IL: Do you think they're right to think that?
A: Not really, because what are we supposed to do, eh? There's nothing about for us to do, we hang about the streets and they move us. What are we supposed to do, sit in our houses all the time, sit and watch the telly? *(16/18-year-old males, Craigmillar)*

Young people also resent the fact the police routinely interpret groups of youths hanging around as 'trouble'. As one sixteen-year-old male reflected: 'If you hang about in a crowd and something happens, they'll automatically think it was you because you're with that crowd.' The conflation of groups of young people on the streets with 'casuals' was a cause of particular annoyance in this respect:

IL: If you could meet the police and tell them what you wanted, what would you say?
A: I'd tell them to get off their high horse and stop accusing all young kids of being troublemakers, cos they're not. Half of the kids on the town are barry [good] people, but because of all the trouble with the 'casuals' and that, all the young people are accused of being troublemakers. If you hang about in a group of people then you're a troublemaker. You might not have done nothing, you might have never offended the police on your life, but you're still classed as a troublemaker for hanging about. *(18-year-old female, Niddrie)*

Though young people by no means consider the policing of groups of youths hanging around to be always in principle illegitimate (see Chapter 6), the dominant understanding of such policing is that it is in large measure both futile and out of proportion. Its overall generative effect is to occasion among young people a mixture of bewilderment, wry amusement and cynicism:

In Princes Street, they just move them from one end to the other end. They get down one end and the policeman shuffles them back up the other end. *(18-year-old female, Niddrie)*

IL: Do you ever get moved on by the police if you're just hanging about?

A: All the time. We always go back and they say, 'this is your last warning. If you come back you're getting lifted'. So we just go back and if they do come they do come, but they never lift you.

IL: Why do you think they keep moving you on?

A: I don't know.

B: It's a waste of time, because we just go back all the time.

IL: Why do you think they do it then?

B: Somebody's been phoning up.

A: They get paid for it, they're no getting paid to go after big crimes, they ken all they've got to do to earn their money is move us on from a street, that's brilliant. (*16-year-old females, Leith*)

The association many young people make between the police and routine control has all sorts of consequences for the (non) reporting of crime. Most importantly, it represents an important background factor against which the police are understood as largely irrelevant to the question of youth victimisation:

IL: Did you ever think of calling the police when you got bother from other groups?

A: No. There was not any point in calling the police. Because with us hanging down there anyway we were just classed as dirt, what they gonnae help us for. (*18-year-old female, Niddrie*)

As a result, few of the young people interviewed had called upon a police service as victims of crime. The accounts of those who had suggest quite strongly an experience which serves merely to reinforce already existing dispositions:

A: Me and Julie, this lassie, we was standing at my old bit [area]. This flasher came past, he only had a jacket on and he kept flashing at us right. So we were near Leith police station and we ran down and told them. They goes, 'you're just telling lies, go home'. So I told my dad, and my dad got on the phone and went mad at the police and they came up and that. So they still said, 'we dinnae believe you' and then my dad's all for them, not believing us. But it was true, what would we make up a lie about a flasher for?

IL: Why don't you think the police believed you?

A: No, they didnae. They just told us to go away and that when we went down because they thought we were silly wee lassies. (*16-year-old female, Leith*)

IL: When you reported the incident [being hassled by a group of 'casuals'] to the police, what did they do?

A: Nothing . . . They just started smiling. They said 'okay, I'll put the word out, I'll see what I can do'.

IL: How did you feel they treated you?

A: They weren't bothered. They had more important things to do.

IL: Do you think they're right to feel like that?

A: No . . . They don't bother about it, they just laugh at you and bother with someone else. Then you feel really stupid when you walk out of the police office. (*16-year-old male, Broughton*)

What though of the generic reasons for not reporting crime to the police? It was noted above that young people develop (collective) knowledge and skills that enable them to minimise the attendant risks of public space, and it is in this broader context that young people's non-communication with the police needs to be understood. Morgan and Zedner (1992a, ch. 2) point out that reporting crime to the police involves young people passing through a triple filter: (usually) disclosing the crime to an adult, having the adult inform the police, and persuading the police to take it seriously. Each of these stages has the capacity to magnify the impact of the original incident. The case might also end up in court where – in a setting perceived as unfamiliar and threatening – young people are called upon to convince lawyers and a jury of the validity of their experience:

A: Aye. I wouldnae phone the police for anything. If my neighbours were getting attacked I'd maybe phone the police for that, but I wouldnae want to get involved. It's not worth it. Cos they make you feel in court worse than what the criminals are. Bloody lawyers and that. It's not worth it. And besides you just get a lot of backlash for it. 'You grass and that, you grass.' Maybe your windows put in.

IL: Is that a real problem?

A: Round here it is. Everybody really keeps to everybody. If I phone the police I'd probably get a kick in. (*20-year-old male, Niddrie*)

Young people's reluctance to communicate experiences of crime to the police is also the product of a widespread belief that reporting crime (or 'grassing' as it is more commonly known) can occasion deleterious consequences. Stories recounting the brutal fate suffered by people who 'grassed' to the police surfaced frequently during the interviews. As one sixteen-year-old female put it: 'Grassing! That's the last thing you do down here, because what you see going on will happen to you.' The importance of such stories is (once again) not so much their proximity to some external reality, but the extent to which they assume a central place in young people's understandings of the dangers of public space. For the circulation of these tales of atrocity among young people serves to sustain beliefs about the amplificatory consequences of calling the police:

A: Aye you cannae really grass people about here, cos you end up getting stabbed or something.

B: If you grass about here . . .

A: They'd smash all your windows, petrol bombs through your windows, kick your door in.

IL: Do you know anyone that's happened to?

A: Aye, this old guy grassed about something over there, old Billy. Got petrol bombs thrown through his window, and got all burnt. Got 90 degree burns all over him. 90 per cent of his body got burnt. (*17-year-old male, Craigmillar*)

Not 'grassing' is also a way of protecting the collective loyalties upon which youthful strategies for safety rest. Collective social practices can only sustain a sense of ontological security for young people if the informal understandings constituting them are harboured from outsiders. It is only by safeguarding their shared knowledge from formal institutions that young people can prevent those institutions from colonising the practices they develop to make practical sense of their marginalisation. The non-reporting of crime is, in other words, one of the few ways in which young people can retain 'control' over relations in public in which they are minimally empowered:

IL: What do you think of people who would tell the police?

A: They should get their throats slit!

IL: That's a bit drastic, isn't it?

B: Well, they wouldnae do any more squealing.

IL: Don't you think it's a bit harsh?

B: There's a few people walking about Lochend with holes in them.

IL: How do you know that?

B: Because I ken the people and I ken who done it to them. (*16/17-year-old males, Leith*)

The overarching generic limitation of formal policing in respect of youth safety is that its institutional logic – to apprehend and convict a culprit – runs counter to the practical logic of young people. By 'handing over' the problem to the police, young people risk magnifying the significance of the incident in their lives and have it take on an existence of its own. To involve the police is to lose control of the situation; it renders young people dependant on the decisions of powerful others, thus making the future unpredictable. Against the backdrop of institutional arrangements that preclude the collective communication of young people's experiences and concerns, it is this above all that explains the practical objective of young people to minimise their contact with the police – something with potentially far-reaching consequences for the possibility of democratic communication between young people and the police.

4 Policing Public Space: The Over-Control and Under-Protection of Youth

Young people occupy a prominent and structured place in the daily workloads and occupational consciousness of police officers. Many of the things officers are called upon to deal with during the course of routine patrolling involve teenagers, especially teenage boys. Noisy and boisterous youths hanging around, vandalism and other acts of petty offending, such matters are the staple diet of police officers when it comes to young people. The following account captures well both the nature of prevailing police–youth encounter and the feelings it so often generates among officers:

> Most of the time we spend with youngsters is prosecuting them or moving them on from street corners. I don't know if it does any good or not. (*Male beat officer*)

My aim in this chapter is to make sense of both aspects of this remark. In addressing the question of how young people's use of public space is policed, I shall explore the range of attitudes evinced by officers towards this aspect of their work, and examine which of these attitudes currently prevails in determining police action towards young people. The chapter also explores that feature of young people's experience of public space which police officers seldom come across: victimisation. I consider how the police experience and understand young people as victims of crime and discuss how officers interpret the fact that so little of young people's experience as victims and witnesses is communicated to the police. In taking up these various issues, my overriding purpose is to understand why young people are over-controlled and under-protected by the police in public places (Anderson *et al.*, 1994).

Before proceeding, two further introductory remarks are in order. This chapter is concerned with police officers' perceptions of young people up until the age of (around) sixteen. In this respect, it returns to many of the issues introduced in the previous chapter and reconsiders them from the vantage point of the police. Given my concern with democratic communication and its prospects, it is also worth noting that the police accounts which follow are of dual significance; of interest not only for their propositional content, but also in terms of what they tell us about

Table 4.1 Competing themes in policing young people's use of public space

	Perceptions of youth, crime and public order	Perceptions of occupational constraints
Orientations to (paternalistic) control	Groups hanging around are 'trouble' Young people are in 'moral danger' Hanging around is a mark of 'parental neglect' Hanging around is 'unproductive' leisure	Public complaints must be dealt with Hanging around is a threat to the police Police task is to maintain order
Orientations to tolerance/non-intervention	Young people hanging around are not a problem Young people want their independence Young people have nowhere else to go	Formal processing is futile and counter-productive Sours police-youth relations Moving groups on is a waste of police time

how police officers talk about their work to a third party (in this case a researcher). We must pay attention, in other words, to both substance and process.

A SENSE OF AMBIVALENCE: POLICE PERCEPTIONS OF YOUNG PEOPLE'S USE OF PUBLIC SPACE

How do police officers understand and relate to young people's collective use of public space? Much of the research on police culture indicates on this point that young people – and especially working class or black males occupying public places – are poorly regarded among officers (Smith and Gray, 1983). This research, however, suggests a somewhat more nuanced picture. It demonstrates, above all, that officers feel ambivalent about both young people's use of public space and the manner in which it is currently policed. The various elements of this ambivalence are set out in Table 4.1.

Three aspects of this ambivalence are worthy of comment. One must note, first of all, that officers understand the relevant issues both generally, in terms of their overall conception of the relationship between youth, crime and public order; and more specifically, as a series of occupational constraints pertaining to police-youth relations. Secondly, one can discern from police accounts two contrasting sets of images about the policing of young people, one geared towards the routine regulation of their collective use of public space, the other anticipating more tolerant and non-interventionist resolutions. Thirdly, in so far as these contrasting dispositions can be located within a single occupational consciousness, they generate a series of moral and practical dilemmas which officers have to resolve on a daily basis. Let us elaborate more fully on each of these points.

One of the most prominent views expressed in police accounts is that young people hanging around in groups are in some way or other engaged in illegitimate activity. Here, officers' objections lie not so much in the effect of young people's behaviour on local residents – they object to the collective use of public space irrespective of whether or not others find it unsettling. Rather, such conduct is taken as a (symbolic) threat to the police's capacity to control the neighbourhood, something requiring a proactive response:

> It doesn't do any harm for the groups of young people to be aware of when the police are in the area ... I think that the police should move on groups from the streets, shouldn't just leave the kids. I'm not talking about speaking to kids and hassling kids but I think that if they're there, they should be made aware that the police are aware of their business. (*Male beat officer*)

For the most part, however, police concerns about groups of youths hanging around focus on specific issues. Foremost among these is the belief that young people's occupancy of public space is a mark of 'parental neglect'. As one male beat officer exclaimed: 'What are the parents doing when these kids of thirteen and fourteen are hanging round street corners until two or three in the morning?' Here, young people hanging around in inappropriate places is mobilised by officers as a means of distinguishing a minority of 'bad' parents from the rest:

> Most of the decent people in Wester Hailes who are bringing up their kids properly, their kids aren't out there standing on street corners. They may be at the bottom of a stair, but it's usually their stair. (*Male area officer*)

One reason why officers take such use of the streets to be a sign of 'neglect' is that they see public places as risk-laden. This is rarely a reference to victimisation, however. Instead, parents are viewed as failing to appreciate the ways in which hanging around exposes teenagers to 'bad company'. Many officers hold what might be termed a 'rotten

apple' theory of young people's collective practices; these being understood as a conduit within which one or two individuals can effect an
undue, negative influence upon an impressionable majority:

> It's quite difficult because some kids won't pay attention, some families
> won't pay any attention, the kids are allowed to roam about. And I think
> that's the problem. They tend to roam about in groups and you always
> find that someone in the group has a bad influence on them. (*Male beat
> officer*)

> The problem is there's a lot of parents about who are not interested where
> their kids are, that's really what it is. The mischief becomes so bad that
> it literally becomes serious . . . like trying drugs and glue sniffing. All
> their pals have tried it, so they just have a wee go at it. (*Male beat officer*)

This individuated understanding of young people hanging around constructs 'the problem' in such a way as to make it amenable to practical
police intervention (thereby obviating the need for more structural resolutions). In particular, it enables police officers to adopt the role of 'surrog-
ate parent', supervising young people's use of public space and promoting
'productive' alternatives to congregating in the streets. As one male beat
officer put it: 'I advise them to go home for their own good.' This paternalistic regulation is aimed particularly at those considered to be in some
kind of 'moral danger':

> IL: Do you think the time you spend with young people is a waste
>   of time?
> A: No not at all, it's useful if we can help them channel their youth-
>   ful exuberance in a productive manner instead of hanging about
>   outside the chip shop. (*Male beat officer*)

> Every single call you go to is different. And if you think you can go
> there and prevent a crime taking place, or prevent some kids from
> coming to some social or moral danger, all to the good. (*Male beat officer*)

A cognate series of police understandings discern young people's collective use of public places as 'unproductive' leisure. In this respect, officers
appear concerned to control hanging around by promoting what are viewed
as acceptable alternatives, such as youth centres, sports clubs or more
private recreational pursuits. This perception is especially pronounced
among officers working in peripheral housing schemes conceived of as
having abundant youth facilities; the reluctance of young people to take
advantage of such opportunities serving merely to buttress an already dim
police view of collective social practices:

They'll say to you, 'we've nowhere else to go, I'm bored, I've nothing to do'. But you must ask the question yourself, surely, if you've got a brain in your head, and there's half a dozen of them there, girls and boys, there must be something they can be doing. You might laugh in my face, but what's wrong with going up to one of their houses and having a game of *Monopoly* or something like that? Something along these lines, or a game of cards, a game of chess . . . If you're bored, if you've so-called got nothing to do, you don't hang about street corners. I didn't hang about street corners. (*Male beat officer*)

'So-called nothing to do.' This encapsulates perfectly the predominant and rather sceptical way in which (most) officers respond to hanging around and its justifications. Here, young people's unstructured use of public space is set against any number of more 'respectable' leisure pursuits and found wanting. It is somehow 'out of place', inappropriate. Young people consequently need to be persuaded, nudged and educated into directing their energies towards more legitimate alternatives.

This however is not the only story to be told. Situated alongside these themes there exist among (albeit) a minority of officers a range of understandings that anticipate more tolerant, non-interventionist approaches to the policing of young people. These conceptions emphasise the importance of the street as a site of young people's autonomy, and conceive of hanging around as a harmless, even 'natural' feature of adolescence:

Kids are bound to want to go out and explore the streets on their own without their mum and dad trailing along behind them. (. . .) They want to go out and explore, do their own thing, which is fair enough. (*Male beat officer*)

It's fair enough if they're hanging around outside school and there are not residents where they are, that's fair enough. There's very few places for them to go. (*Female area officer*)

This appreciation of young people's lot appears in many cases to be based upon officers' own youthful experiences. As one beat officer reflected: 'When I was a laddie I used to spend half my time standing about on street corners getting moved by the police.' This can even result in a kind of 'empathy from memory' with officers recalling experiences from their own adolescence to bring home the point:

I hung around plenty of street corners when I was fourteen, you know. There's bugger all else to do. I can understand. Okay, let's face it. Youth clubs aren't everybody's cup of tea. They do a good job I'm sure for a lot of people, but some kids like their independence, they want to be free of some bloke walking about saying, 'right, we're going to have a game of football now. You split into teams'. They don't want that. So they're going to hang about street corners. Quite honestly, if I see half a dozen fourteen year-olds standing on a street corner and they're not doing anybody any harm, they're not making a nuisance of themselves, if they're just mucking about, fine, just walk past them. (*Male beat officer*)

We have, then, two sets of images regarding young people's collective use of public space, one suggesting the need for police intervention, the other pointing towards tolerance. But how, if at all, do these respective conceptions shape the everyday practice of police work? For answers to this question, we must turn to the organisational possibilities and constraints within which these dispositions are mobilised.

'PIGGY IN THE MIDDLE': POLICING YOUNG PEOPLE'S USE OF PUBLIC SPACE

The recent history of police–youth relations in Britain is replete with examples of young people's use of public space being proactively policed. In areas of long-standing tension, we have come to expect that police officers anticipate trouble and move young people on 'just in case'. Certain symbolic locations – Brixton's Railton Road comes readily to mind – have regularly attracted police suspicion.

A number of the police officers interviewed for this research clearly have some sympathy with these styles of policing, believing that the police ought to respond to the 'problem' of youth by routinely and proactively moving young people on. But this is very much a minority view. There is little testimony to suggest that a dominant perception of hanging around as 'unproductive' leisure occasions the proactive policing of young people's use of public space.[1] For the most part, officers spoke of being 'too busy' to move on groups of youths, or of not wishing to generate unnecessary work for themselves. As one beat officer put it: 'Trouble finds you quickly in this job without you looking for it. It's in moving them on for no apparent reason that you can actually find yourself getting problems.' So long as such groups are not seen as behaving excessively, it seems officers are content merely to 'keep an eye' on them – as one commented: 'At least we know they're there and they're not up to mischief.'

Yet young people's occupancy of public space is an issue for the police.

In a recent survey, for example, no less than 44 per cent of eleven to fifteen-year-olds in Edinburgh reported being 'moved on or told off' by the police during the previous nine months (Anderson *et al.*, 1994, ch. 5). So why are the police so embroiled in forms of policing in which they themselves express little interest? In short, because they are responding to the complaints of local residents. A requirement to act is generated by a combination of local public demands (the informal democratic structure), coupled with an officer's occupational desire to minimise the adverse consequences of his or her actions (the work structure). As one officer tersely put it: 'We're a disciplined body. If I don't respond properly to a complaint I'm in the shit.'

In present organisational circumstances, 'responding properly to a complaint' means moving young people on. Officers here have scant room for manoeuvre and their own evaluations count for little in determining the police response. Breaking up congregations of youths represents by far the easiest way for them to head off further calls from the complainant and thereby avoid any subsequent trouble from their 'bosses' (a formal complaint from the young people is extremely unlikely, something police officers are all too well aware of). Even when the police have some sympathy for young people's plight, and believe the allegations against them to be unfounded, organisational constraints require officers to resolve their dilemma in ways prejudicial to the young people concerned:

> You might know yourself that the kids aren't causing any hassle whatsoever but you have to look out for number one to a certain extent. If you go along and say, 'these kids aren't causing any hassle, I'm just leaving them where they are', they phone up here and say, 'I phoned the police about these kids, the policeman has come down and has done nothing about it'. A lot of hierarchy being the way they are, I'll be the one who gets into trouble. They're not interested in the fact that I say, 'wait a minute, they weren't doing anything wrong, the guy who phoned up is just a pain in the arse'. Their argument is, 'they're obviously annoying somebody, so they've fulfilled the charge of a breach of the peace'. You can't win. We're in a very awkward position. I think it's wrong. We should be able to say these folk are causing no problem, we're leaving them where they are. But at the back of your mind you're always thinking, 'well, if I do nothing here I'm the one who gets it in the neck'. Which is wrong, but it's the system. (*Male beat officer*)

Nor are these fears entirely ungrounded. The organisational constraints impinging upon police officers can be all too real in their consequences. Thus, in the following account an officer – having explained how he had come to know fairly well a group of young people subject to frequent nuisance complaints – recalls the following incident:

> This woman complained again and I went up and they were just sitting there. So I radioed in and said, 'these youths are not causing any riots, I've had a talk with them, they're not making any kind of noise, I'm not moving them on'. The next day I was hauled in front of the sergeant and he said to me, 'what are you doing about it? Those youths should have been moved'. I said, 'when I got there there was no problem, it was all quiet; we have no authority to move them on if they're not committing a breach of the peace or blocking the footway'. And he said, 'well, I'm telling you to move them on'. I said, 'well, I tell you what. You go and move them on, because I'm not' and he said, 'well, I'm telling you, because the chief inspector says so'. And I said, 'well you'll be the right one to tell the chief inspector you can't do that'. And he said, 'well I'm telling you to do it'. And I just walked out of the office. The following day I was up in front of the chief inspector, three days later I was moved. (*Male area officer*)

Police officers then can experience some real occupational binds regarding how best to deal with groups of youths hanging around. For officers ill-disposed to such groups, but who view moving them on as a fairly futile enterprise, these binds are frustrating enough (see below). But among those who manifest some sympathy for young people's lot, these frustrations take the form of genuine moral dilemmas. For irrespective of how they assess the justice of the situation, officers find themselves compelled to move on the group of youths concerned. As one beat officer put it: 'They may have a valid argument, but at the end of the day, if they're told to move then they've got to go.' What is more, many officers appreciate that – by being the 'piggy' that only tries to catch the ball when one side throws it – their actions may serve to sour police relations with young people:

> Okay, they're playing football in the street. We go along to these calls, I don't want to go, I don't want to stop kids playing football in the street. But on the other hand you get a 65 or 70-year-old woman phoning the police who says, 'there are kids playing football in the street, I want them moved on'. We're just piggy in the middle, we're the suckers who've got to go along and say, 'right boys, you can't play football here'. So no wonder a lot of them . . . I wouldn't say don't like us, but that's our job. (*Male beat officer*)

Two brief comments on these processes are relevant here. It seems, first of all, that under the guise of responding to the manifest demands of the 'public', police practice helps constitute a situation in which young people are excluded from determining how public spaces are to be used. In this respect, the police are in the business of maintaining an order which is validated by certain locally powerful (and vocal) audiences, rather than democratically negotiated by a full range of interested parties. Managerialism, with its failure to acknowledge the inequalities in bargaining power that pertain between different policing constituencies, and its emphasis on the police meeting overt consumer demand, seems set to exacerbate these tendencies. Secondly, and as many police officers themselves recognise, these prevailing police practices can exact a considerable toll on the quality of police-youth relations. In particular, they have the effect of reducing contact between young people and the police almost entirely to a series of encounters characterised by the 'paradox of face' (Muir, 1977); situations, that is, in which police officers 'communicate' only one message ('move on'), and where mutual stereotypes inimical to any possibility of genuine dialogue are generated and sustained.

PANELS, PAPERWORK AND PEDAGOGY: THE APPEAL OF INFORMAL SOCIAL CONTROL

Police officers, then, are required to 'do something now' about groups of youths hanging around (Bittner, 1990, ch. 5). But what precisely is the nature of this 'something'? What resources of order maintenance are mobilised by the police and how is this determined? There are occasions when the police deal with troublesome congregations of youths by mobilising the full weight of the criminal law. This research suggests, however, that these occasions are relatively rare. Police officers, it seems, consider enacting a formal charge (such as breach of the peace) only as a last resort, confining such action to circumstances where a group of young people persistently refuse to move on:

> If they refuse to move, then you've got a problem and you have to be seen to be taking some form of action. Because if you don't that's going to encourage the rest of them to congregate at a particular trouble spot and the problems then could escalate. (*Male area officer*)

IL: What if they're there half an hour later?
A: Just move them on again. It wouldn't go on indefinitely. I would have to take some sort of action about it. Initially I'd note names and warn them, but it is an offence not to move on when asked to by a police officer in uniform. (*Male beat officer*)[2]

This reluctance to mobilise the formal machinery of social control is in part a product of how the police see the issue at hand. In the overall scheme of things, groups of youths hanging around are considered by the police to be a relatively trivial matter, and the policing of such groups is viewed as a distraction from the pressing business of 'real' police work. Against this backdrop, it should come as no surprise that formal resolutions are thought inappropriate:

> Basically I think that would be a bit harsh, locking them up for failing to move on at the request of the police. Only in excessive situations would we do that. We've got better things to do than locking youngsters up. (*Male area officer*)

> If they came back time after time after time you would charge them or put something on paper as far as an obstruction was concerned or a breach of the peace. But it's not really worth it at the end of the day, you're just creating problems for everybody. The best solution is to try and iron it out as best as you can on the night, and deal with it from there. If you can build up some kind of trust between yourself and them things will work out better in the long run. If you keep on hassling them all the time they'll probably get worse. (*Male beat officer*)

These dispositions are reinforced in a whole manner of ways by the organisational constraints within which police officers work. Formal action is, for example, liable to mean paperwork for the officer involved, something which runs counter to a well-documented tenet of police occupational culture. It also increases the chances of an officer being rendered accountable for his or her actions: what Ericson (1982) calls 'patrolling the facts' is much easier in the absence of any written documentation. The requirements of an independent prosecution system may also serve to dissuade officers from pursuing a formal course of action:

> It's a vicious circle, unless someone actually point blank refuses to go. Fair enough you could say they were failing to desist but all policemen know that if you were to write that down on a bit of paper and send it to the Procurator Fiscal, it wouldn't wash unless you had something else to back it up. I think the courts these days are so busy that things like that will just get red-penned and thrown away. (*Male beat officer*)

A further, and significant, aspect of the legal structure encouraging the informal policing of young people is the organisation of juvenile justice in Scotland, and in particular the welfare-based children's hearing system (or panels).[3] Police understandings of children's panels relate particularly to the small minority of youthful offenders who officers believe to be in need of formal (and tough) sanctions. In respect of such offenders, the system's social welfare orientation is overwhelmingly viewed as excusing those who should be held fully and individually responsible for their actions:

> I've seen a lot of fourteen-year-olds who are bigger than me, but they think 'oh, he's only fourteen, he's just a young boy and he comes from a broken home'. But to me that's not an excuse because I know a lot of people who come from broken homes and who don't commit crime. They would never dream of committing crime because they know the difference between right and wrong. It seems to get used too much as an excuse, and I think if we were to deal with the individual rather than trying to look at his social background, it would be much better. (*Male beat officer*)

Police views of children's panels are thus largely a product of their (classicist) diagnosis of juvenile crime and its causes. As one female officer put it: 'What the panel at times doesn't seem to recognise is that some of the kids they are dealing with are tomorrow's major criminals.' Here, officers' understandings are constructed – to the exclusion of almost all else – around the paradigmatic case of the fifteen-year-old recidivist who receives a 'slap on the wrist' and leaves the hearing with a beaming grin on his face:

> There's this sort of 'softly softly' approach. You get wee Johnnie breaking into half a dozen houses and he's only fifteen, so he goes up in front of the panel and they just tell him, 'don't do it again'. And he goes away thinking, 'well, that wasn't that bad, was it'. It's like the first offender syndrome. If you're lenient with them then they might go away thinking, 'that wasn't that bad, I'll just go out and do it again'. Or if you're hard on them, they might say, 'I'm not going to do that again'. (*Male beat officer*)

From this vantage point, police criticisms of the panels focus upon two aspects: the perceived dearth of adequate powers available to panel members (what one officer referred to as lacking the 'big stick'), and an absence of sufficient gravitas in the proceedings. For these reasons, panels are thought of as unable to enact a sufficient deterrent effect upon the future behaviour of juvenile offenders:

> I'm afraid I strongly feel that the children's panel system is not a deterrent for a child. Any child going to a panel they're not in fear of

the members of the panel. They know that they can't get locked up. (*Male area officer*)

This perception is (again) reinforced by a number of more occupationally specific concerns. In addition to the time and paperwork it necessitates, referring a case to the reporter serves to terminate an officer's formal involvement in the proceedings. As one beat officer put it: 'That's it, I charge them and that's the last I see of them. I don't have any other role in the whole procedure.' Many officers, it seems, experience this state of affairs as frustrating, either because it reduces the police role to what one described as a 'reporting agency', or because they believe a more active police presence on the panels would be beneficial:

I feel it would do no harm if a police officer, one police officer, was part of the children's hearing system and can be there and seen as a member of the police force who is actually there in uniform. He can ask questions and make sure that a child will not mislead the panel, as some of them are certainly capable of doing. (*Male area officer*)

For all these reasons, many police officers come to view the processing of those under sixteen through the formal juvenile justice system as a pointless, even counter-productive exercise.[4] This is especially so if officers are dealing with those apprehended as teenage recidivists:

You're going in front of panels where kids of fourteen or fifteen have been involved in quite a chequered career and they're getting away with it. You just say what's the point. They're not solving the problem, just adding to it. (*Male beat officer*)

When set against these constraints, and the frustrations they entail, the option of keeping young people under sixteen out of the formal system and dealing with the matter on an informal basis is, for many officers, an attractive one. This course of action has the merit of facilitating the delivery of an informal lecture to the offender consistent with an occupational definition of the offence's 'seriousness', as well as enabling them to monitor the progress of the situation over coming weeks and months. It also allows officers to investigate the family situation and assess the chances of that young person pursuing the 'right path' once they leave school:

I honestly just generally sit down and chat with kids really. Try and show them the error of their ways as it were. And I sometimes have followed up with a phone call to their parents, maybe six weeks later to find out what's going on. It's not policy but that's about all I can do. (*Male beat officer*)

What is more, by keeping young people under sixteen away from children's panels, and withholding what is viewed as the 'big stick', police officers are able to deploy the threat of a harsh 'post-panels' criminal justice system as a 'bargaining counter' during the course of an informal disposition:

> I'll say to them, well, look, you're now fifteen years of age and committing a crime of theft. Next year or in four months when you're sixteen, you're going to be treated in the eyes of the law as an adult. Should you commit the same crime again I don't require to come up here to speak to your parents. I don't require them to be present when you are cautioned and charged. Do you realise that you can be detained or arrested and taken to a police station. (*Male area officer*)

It appears, then, that young people's collective use of public space is subject largely to a system of informal social control, one enacted by local residents and undertaken by the police (cf. Meehan, 1993). If young people get out of hand, the machinery of the criminal law is available and sometimes resorted to. But for the most part formal sanctions function as just one of the levers officers use to expedite 'on the spot' order maintenance. This amounts to what one might call pedagogic policing. The police's primary concern is to keep young people 'in place' by monitoring their activities and encouraging where necessary alternative and more 'wholesome' ways of passing the time. It is a practice based, not on mutual dialogue, but on 'communicating' to young people a series of messages about the norms of local public order, the places they can and cannot use, the people they should and should not be seen with, and the role of the police as ultimate arbiters of legitimate conduct (cf. Cohen, 1979).

YOUNG PEOPLE HANGING AROUND: A PROBLEM FOR THE POLICE?

Most police officers at some time or other confront the following question: what can the police do about the disputes generated by groups of youths hanging around? The answer in short is very little. And it is the practical realisation of this which generates among officers what is perhaps the most deep-seated aspect of their ambivalence regarding how young people are policed. One of the most common refrains expressed by police officers about the policing of congregating youths is that it represents a waste of police time. For some this view is borne, not so much of ambivalence, but of frustration. Here, officers sense young people as being practically attuned to the limits of police powers and unwilling to heed police instruction. As one officer bemoaned: 'A waste of time definitely. It's in one ear and out the other. They'll be back in half an hour because they know the score. They've done what you've asked and if they come back again all you can do is start from scratch.'

The dominant view, however, *is* best captured by the term ambivalence. Here, police involvement with problems arising from groups of youths hanging around is perceived as no more than a temporary palliative. The police, it is thought, can at best merely 'keep people happy for the night' by containing the disputation within acceptable bounds:

IL: Does it [moving on groups of youths] ever solve the problem?

A: No, I don't think it's going to solve the problem at all.

IL: What does police intervention achieve then?

A: I don't know. It's all part of it. The police are there and the youngsters know the police are there. If the police weren't there I would probably think the situation would be a lot worse, because they would be able to do what they wanted and they would know that no-one could do anything about it. If we know they're there and they know we're there, it keeps things at a good level. (*Male beat officer*)

Police officers recognise that their intervention seldom gets to grips with the problem at hand. As they see it, the police role is crisis intervention. They move the 'problem' elsewhere and secure for local residents some temporary respite from local youths. But they accomplish little else that is positive. Some officers even consider this kind of intervention to be counter-productive, believing that it amplifies already existing tensions:

If we say we've had a complaint and they say, 'that's that old so and so from whatever house'. I say, 'no names, no packdrill, you either button it or go away'. You wait ten minutes later, then the window's been tagged and they're off. Then you've got to try and find them, so sometimes it can just antagonise the situation by going in there trying to deal with it. (*Male beat officer*)

It gets their back up and I know how I would feel if I was getting hassled like that. I'd want to go somewhere else and I'd start gathering somewhere else and then the police would come along there and shift me from there. And I would say, 'well, I'll go and stand here'. And I would go and stand there and eventually get shifted from there. And eventually I would get so fed up I'd just keep moving and I would make a point of being boisterous. (*Male area officer*)

A constituent feature of this understanding is the sense that police intervention generates resentment among the youths concerned. As one female
officer remarked: 'They think we're just coming and telling them to shift,
not listening to anything they say'. In this respect, many police officers
evince an acute appreciation of the hostile dispositions that prevailing
police practice can produce:

> I would resent it as a young person. If I was just standing there with a
> group of my mates, just chatting maybe, having a laugh, telling stories,
> whatever they're doing and a cop comes up and says, right, move on.
> Why? What have I done? You're obviously going to resent it. (*Male area
> officer*)

> Yes, even though we try and explain to them why we're doing it,
> because a complaint has been made. They I think, generally speaking,
> think that we are doing it off our own back and it obviously doesn't help
> the relationship between the police and youths. (*Male beat officer*)

Of all the police perceptions that point in the direction of non-intervention,
the belief that police involvement is a waste of time is perhaps the most
widely and strongly held. Yet it rests uneasily alongside an equally embedded set of understandings which consider the regulation of youth practices to be quite properly a police task. A police-centred view of how best
to deal with congregating youths represents a fairly stock theme within
police accounts, surfacing time and again in refrains such as: 'If the police don't do it, who's going to?', 'Somebody's got to keep the peace'
and 'The shit stops here'. Such comments suggest that police officers find
it hard to think about youth social practices outside of an occupational
paradigm signifying 'disorder'; one which enables them to sustain the
resigned, indeed somewhat apocalyptic, conclusion that no other agency
is capable of undertaking the required task – that of maintaining control:

> A:　If they cause a nuisance you've just got to say, 'enough, time to
> 　　go, goodbye' and so on. And they'll be muttering under their
> 　　breath at you that you're an old sod or whatever, but you've just
> 　　got to accept it. It's what the job is.
> IL:　Do you think it solves the problem?
> A:　No, not in the slightest. Moving the kids on from street corners
> 　　and telling them to stop playing football? Not in the slightest.
> IL:　Do you think it's a police job?
> A:　Well, moving them on if they're causing a nuisance, yes, but again
> 　　that's what we're here for I suppose. (*Male beat officer*)

Here, succinctly put, one finds a perfect encapsulation of police ambivalence towards the policing of young people's unstructured use of public space. This ambivalence couples a sense of *futility* in respect of police engagement with the issue, with a *fatalism* about the prospect of any more embracing (non police-centred) remedies. It creates among officers many frustrations and dilemmas, dilemmas which currently find concrete resolution in the organisational requirement to 'do something now' in the face of local (and vocal) public demands. The principal consequence of this is the transformation of what is in effect a series of disputes about the legitimate use of local public space into a problem of 'law and order'. And herein the lies the crux; for once transposed into this 'structure of attitude and reference' (Said, 1994), the issue permits not only of no negotiated, democratic solution, but of no lasting settlement at all.

THE POLICE AND YOUTH VICTIMISATION: UNACKNOWLEDGED, UNDER-PROTECTED

I don't think it's too much of a problem, not victimisation of youngsters, not really. (*Male beat officer*)

This quotation reflects what is perhaps the prevailing view among officers regarding youth victimisation. Young people rarely present themselves to the police as consumers requiring a service and their experiences as victims consequently have little impact on the routine workloads of police officers. The contrast with young people in 'trouble' could not be more stark. As one officer put it: 'It isn't a problem. You know it goes on, but it's not reported to us as often as it is happening. So unless we're told about it we're not going to look for victims.'

In an occupational culture which privileges an experientially-based 'common sense', this can be of some significance. Research on police culture has consistently documented that officers claim a 'we know best' expertise regarding matters of crime and policing (Holdaway, 1983; Fielding and Fielding, 1991). Yet such a claim does not appear to extend to the victimisation of the young. Lacking practical knowledge, officers are reluctant to speak with confidence about this aspect of the crime question. As one officer commented: 'We don't know exactly what's happening out there. We only hear about a very small percentage of it.' The police, it seems, approach the issue of youth victimisation with evident caution – dimly aware of the existence of a problem, yet unsure of its magnitude and significance:

IL: How big a problem do you think it is, young people's victimisation?

A: I think it's worse than our books show, definitely. (. . .) Just talking to the kids in general, they're very loathe to report things. Okay, it's maybe only minor assaults, or wee sorts of battles in the street, but they won't report it to us because there's gangs involved and they're afraid it'll go further. (*Female area officer*)

It's hard to say whether it [youth victimisation] ever all comes to light. This is the problem. A lot of it's probably happening. I mean, how much crime goes undetected? How much crime goes unreported? I don't know. (*Male area officer*)

One consequence of this is that when police officers either confront, or reflect upon, the question of youth safety, they do so in terms of their more familiar occupational experiences and concerns. Thus, a number of officers did consider young people to be at risk in Edinburgh's city centre (especially at night), this being one locale in which the police are likely to encounter young people as victims irrespective of whether or not the incident is reported:

When you've got such a large number of young people coming into town, a certain percentage end up being victims, obviously. Again, assault and robberies, that kind of thing. There's a tremendous amount of fear within young people in the town centre of groups of gangs and the young people tend to be very, very wary of these people. (*Male beat officer*)

IL: How big a problem would you say young people's victimisation is?

A: I'd say it's a major problem in Edinburgh. (. . .) I wouldn't go up the town myself after ten on a Friday or Saturday night, I really would avoid it, unless I was working. I would make a conscious effort to avoid it . . . if you're going up town when you're sixteen wearing a nice leather jacket, people will rob you of that leather jacket. It's not an epidemic yet, but it's not far off it. (*Male beat officer*)

Recognising this context of experience is vital if we are to come to terms with how police officers understand young people as victims of crime, for it has great bearing on whether or not young people's victimisation is taken seriously by the police. As recent criminological research and reflection has shown, the status of 'victim' is one that has to be earned, and the

ease with which this is accomplished differs markedly among social groups
(Walklate, 1989). Some groups – the elderly are a prime example – fit
easily into prevailing conceptions of what Christie (1986) calls the 'ideal
victim'; while others – such as victims of rape and sexual assault – have
had to engage in a long and continuing struggle in order to have their
experiences acknowledged as worthy of police attention.

Young people have long been positioned outside the boundaries of the
'ideal victim'. Official and popular discourse about crime tends to view
young people as 'trouble', rather than as regular users of public space
vulnerable to its attendant risks.[5] Among police officers, this dominant
public mood is reinforced by routine contact with young people in circumstances of conflict, a pattern of experience which significantly colours
how young people's victimisation is viewed. What results is a climate of
attitude and experience which enables officers to generate and sustain a
distinction between 'legitimate' and 'disreputable' victims:

> I think the company they keep has a lot to do with it . . . If they say,
> 'I was out on the piss looking for a fight and got jumped', tough shit.
> But if the guy's walking along the street and he gets jumped for no
> apparent reason, the guy's not been in bother before and not looking
> for trouble, then of course your attitude to him is going to be different.
> It's difficult to keep a straight attitude to everybody once you've found
> out the circumstances or the background to it. It's not easy to keep the
> same attitude towards them all. (*Male beat officer*)

This bifurcation is pivotal to the way in which officers think about young
victims and is worth elaborating upon. It surfaces most often in respect of
groups of young people hanging around. Encounters with such groups
constitute, as we have seen, a large amount of current police dealings with
young people, and as such, they provide an interpretive framework through
which the police assess young victims. This framework has two effects. It
results, first of all, in the dismissal of much teenage victimisation as 'kid's
stuff' – trivial incidents (encountered during a passing adolescent phase)
which have no either immediate or lasting impact upon the quality of
young people's lives:

> I suppose you get them complaining about each other in terms of petty
> assaults and things like that, but these are the kinds of things that you
> don't submit reports about. Kids will be kids. No doubt there will be
> times when it's probably more serious, but you just treat it as though it's
> just kids and I think most of the time it's just kids being kids. (*Male area
> officer*)

IL: Would you say that it was a big problem, young people's victim-
     isation?
A: I wouldn't say it's a big problem, no. I think there's more inter-
     school rivalry than anything else. In most cases, it would be by
     youngsters from a different area or locals doing it to youngsters
     from a different area passing through. I wouldn't say it's a major
     problem. (*Male beat officer*)

This framework gives rise, secondly, to the view that young people's
victimisation is in some way or other their own fault. As Christie (1986)
notes, an 'ideal victim' must neither be complicit in the circumstances
leading up to the offence, nor have prior knowledge of their assailant.
Young people rarely, in the circumstances of inter-group rivalry, fulfil
these criteria. By hanging around in groups they are deemed guilty of
contributory negligence. Their victimisation is, as one officer put it, 'a
problem of their own creation'; a further and only to be expected consequence of mixing with 'bad company':

They know what their friends are like and what's going to happen when
they get involved with that type of people, it's going to lead to crime,
to somebody getting hurt. If they go out with so and so and they know
he's a bit of a tough nut, situations arise where they get involved in
fights or gang fights; and they're not as tough as he is and they get a
doing or end up doing somebody in or having to do something they
wouldn't otherwise do to prove how tough they are, that they're part of
the team or the gang. (*Male beat officer*)

The process of distinguishing between 'legitimate' and 'disreputable' victims operates in two further ways that are worthy of comment. It is, first
of all, gendered in significant respects. Some police officers view the risks
of public space for young women as entirely the responsibility of potential
male assailants. As one male beat officer put it: 'The reason for violence
is always the fact that it's the assailant, the guy that attacks the woman,
it's not her fault, it's his fault.' Others however, by positioning young
women's safety in the domain of sexuality, come to view the victim as in
some way responsible for her plight:

A: From a male's point of view, some of them I would say are asking
     to be sexually harassed because of the lengths of the skirts. You
     could turn round and say it's just the fashion, but they have to sort
     of come and go a bit and remember that because they're a young
     lady they're going to be a bit vulnerable there. Because basically
     it's the animal instinct in the guy.

IL: Do you think it's right that girls should have to worry about what they're wearing when they leave the house?

A: No, I don't think it's right, but there again one has to sort of not dress too over the top. I'm talking about bordering on the tarty sort of level. I'm not saying they should have to say, 'oh wait a minute, I'd better not put that on I might get raped', but then again, they've got to have a wee bit of decorum as it were. Maybe it's my old fashioned point of view, but then again they've got to watch, because there are these sexual deviant types out there, I'm not talking about guys like you and I. You've got to think about the weirdos. (*Male beat officer*)

This account provides due illustration of how the process of bifurcation works to the detriment of young people. Such is not always the case, however. There are circumstances in which young people are constructed by the police as 'legitimate' victims. The view that crime against young women is the sole responsibility of the male assailant provides one example. But there are others. Most commonly, this categorisation is accorded to young people minding their own business who find themselves innocently caught up in the violence of their peers. As one officer remarked: 'They're people who never have been in groups and they're looked upon as soft targets if you like. They go up the town and for one reason or other they get filled in by somebody, usually groups of youths.' Sometimes, class is used as the relevant distinguishing category, with middle-class teenagers being viewed as the prey of 'rougher kids' from nearby estates. As an area officer whose 'patch' crossed the spatial divisions of poverty put it: 'Some of your streetwise kids from Wester Hailes will certainly pick upon these kids from the good class areas.' For others, the label 'legitimate' victim takes in those victimised for either wearing the 'wrong' clothes, or for being where they do not 'belong':

IL: Do you think young people bring these sorts of things on themselves?

A: Very seldom, I would say. As I said before, just probably what they're wearing or what area they come from is more to do with it than anything else. (*Male beat officer*)

These accounts demonstrate that current patterns of police–youth contact can have important effects on how young people's experiences as victims of crime are understood by the police. A dominant paradigm of youth as 'trouble' becomes a lens through which police understandings of youth victimisation get filtered. This of course can operate to the benefit of those

believed to be 'innocent' victims; but for the most part it serves to prejudice the interests of young people *vis-à-vis* policing. It minimises the impact
that questions of youth victimisation have upon the police's occupational
consciousness (and policy agendas), and undermines the claims that young
victims are presently able to effect over police time and resources. So long
as this continues, young people will remain under-protected as users of
public space.

POLICE PERSPECTIVES ON REPORTING CRIME

> I honestly can't remember the last time any youngster has volunteered
> any information to me regarding an incident. (*Female beat officer*)

Criminological research has emphasised time and again that the successful investigation of crime requires information to be forthcoming from the
public. It is estimated that between 77 and 96 per cent of crimes recorded
by the police are initially reported to them by a member of the public
(Bottomley and Pease, 1986, p. 34). Research on police work has also
pointed out that the willingness of people to cooperate with the police
varies among social groups, with young people – and especially black
youth – being among the most reluctant to come forward (Kinsey *et al.*,
1986).

The police officers interviewed for this research are all too aware of
these issues. They know that relatively few young people are willing to
communicate information about crime to the police. It is an almost daily
occurrence for them to be confronted with a determined, silent teenager
adamant that he or she 'saw nothing'. The following accounts provide
some flavour of this:

> There's an unspoken law, you don't 'grass'. Every youngster you get
> in now, they don't 'grass', that's what they'll say to me. (*Male beat
> officer*)

> I think quite often you're banging your head off a wall sometimes
> asking them, although we do always ask, but nine times out of ten
> you know what the answer is going to be before you ask the question.
> (*Male beat officer*)

In making sense of how the police understand this phenomenon, it is
useful to recall the distinction (introduced in Chapter 3) between generic
and specific reasons for non-reporting. A number of officers discern young
people's lack of communication in generic terms and manifest a grounded

recognition as to why young people keep their experiences from the gaze of the formal criminal justice system. In this respect, police understandings are dominated by two themes – fear of reprisals, and inconvenience and intimidation at the hands of the courts – both things which are perceived to happen most often to 'innocent' victims:

A: You go and talk to them, 'what did you see?'. 'I didn't see anything.' 'But that's your mate lying there.' For several reasons, you don't want to be a 'grass' and they're also scared of the person who's done the initial crime, they could be the next one. Or if they've got to give evidence in court, they hate going up to court and I can't say I blame them. It's a total nightmare up there.

IL: Do you find it frustrating?

A: Yes, but you can also understand their attitude. They say, 'if I tell anyone I'm going to get a doing, my tyres are going to get slashed, my family's going to get victimised because I spoke against that guy for doing it'. It's going to make you think twice. Of course you can understand it. (*Male beat officer*)

Let us examine fear of reprisals first. Here, many police officers evince a marked appreciation of the everyday reality of young people's lives. As one officer remarked: 'They go to school with these people. They are walking along the street every day and they'll see them, so whoever it is they grass on is going to bump into them sooner or later'. In particular, officers understand that in circumstances where young people are in routine contact with one another, the consequences of involving the police can be both immediate and lasting:

When you approach a victim of a crime and ask them if they know the identity of the persons, nine times out of ten they do but they are very reluctant to come forward and volunteer any information because they're terrified of the reputation these gangs have ... Edinburgh being a small place, young people want to concentrate in the town centre, St. James [shopping] centre, Waverley Market, the Bridges, wherever; and they know if they turn round and shop people who assault and rob them, they're terrified they're going to meet them again. There's every likelihood that they're going to rub shoulders with them again in the future. This is where the tremendous fear is. (*Male beat officer*)

These accounts suggest that officers share many of young people's concerns *vis-à-vis* reporting. In particular, they demonstrate an acknowledgement among officers of how reporting victimisation to the police can – by invoking reprisals – amplify the consequences of the original incident:

In certain circumstances when the police get involved it just makes
the problem worse . . . I've seen it happen where he [the offender]
just goes back and assaults the person again. Whereas if the police
aren't involved they might not. What does the victim do in those circumstances? (*Male beat officer*)

With respect to appearing in court, officers have a large measure of sympathy for both young and adult victims alike. Central to this is what the
police view as a shared experience. Officers, like victims and witnesses,
encounter much of the frustration and anxiety that accompanies both mill-
ing around for long periods in courts, and the ensuing process of giving
evidence. This occupational disquiet is easily transposed into empathy for
those 'innocent' victims and witnesses who suffer a corresponding fate:[6]

There's definitely an intimidating thing about going to court. I feel sick
before I go into court, it's a horrendous thing, I must admit. As soon
as I stand up in the witness box I'm fine, but the feeling before you go
into court is horrendous, it's not a nice feeling at all. The whole thing
about officialdom, for a lot of people it's too much hassle for them.
(*Male beat officer*)

These dispositions, rooted as they are in experiences with which officers
condole, intimate a certain appreciation of the reasons why young people
choose not to involve the formal criminal justice system in their lives.
They also suggest, interestingly, that not all officers hold a police-centred
view of youth victimisation. Some, it seems, are cognisant of the limits of
what the police, and the criminal justice system more generally, can do to
ensure young people's safety in public. This may even result in a working
respect for young people's decision not to report crime:

I'll never, ever pressurise anybody into being a witness. They've got to
live there twenty-four hours a day. It's not easy, if you're frightened
about people nearby or in the area. I don't think you can browbeat them
into it. (. . .) We can't protect them twenty-four hours a day, however much
other people may say so. I think that's a fact of life. (*Male area officer*)

These understandings must be situated, however, alongside a further series
of accounts which consider young people's reluctance to report crime to
be more specifically associated with the police. Here, a history of poor
experiences of the police is seen as particularly relevant. The following are
typical:

It's a possibility that they don't want to help us. Even stemming back
from our younger days if you kept getting moved by the police you'd

not bother telling them: 'I saw nothing, I turned my back at that particular moment.' (*Male beat officer*)

You hope that someone will step in and give you a hand. But if that person walking along the street had dealings with the police before and they weren't treated very well, they might say, 'stuff them' and walk off. (*Male beat officer*)

Within this frame of reference, a number of officers clearly connect a reluctance to help the police with a passing adolescent phase during which young people are, and want to be seen as, 'anti-authority'. Against a backdrop of police–youth encounters marked by the 'paradox of face', such an explanation is both apparent and appealing. But its effects – from the standpoint of democratic communication at least – are detrimental. For it enables officers to dismiss young people's perceptions as transitory and unworthy of any serious consideration (thereby enacting a police variant of popular approaches to many youth issues). It also rationalises a paternalistic desire to 'educate' young people about the importance of helping the police:

I think with young people there is an attitude that you don't want to be seen talking to . . . I think it comes down to authority figures. I think people go through a stage where they think they're rebelling against authority, they might never actually do it, and the police come top of the league as far as authority figures are concerned, then you work your way down to social workers etc. So I often think maybe it's a thing against authority, they don't want to be seen cooperating with the authorities. (*Male beat officer*)

It is possible then to detect a certain ambivalence among officers. On the one hand, we find sympathy for young people's decision not to report crime; while on the other, we encounter a more dismissive cast of mind. But which of these attitudes predominates within the police? I believe it is the latter which asserts itself. Ultimately, police officers subscribe to a police-centred view of youth victimisation which holds low levels of reporting to be a problem in need of some remedial attention. This is so for two reasons. In the first place, officers experience young people's unwillingness to pass on information as a source of considerable frustration, both in terms of the impediments it places in the way of a successful prosecution, and because of the limited steps officers may employ to deal with the situation:

It can be quite frustrating, yes, because it makes our job a lot harder, you know. You are maybe looking to solve a crime which you want to solve because every policeman, no matter what some people say, they always want to get to the bottom of it, you know. There's nothing better at the end of the day than getting whoever has committed the crime and put them in front of the court. So, obviously, every obstacle that's put in your way, whether deliberately or not, by these people makes it more awkward and obviously that's frustrating. (*Male beat officer*)

The second reason is also suggested by this account. It reminds us that police culture is one in which arrest and prosecution are highly prized. The police view themselves as offering one central service to victims (what one officer called 'trying to detect the offenders') which young people are unwilling to take advantage of. No matter that this service is the one most likely to dissuade teenagers from calling for police assistance – arrest and prosecution being the outcome which amplifies most the consequences of the original incident. From the police vantage point, young people are seen as as doing themselves a great disservice. As one officer put it: 'I mean they're the losers, we're not the losers, I would say, as such. Albeit we haven't got the person for the crime but that's a numbers game in some respects, but the victims themselves are the losers because they're not willing to come forward.'

The corollary of these police-centred understandings is that officers endeavour to promote increased levels of reporting. Young people's reluctance to pass on information sparks a variant of what I earlier described as pedagogic policing, a practice oriented to steering young people out of their 'socially unaware phase'. These efforts can take a number of forms. They are embodied formally in police–school liaison schemes. More routinely they take the form of officers 'making themselves known' to local teenagers. In either case, the object of the exercise is to generate trust between young people and the police; something which evokes those halcyon days when adolescents knew and respected the 'local bobby':

In that way the kids actually do see you in a different light and then they realise you're just another member of the human race, you're not the pig they all refer to you as. I know fine that I can get information from the kids that I've got to know fairly well. The kids have on occasions asked to see me because of something that has occurred but that has only happened through hard work by myself in getting to know the kids. (*Male area officer*)

It is in the context of this attempted 'trust building' that a final set of police frustrations regarding groups of youths hanging around is to be found. Already situated in a register of experience and apprehension signalling 'trouble', this practice now comes to be viewed as an obstacle to police efforts to tackle juvenile (and other) crime. As one officer rather disparagingly put it: 'Oh yes, this is the thing. You can't grass on your mates, and all this'. Faced with this situation, many police officers make strenuous efforts to break down young people's collective wall of silence. A number of officers suggested, in particular, that they endeavour to elicit information outside of situations (characterised by the 'paradox of face'), where young people feel compelled to display their invulnerability *vis-à-vis* the police in front of their peers:

I think if you get a young person on a one-to-one basis, or two of them, any more than that and they're not going to speak to you at all, because they're going to try and live up to their friends, this code of not grassing and things like that. If we know they're part of a group that hang about, we can go to their house and speak to their parents, ask them if they know anything, what happened, and generally they're not too bad. If their parents are there they encourage them to speak as well. (*Male beat officer*)

They all do it. They'll all grass, but they just don't want to admit it and they don't want to be seen to be, so you've got to attack it in a different way now. You've got to make sure they're not seen to be a grass when they're actually doing it. (*Male beat officer*)

These perceptions of course have a rational kernel. There are situations where young people generate excitement, and raise their self and peer-esteem, by 'acting up' in front of the police. This is one of the constituent features of encounters marked by the 'paradox of face'. However, by taking such a wholly negative view of these youthful understandings, prevailing police perceptions fail to appreciate how these collective practices and loyalties help to protect and empower young people in circumstances of routine danger and structured marginalisation. As such, they serve as practical testimony to how the absence of democratic communication makes a broader appreciation of the relationship between young people, crime and public space difficult for officers to develop and sustain.

5 Transitions in Trouble: Fragmentation, Inclusion and Marginalisation

Everybody wants to better their self, everybody. They all want to be better than the next, it's all wrong. It's competition. Keeping up with each other, man, it's raj [stupid], it disnae make sense. (*23-year-old male, Niddrie*)

Young people's transitions are in trouble. The growth of youth unemployment, a dearth of adequate training schemes and cuts in social security have all meant that young people leave full-time education facing an uncertain future. At best, young people's foothold in the job market seems precarious. For many it is simply non-existent. Insecurity, poverty and divisions between those in and out of work increasingly mark the condition of contemporary youth.

The effects of prevailing economic conditions on the quality of young people's lives are as profound as they are varied. My purpose in this chapter is to focus on one particular aspect of the issue, that of how various post-sixteen transitions shape young people's experiences and understandings of public space, crime and policing. My aim is to set out and examine the ways in which young people and police officers make sense of these changes, and to assess the impact of different transitions on the possibilities for democratic communication between young people and the police.

In respect of these matters, the accounts presented and elaborated upon here are of a somewhat different temper to those discussed so far. Hitherto, we have been concerned with the ways in which young people reflect on their recent past, and with police officers' perceptions of young people up to the age of around sixteen. Now, however, we are confronted for the most part with the attempts of young people and police officers to obtain a practical grasp on a series of processes that are current, and whose outcomes are far from clear. This provides the relevant accounts with a conjectural and somewhat uncertain character. The analysis thus endeavours to take heed, both of the propositional content of these accounts, and of their indeterminate nature.

FRAGMENTING SOCIAL PRACTICES, 'RAGGED' TRANSITIONS

For many young people, the most immediate effect of leaving full-time education is the abrupt termination of their reliance upon, and unstructured use of, public space. As perhaps the dominant focus of young people's lives, school provides the practice of hanging around in groups with much of its coherence. It furnishes young people with a set of routines, a group of friends and a basis for their identity. The end of school thus has some devastating effects upon the informal loyalties and understandings that sustain the business of congregating in public:

IL:　What sort of places did you used to hang out?

A:　Down by the old railway. They've made it into a park. We used to go there. We used to drink there and everything. We used to sit down, have a laugh and that. It was barry [good].

IL:　What's different now, why don't you go down there any more?

B:　We've all split up, everybody has all split up. If you go down just yourself it's not so good. (*16/18-year-old females, Leith*)

In the aftermath of leaving school, hanging around begins – in a whole manner of ways – to lose its homology with young people's preoccupations and concerns. One might note first the onset of responsibilities – such as those of work or family – which render collective practices both more difficult to pursue and largely irrelevant to young people's new found circumstances. Thus, to recall for a moment the case of 'football casuals', even the most diehard 'members' are seen as outgrowing their formerly prevalent activities; either because they 'settle down and have bairns', or because their routines and outlook are transformed by the demands of work:

There's a guy in Penicuik called Crazy, that says it all. He was really pretty bad. He was sort of the top man and he was pretty young for a top man. I think he was about seventeen when he was top man. He's nineteen now and he's totally given up, just like that. He's in a job now, and he doesn't want to lose it through a stupid fight. (*16-year-old male, Gorebridge*)

Material changes such as leaving school, or starting work, are accompanied for many by a developing sense that hanging around the streets is no longer appropriate behaviour. This was a persistent theme among the young people interviewed, cropping up time and again in refrains such as 'I grew out of that years ago' or 'It's kids stuff'. One of the best illustrations of this is the incredulity young people express towards those deemed to have persisted unduly with their 'childish' endeavours:

IL:	Do you still spend a lot of time hanging about the streets?
All:	No.
A:	I ken a boy that does it and he's twenty-three-years-old, a boy called Tommy, have you ever heard of Tommy and John.
IL:	Do you think he's a bit old to be doing it at that age?
A:	Well, do you not? (*16/18-year-old males, Dalkeith*)

An integral feature of the fragmentation of hanging around is that the petty delinquency which can make congregating in public places such fun begins to lose its attraction. As one twenty-one-year-old male recalled: 'We used to be a wee bit wild you know, me and my pals, we used to smash windows, kick in cars, put darts in car tyres, broken bottles, things like that. We used to do that, but that was in the past. Now I've grown up a bit. It's just calmed down.' Most young people, in other words, simply grow out of crime (Rutherford, 1992). One aspect of this is the practical realisation that, once you pass sixteen, acts of petty offending are likely to prompt a more serious and formal response from the criminal justice system; something which seems out of proportion to what young people view as transient events:

IL:	When you say getting into crime, what do you mean?
A:	Just breaking into places and that. Not shops and that. Warehouses. For a laugh, like.
B:	We stole a big charity bottle once, we werenae proud of that like. It wasnae actually out a church, it was a church's bingo place. It wasnae nothing to brag about. We got charged for that.
IL:	So what's the difference when you get to sixteen?
B:	Because you're older, you dinnae do wee bairnish [childish] things, and you get put away, no-one wants to be in jail, no danger. (*16-year-old females, Leith*)

A:	I used to be a thief like but I stopped when I was sixteen. Fifty-four charges between when I was thirteen and sixteen, but I've never been in trouble since.
IL:	Why?
A:	Well when you're thirteen to sixteen, you ken you're just going to go to the panel, 'slap, slap, don't do it again you naughty boy' all that kind of shit. But once you're over sixteen ken, you just end up in Glenochil or Saughton [prison]. (*17-year-old male, Niddrie*)

These accounts suggest that young people are able to generate some reflexive distance on the practices that used to structure their lives, something which is vital if mutual dialogue about matters of crime and policing is ever to accomplish anything positive. They also demonstrate that the identities provided by hanging around are both fleeting and possessed of illusory coherence. Defensive loyalties to place or football club – and the narratives of exclusion which constitute them – are, it seems, a product of the informal pressures generated by what Matza (1964) once called the 'situation of company'. As one erstwhile 'casual' reflected: 'I've nothing against other teams really, it's just that you're with a group and if you dinnae go you're called chicken and all that, so you just tag along. I never actually got into fights.' The following account offers a graphic retrospective on these pressures:

> It's a very hard place to make pals in, unless you've got the reputation of being a fighter. If you've got a reputation of being a fighter, everybody wants to be your pal. But if you're just a fucking idiot, everyone just ignores you: 'Oh he's raj him.' It's the same everywhere, the same at school, it all starts when people are young. That word 'coward' should be taken out the bible and all. Young laddies getting called cowards: 'If you don't do it you're a coward.' It should be taken out of the dictionary, that word, because there's no such a thing as a coward. A coward is an intelligent person as far as I'm concerned. It's your brain telling you not to do it. But other people are telling you to do it, so you fucking just do it to be in the gang and that. It's all wrong, it's all wrong. (*23-year-old male, Niddrie*)

The fragmentation of young people's collective use of public space can for many be important in and of itself. But it also signals a more general differentiation of young people's experience, the crucial determinant of which is access to the labour market. In recent decades, the paradigm of full employment that marked much of the post-war period in Britain (for young men at least) has fractured, to be replaced by a series of what Wallace (1987) calls 'ragged' transitions. Increasingly, young people's experiences of the job market comprises intermittent and uncertain periods of work, training and unemployment (Coffield *et al.*, 1986). And increasingly, this circumstance generates among young people new and sharper divisions, new and more pressing problems, and a search for new forms of identification (Willis, 1984a and b; Banks *et al.*, 1991).

In the rest of this chapter, my task is to make some sense of how young people and police officers come to terms with the impact these economic conditions have on young people's experiences and understandings of crime and policing. To this end, I shall mobilise a distinction between what I term *inclusive* and *marginalising* youth transitions. This distinction is far from exhaustive, and more precise categorisations could no doubt be drawn within each of its terms. But for present purposes it will suffice. For it alerts us to the difference between those who proceed to full-time employment or education (inclusive transitions), and those who experience youth training and unemployment (marginalising transitions). It draws attention to how the age-based marginalisation of youth is superseded by a process of differential access to allocative and authoritative resources.[1] And it enables us to obtain some interpretive purchase on the criminological consequences of different post-school trajectories.

THE MEANINGS AND EFFECTS OF INCLUSIVE TRANSITIONS

The principal effect of inclusive transitions is to 'embed' young people in a network of contacts, opportunities and routines which constitute them as 'part of' society (Hagan, 1993). The chief vehicles of this social embedding are further or higher education and work. These warrant the description 'inclusive' because they hold out the prospect, either immediately or at some future date, of greater access to allocative resources. In so doing, they provide young people with reason to think beyond the present.

Further and higher education constitute something of a 'limbo-land' between school and future employment. They delay the onset of the rigours of work and hold in abeyance the financial independence it brings. This temporary suspension of economic security is not without its compensations, however. Not only is it traded against the prospect of a future career, but it is also coupled with a measure of social and cultural autonomy. Educational transitions provide a space in which young people can develop and sustain new identities. In the immediate term, many of the difficulties associated with this surround obtaining access to cultural outlets (such as pubs and clubs) that are off limits to young people under eighteen:

IL: How has your social life changed since you left school?
A: More clubs and stuff, but not that much. But you've got to be eighteen to get in or twenty-one. There's nowhere for under eighteens. I'm sixteen and I dinnae look any older, and so it's hard for me to go places where all my friends are going.
IL: What sort of things would you want that there isn't at the moment?
B: More social clubs for young people. Discos where you dinnae

have all the wee bairns running about. Folk over sixteen and under eighteen can get into without all the wee bairns running around. (*16/17-year-old females, Gracemount*)

Securing employment, the second path to an inclusive transition, has a number of significant corollaries. Most importantly, it provides young people with the key to greater allocative (though not necessarily authoritative) resources, and it transforms them from vicarious into direct consumers. It can also allow young people to secure for themselves autonomous domestic space, thus enabling them to reduce their routine reliance upon public space, and develop identities centred around the home.

Perhaps the most immediately apparent effects of work are associated with its disciplinary rhythms. Work significantly disrupts young people's received routines, serving both to limit the amount of 'free time' they have available and to transform its meanings. One pivotal aspect of this concerns the enhanced value that comes to be attached to the 'weekend':

IL: How do you find your lives have changed since you left school?
A: I've changed what I do at weekends and that now, cos the weekend is more important cos I'm working.
IL: In what sort of ways?
A: Well, you sort of look forward to weekend, whereas at school you got out at four o'clock and had the rest of the day. Now it's five o'clock you get out of work and you get home about five-thirty and have your tea and only have a few hours. (*16-year-old male, Penicuik*)

Inclusive transitions are crucial in transforming how young people use, and understand, public space. On the one hand, young people's spatial horizons expand to encompass more and more of the city; the city centre, in particular, begins to figure more prominently in their everyday life, whether for purposes of work, study, consumption or entertainment. On the other, the immediate locality – once invested with such meaning, and once so central to young people's routines and identities – begins to lose much of its material and imaginative importance. This is most evident, as I indicated earlier, in the almost complete eclipse of young people's unstructured, expressive use of public space. When young people obtain access to cultural resources such as pubs and clubs, the streets are no longer needed as a site of compensatory leisure:

IL: How much has your social life changed since you left school?
A: I go to some night clubs on a Friday, Saturday. Go to the pub. I just go out with my mates.

IL:　Do you go into the city centre at all?

A:　On a Friday night I'll go to a pub then I'll go to a club, same on a Saturday. And on a Sunday I'll just stay in bed. That's my weekend for you. (*17-year-old male, Dalkeith*)

Two aspects of these transitions warrant further consideration. Let us look first at how this time–space concentration of the use of public space impacts upon the experience of criminal victimisation. In the case of teenage men, this can be quite marked; the demise of congregating in groups serving to focus and delimit their routine exposure to the risks of being out in public. For teenage women, however, the break is – as Stanko (1990) has pointed out – rather less pronounced, with the attendant possibility of sexual harassment and intimidation continuing to shape young women's experiences, use and understandings of public places.

This can be illustrated by examining evidence from two crime surveys conducted around the time of this research, the 1988 British crime survey (Scotland) and the Edinburgh crime survey. The British crime survey found that victims of offences against the person are for the most part young and male, with sixteen and seventeen-year-old males comprising no less than 29 per cent of victims of assault and 14 per cent of victims of threatening behaviour (Kinsey and Anderson, 1992, ch. 4).[2] Similarly, the Edinburgh crime survey shows that a disproportionate amount of offences against the person are concentrated in the city centre, an overwhelming majority of which (for example, 85 per cent of assaults) occur after nine o'clock in the evening (Anderson *et al.*, 1990, ch. 5).[3]

The British crime survey also explored – in a manner relevant to my present concern with inclusive and marginalising transitions – some aspects of the relationship between class, place and male violence. It found the use of public places is related both to age and affluence – with 45 per cent of males earning between £10–20 000 per annum having 'very active' social lives (defined as going out three or more times a week), compared with 34 per cent of those under £10 000. It also shows that those with 'very active' social lives are three times more likely to be a victim of an offence against the person (12 per cent) than those who venture out less frequently (4 per cent).

However, it was the nature and impact of these offences that suggested the most telling class distinctions. Those earning between £10–20 000 are more likely than those on a lower income to be victimised by an unknown assailant, and outside the immediate vicinity of their home. They are less likely, however, to be victims of incidents involving a weapon, or to suffer serious injury or lasting emotional effects as a result of their experiences

(Kinsey and Anderson, 1992, pp. 44–6). One of the principal criminological consequences of inclusive transitions, it seems, is that young men at least come to experience routine danger most frequently at the hands of strangers, in city centre public spaces, during weekend nights out.[4]

In this context, the reservoir of memories and apprehensions about public space young people inherit from their early teens are no longer sufficient. New risks and experiences have to be accommodated, new ways of coping need to be found. Young people's cognitive map of the city is consequently redrawn to take account of these dangers, and new collective and individual routines for managing safety in public are forged, such as going out with friends, avoiding 'dangerous' streets, pubs and clubs, and taking taxis home (Anderson *et al.*, 1990; Stanko, 1990). A revised practical knowledge of the city and its sources of trouble slowly emerges. Thus:

> We dinnae go up Rose Street, cos we had a bit of trouble there with some guys. We got jumped. He wanted my leather jacket. It was 'casuals' ken, Hib's 'casuals'. I was walking down Rose Street and the guy came up to me, and just kicked me right there and I folded. He's trying to get my jacket off me. I got up and said, 'I'm no wanting any trouble', started walking away. So me and my mate started walking away and he starts following us, trying to push us. He was drunk. My mate said just go away before trouble starts ken, and he's turned round and punched my friend in the jaw. Then he punched me and kicked me in the head. I got up and Tony, my friend, tried to grab the jacket off him, cos he was trying to get me jacket and he slashed the jacket, wush! It was a nice jacket, fifty odd pounds, just slashed it. (*20-year-old male, Craigmillar*)

A second feature of inclusive transitions, one implicit in the foregoing discussion, is that they provide young people with access to a range of allocative resources – money to spend, the chance to consume, go out and so forth. In this sense, inclusive transitions constitute a move towards what Habermas (1975) has called 'civic privatism'; that is, they offer young people the seductions of consumer capitalism, while providing them with few opportunities (beyond the acquisition of formal political rights) to participate meaningfully in institutional processes of public decision-making. Put bluntly, young people become consumers but not citizens.

To the extent that this privileging of consumption over citizenship is a key feature of late-modern society (Bauman, 1987), it is crucial in understanding the alienation from the political process evinced by young people. The accounts generated by this research provide merely a flavour of this, but they point overwhelmingly in one direction: 'What politics,

it's rubbish man. It's a load of crap.' Such cynicism – which has been a
fairly consistent theme of recent youth research in Britain (Furnham and
Gunter, 1989; cf. Bhavnani, 1991) – is most apparent in respect of conventional party political processes, whether national or local:

IL: Did you vote in the last council elections?
A: No. It's not worth it. I won't be voting again either.
IL: Does it make any difference who you vote for?
A: No cos she [Margaret Thatcher] always gets in anyway. I hate her.
She needs a bomb stuck up her arse.
IL: What about if the Labour Party got in. Would that make any
difference?
A: No, cos they're even worse. (*21-year-old female, Craigmillar*)

IL: What about national politics?
A: Just all half wits, dreary old men shouting yeh! yeh! yeh! I certainly don't have a lot of time for any of them. They just talk a lot
of drivel. There's nothing that really affects me. (*20-year-old male,
Niddrie*)

These somewhat resigned understandings of politics are reinforced among
some by the more concrete impression that young people's concerns are
excluded from the political process – a perception encapsulated in the
comment of one eighteen-year-old female that: 'Nobody's prepared to
listen; they think we're all the same. You're all classed as riff raff.' The
effect of such beliefs is that any interest young people develop in politics
is always already tinged with the realisation that they lack any political
'clout':

Who's going to listen to you if you're sixteen years old? All right,
you're sixteen, you've got nowhere to go, what can we do about it? And
it's not just hanging about the streets, it's a lot of things. (. . .) You could
write to the council, to your councillor. He'll listen to you, fair enough
but there's nothing you can do. A lot of sixteen-year-olds demanding
rights and stuff they're going to say: 'So?' If we had somebody on
our side who was powerful it would maybe help. (*16-year-old female,
Portobello*)

Inclusive transitions, then, by no means enable young people to participate in, and effect meaningful influence over, the formal political process, whether in respect of the police or any other institution. Inclusive
(and, for that matter, marginalising) transitions constitute a passage into
the mechanisms of a 'thin' democracy (Barber, 1984). The formal rights

of citizenship are acquired, but little else. By the time they leave school little institutional effort has been expended in helping young people 'grow into' the rights, entitlements and obligations of a democratic citizen. Quite the reverse in fact. The sometimes subtle, sometimes explicit, but ultimately enduring message currently offered to young people in Britain is that they are Other; a problem to be managed or solved, not citizens in the making with demands to voice. It should thus come as no surprise to find that young people acquire the trappings of citizenship that a 'thin' democracy has to offer with an already marked apathy (not to say antipathy) towards prevailing political institutions and processes. Any attempt to enhance democratic communication between young people and the police will have to come to terms with this evident reality.

THE MEANINGS AND EFFECTS OF MARGINALISING TRANSITIONS

> Money is the thing. Without money you're nothing. (*23-year-old male, Niddrie*)

The foregoing remarks about inclusive transitions and citizenship hold as – if not more – strongly in respect of those young people who undergo marginalising transitions. But marginalising transitions offer none of the material promise associated with higher education and work. Rather, those whose post-sixteen experience comprises intermittent periods of unemployment, training schemes and casual work face an uncertain future; a future in which the age-based exclusions of youth are superseded by a class-based deprivation of all kinds of allocative and authoritative resources.

Youth unemployment traps young people in a state of 'suspended animation', extending their status as dependent 'adolescents'. Instead of the positive 'limbo-land' of further and higher education, unemployment ushers in a period of sustained insecurity with little prospect of a different let alone better future. And instead of the financial independence connected with work, unemployment brings poverty and social exclusion. It also prolongs young people's reliance upon their parents (with all the stresses that entails) and precludes young people's entry into the world of consumption (Willis, 1984a; Wallace, 1987, ch. 4). The following accounts provide some flavour of this:

A: £29.50, then £33.00! Slave labour.

IL: Do you have to pay for digs?

A: A tenner. And I've got five pound for my catalogues, and that.

B: My mum disnae take digs from me.
IL: Are you still staying at home?
C: Aye. (*17-year-old females, Craigmillar*)

YTS is just to get young folk off the street and onto Maggie Thatcher's slave labour. £28.50 a week! What could you buy with £28.50? (*17-year-old male, Craigmillar*)

Youth unemployment has a number of immediately felt effects. In the first place, jobless teenagers confront a climate of feeling that is in numerous ways hostile to them. As one twenty-year-old male put it: 'The worst thing is people's attitude towards unemployed people. They think we don't want to work, we're lazy, dole scivers.' There is, moreover, a widespread sense that local employers discriminate unjustly against young people from Edinburgh's peripheral estates: 'My mate went up for a job interview and as soon as he says he was from Niddrie they said, "We'll get in touch." But he's never heard. It's just where you come from. If you come from Niddrie, it's got a bad reputation . . . But you cannae judge a book by its cover, you cannae tell what a person's like just by where they come from, ken what I mean?'

Unemployment also deprives young people of access to a range of leisure activities that the transcendence of an age-based marginalisation would otherwise make available to them. Here, the felt consequences of joblessness can be at their most acute for young people, especially given that their working peers now enjoy the very amenities from which the young unemployed are excluded. This aspect of a marginalising transition troubles many jobless teenagers:

IL: Is there anything to do for young people round here?
A: They've got the complexes like Megabowl and that down there. That's no good to us, we're only making £29.50 a week. You can spend that in twenty minutes down there, ken what I mean. (*17-year-old male, Craigmillar*)

It's shocking, there's nothing in it for any person here. What do we do? Come up here [the unemployed club] every Wednesday, that's it. (*19-year-old male, Niddrie*)

Exclusions such as this have all kinds of consequences for how unemployed young people use the city and its facilities. Denied the purchasing power needed to use, or even get to, other parts of the city (and most importantly the city centre), unemployed youths are for the most part confined to the communities in which they live (something exacerbated in Edinburgh by the sharp spatial segregation of the city, and the concentration of social deprivation in the city's peripheral housing schemes). As a result, the 'locality' tends to retain a prominent place in the lives of marginalised young people, both as the site of routine activities and as the basis of their identities. At least three manifestations of this are noteworthy.

First, unemployment can restrict young people's lives to the home. A striking case in point of this concerns young single mothers, whose 'confinement' is a consequence of having to bring up children with little or no material assistance. As one teenage mother put it: 'I got these two. It's hard getting baby sitters for two babies.' For others, lack of income and a dearth of local facilities are paramount. In either case, however, the effect is the same; to generate among the young unemployed a privatised, isolated and humdrum social existence:

IL: Is there enough to do round here?
A: Nothing but sport, pure boredom. That's what's caused all the drugs, no place to go or anything.
IL: How do you pass the time?
A: Watch the telly, that's it. (*19-year-old male, Niddrie*)

IL: What sort of things do you do in your spare time when you're not here?
A: Lie in my bed.
IL: Has your life changed at all since you left school?
B: From bad to worse.
IL: Why do you say that?
B: Oh, just that there's nothing to do about Niddrie. You just need a bit more money and that. (*16/18-year-old males, Craigmillar*)

The spatial confinement of unemployed youth can also prolong their dependence on the collective, unstructured use of public space. For unemployed teenagers, and teenage men especially, congregating in the streets or around local shops is a way of feeling important, exchanging the latest 'news' and generating occasional bouts of excitement. However, as age-based exclusions are replaced by those of class, the experience and meaning of hanging around changes markedly. No longer is it to do with messing about with friends, exploring the urban landscape or generally 'having fun'. Rather, hanging around the streets becomes a culturally inappropriate way of killing endless time (Willis, 1984b):

You dinnae ken how bored you can get just walking about all day. It's unbelievable. You start getting into a certain frame of mind where nothing matters. (*18-year-old female, Niddrie*)

It appears, thirdly, that marginalising transitions can both concentrate and intensify young people's experience of victimisation. Recalling the 1988 British crime survey (Scotland), we find that male victims of assault in receipt of less than £10 000 per annum are more likely both to know their assailants, and to be attacked in the immediate vicinity of their own home. In 32 per cent of cases of threatening behaviour, for example, victims in this income bracket knew the offender well, compared with 2 per cent of victims earning more than £10 000. Poorer victims of offences against the person are also more likely to be involved in incidents occasioning either serious injury or greater emotional impact (Kinsey and Anderson, 1992, pp. 44–6).

These findings suggest that one of the principal criminological consequences of marginalising transitions is to render young males more susceptible to (serious) violence in local public spaces. It may even be that such violence is a product of – not to mention a contributor towards – the pressures that unemployment brings (Campbell, 1993). These pressures, and their effects, are captured perfectly below:

> People have got a lot of problems. Like if I go out and drink, it's just to forget for a wee while, have a good time, just dinnae think about all your problems, just drop them just for the one night. Just get drunk. But then you start remembering things, cos when you're drunk you get all sentimental and you start thinking about it, and then one thing leads to another and you get arguments breaking out, and then suddenly because you're drunk, you get aggressive, your moods change really fast when you're drinking. That's how fights break out, and then things get thrown about the place, and if somebody gets scaled accidently, then they're going to get up and punch you. It just happens. (*18-year-old female, Niddrie*)

The pressures of youth unemployment can have effects of an altogether different kind, however; giving rise to illegitimate and on occasions desperate modes of survival among unemployed youth. It is of course a truism to say that not all unemployed teenagers take drugs, participate in the informal economy, or turn to crime. Yet unemployment – especially if prolonged – undoubtedly makes it more difficult for young people to avoid 'transitions in trouble' (Farrington *et al.*, 1986; Box, 1987). One twenty-year-old male's description of the peripheral scheme in which he lived provides some indication of this: 'It's all right round here if you've got a job. If you havenae got a job, you start going a wee bit crazy. Folk on the b'reau [social security], they'll go downhill, they'll steal, things like that. That's what worries me.'

It is here that the discrepancy between inclusive and marginalising transitions is perhaps at its most marked. Rather than embedding young people in a network of legitimate contexts and relationships, marginalising transitions accomplish the exact opposite. They create circumstances in which young people can all too easily find themselves caught up in illegitimate routines and opportunity structures. What results is a set of practices that combine the prospect of 'escape' – whether of a material or imaginary kind – with some overwhelmingly detrimental consequences. Young people's involvement in drugs provides a pertinent case in point:

A: If you're in Bingham and you want to be somewhere else, you just hallucinate. We were in Bingham but I though I was in Niddrie. God, it's barry [good]. There was this hill right, and it was a big high hill and this escalator took us up the hill. It was barry. And then we thought we seen a barbed wire fence but it wasnae, it was just in our imaginations. Just when went down. It was barry.

B: I just smoke hash and that's enough for me. And drink. Drink and smoke it at the same time, that's awful.

C: It's horrible. You feel like you're being sick and cannae stop. You've nowt left in your stomach and you're trying to be sick. (*16-year-old females, Niddrie*)

For some marginalised youth, the 'escape' offered by the local drugs market has a more material meaning; holding out the prospect of an income and associated lifestyle that the vast bulk of young people have no possibility of achieving by legitimate means. As one twenty-three-year-old put it, commenting on the drugs market in one of Edinburgh's peripheral housing schemes: 'They're local people. It's people from outside who are supplying the stuff, it's local people that are dealing it and taking the drugs. It's like a fucking supermarket isn't it? You've got to go to shops to buy your food, you've got to go to some houses to buy drugs.' Profiting from this 'supermarket' may for some constitute the only available means of acquiring material success and the 'respect' that goes with it, even if such 'betterment' is secured at the expense of others:

Drug dealers are respected by a certain majority of people because they've got a nice car, a nice house, they've got plenty of money. It's how much money, not who you are. You're street-wise if you've got plenty of money. You're bettering yourself and all that shit, ken what I mean? It's all wrong. There's ways of earning money legal but you can earn a fortune out of drugs if you go about it the right way. But they should all be hung, drawn and quartered as far as I'm concerned. The whole lot of them. The bastards, especially hard drugs. (*23-year-old male, Niddrie*)

Dealing in drugs is of course not the only means for unemployed teenagers to survive, or escape, poverty. Participating in, or benefiting from, others forms of economic crime can also be attractive options for the unemployed. For some, the potential benefits of such lawbreaking can give rise to some pressing moral dilemmas. As one unemployed young woman put it: 'There's a split sort of loyalty here. I can go out and I ken people I can buy clothes dead cheap, cos they came off the back of a lorry as they say. I mean that's good for me in one way, but ken it's not right to go stealing and breaking into things in other ways.' For others, however, the benefits of economic crime make it an all too tempting way of easing – and maybe even transcending – material disadvantage:

Cheque books. Even when they've been reported stolen. Me and this lassie Julie, we went down to Cameron Toll [shopping centre], and took out something like £1500 in instant credit in Cooksons. We also took them to London with us as well, cos that's the easiest place in the world. You know the change bureau, well see if you keep a cheque under £50 they dinnae phone up. It's their own stupidity. And you get to know all this. (...) You usually just buy things with the books, like TVs and videos and anything that's easy to sell. Cos then there's no comeback sort of thing. (*19-year-old male, Broughton*)

A final example of surviving unemployment and poverty is that of (male) prostitution, a single account of which was generated during the research. For the nineteen-year-old male involved, what he called 'going up the hill' was very much a 'last resort'; the culmination of a whole series of 'ragged' transitions: 'I went on a YTS catering, I was on that for about eight months and then I packed it in. Then I went back to the voluntary, then I got ET [Employment Training] when the ET came in, but it was just slave labour again, I wasn't treated with any respect so I packed that in. I've had odd jobs like in chip shops, looking after an old man who was disabled, looking after bairns. When I moved into Leith I started dabbling in drugs or prostitution as well, like going up the hill, and I still do it. Monday was the last time I was up there.'

Here, prostitution is considered as merely the latest in a long line of dead-end training schemes and casual jobs. And as jobs go it has things going for it, whether that be flexible working hours, meals out, or the occasional gift of expensive clothes. Such perks, however, are few and far between, and they provide scant compensation for having to endure such things as violence from pimps and unwanted clients. Thus:

A: When I'm up that hill when I get in the cars, it's like, 'I must be
      something else' ken what I mean. I know he's just thinking of me
      as just another . . . not even thinking of me as a face probably, but
      you have to get a wee bit of a good expectation when you get in
      the car sometimes. Think to yourself, 'I must be amazing'. You
      have to coax yourself up sometimes. And sometimes you just
      think, 'ah! I can't be bothered with it'.

IL: What do you do when you feel like that?

A: You just go through with it. You just shut your eyes. Sometimes
      I just stop halfway through and say: 'Stop, I cannae handle this let
      me out the car.' (*19-year-old male, Broughton*)

Extreme though it is, this example illuminates very well the double-edged
nature of all these illegitimate means of dealing with the boredom, poverty
and hopelessness ushered in by unemployment. On the one hand, these
practices hold out the promise of 'escape', however temporary or illusory
that may turn out to be. But on the other, they bring with them troubles
which themselves have to be managed and coped with. And for the most
part, it is the damaging and brutalising aspects of these practices that win
the day: the 'solution' ends up being the problem.

POLICING YOUTH TRANSITIONS: RECONFIGURATIONS OF FORCE AND SERVICE

Let us now turn our attention to the relationship between policing and
youth transitions. In what ways do officers orientate themselves to various
post-sixteen trajectories? How are young people's experiences of the force
and service dimensions of policing reconstituted in the years immediately
following school? These questions, the answers to which impact in important ways on the possibility of democratic communication between young
people and the police, are my concern in the rest of this chapter.

Perhaps the most immediate consequence of the fragmentation of hanging around is a marked reduction in many young people's routine contacts
with the police. The extent of this can be gauged in part from the findings
of survey research conducted recently with both adults and young people
in Edinburgh (see Table 5.1[5]). This overall reduction is by no means the
only effect, however. The fragmentation of hanging around is accompanied
by an overall time–space concentration in adversary police–youth contact. The routine policing of youth becomes for the most part focused on
regulating the city centre on a Friday and Saturday night. Thus, the Edinburgh crime survey found that 49 per cent of sixteen to thirty-year-olds

Table 5.1   Young people's adversary contact with the police

	Moved on or told off	Stopped and questioned	Stopped and searched	Stopped in a vehicle	Arrested or detained
11 to 16	44	25	13	n/a	10
16 to 30	n/a	9	4	18	n/a
Male 11–16	55	31	19	n/a	13
Male 16–30	n/a	10	4	18	n/a
Female 11–16	32	19	6	n/a	7
Female 16–30	n/a	2	0.5	7	n/a

stopped and searched, and 47 per cent of those stopped and questioned, were apprehended in Edinburgh city centre (Kinsey, 1992, ch. 2). The following account gives some indication of these changing patterns of experience:

> Normally prior to nine o'clock you'd be busy with say ten to sixteen-year-olds. After that time, maybe the sixteen to twenty-one-year-olds. They don't seem to appear a great deal earlier, I mean, they're there but they're not really causing us a problem. (*Male beat officer*)

The transition from school then can mark a significant turning point in many young people's experiences and understandings of the police. And like all turning points, this one takes young people off in some markedly different directions. The years immediately following the end of full-time schooling tend to mean far less frequent contact with the police for the majority of young people, coupled with more sustained and serious experiences for a small minority. This is certainly how the police construct it:

> What you find happens is that around twelve, thirteen, fourteen there's usually a mass of them and they're playing football, hanging about the street, maybe involved in petty shoplifting, which is a silly phase they go through, a bit of bravado. But when they get into their later teens, you are dealing with a hard core if you like, because you get the same ones over and over again. They tend to be the ones that have diversified from being just a nuisance to breaking into cars or stealing cars, or breaking into shops. So they've gone towards a criminal life if you like. (*Male beat officer*)

In order to make sense of these differentiations and their policing consequences, let us return to the distinction made earlier between inclusive and marginalising transitions. And let us examine how these respective post-school trajectories impact upon young people's experiences of, and dispositions towards, the police. Might it not be that such differentiations bring about a reconfiguration of service and force, whereby the bulk of young people are constituted as 'consumers' of policing, while a minority become what police officers call their 'regular customers'?

THE POLICE AND INCLUSIVE TRANSITIONS: BECOMING A 'CONSUMER'

In the overall scheme of things, the police have a minor part to play in easing young people's path towards an inclusive transition from school. Such transitions, as we have seen, are facilitated largely by education and work. But this is not to say that the police have no role at all. Many police practices in respect of teenagers – such as those mobilised under the sign of 'community involvement' – have as their principal aim the production of 'good' citizens. These practices are for the most part directed at youth in general, such as in police–school liaison schemes. But they take on a certain urgency when it comes to that fraction of young people considered to be on the verge of crime, yet still capable of being 'saved'. Here police officers often see their 'rescue mission' as critical.

The formal dimension of this 'mission' is embodied in the person of the juvenile liaison officer. JLOs are crucial in determining whether or not a young offender is processed into the formal criminal justice system, and in this context, an offender's future depends much on whether or not he or she is thought of as redeemable. In respect of those who are, the JLO's principal task is to encourage them away from trouble and onto the 'right' path out of school:

> My job is to give them a talking to, try to point out the seriousness of their actions. I have their parents present always, and we have a very high success rate. It gives the children a chance to tell me their problems and it gives the parents a chance to bring up anything that's happened since the last offence. (*Male juvenile liaison officer*)

Pedagogic practices – as we noted in Chapter 4 – can also be employed on a more informal basis by police officers. In the course of their routine dealings with young people, officers have ample opportunity to proffer pertinent 'career' advice. This frequently amounts to providing young people with what one officer described as 'general commonsense guidance' about their future:

I normally stress to them, 'now look, this time next year you'll be looking for a job. Would you employ anyone who has committed a crime of theft? Would you then regard them as trustworthy?' They obviously answer, 'no, I wouldn't'. Well, then I would say, 'well why should someone employ you if you've had a previous finding of guilt for theft'. If the kid is just on the fringe of crime, I would say there's a good chance of that kid listening to you. (*Male area officer*)

Various aspects of this pedagogic policing are noteworthy. It is evident, first of all, that police officers conceive of these practices as a one-way process of instruction; one in which young people are constructed as empty vessels into which sound police advice can be poured. The emphasis here is on moulding young people into 'good' citizens by instilling in them a complex of appropriate attitudes; something which rests – rather ironically given how the police pride themselves on a down-to-earth pragmatism – upon an idealised, voluntaristic understanding of how young people are to make inclusive transitions.

The pedagogic enterprise also involves a bifurcation. It is about dividing young people up into those who can be saved and those who cannot. And it is about expending effort (for understandable occupational reasons no doubt) on young people thought amenable to constructive change. As one officer put it: 'If I feel that they're receptive, I'll have a go. There's others who just won't listen so I wouldn't waste my breath.' The police's central preoccupation, in other words, is with protecting the 'good apples' from the contaminating effects of a 'bad barrel':

A: There are occasions when you're dealing with kids who are just starting out in crime, say, or have just done something stupid. You help them.

IL: What does that mean in practice?

A: You can advise them. Quite a few of the kids we get go into shoplifting, for example, because the other kids in school do it. It's well worthwhile taking a bit of time out to chat to these kids. I think quite a lot of them listen to what you say. We're talking about kids here from respectable backgrounds and going to good schools. (*Male beat officer*)

This process is, thirdly, gendered in significant respects. Police admonition is aimed primarily at steering male adolescents out of trouble, and it is against this backdrop that young women tend to figure in police occupational consciousness. Teenage girls are understood largely in terms of the impact they have on the behaviour of male peers. As one officer put it: 'I must say I don't have a lot of dealings with young girls, but I can guarantee that the guys that are with them will be committing some crime.' In respect of younger teenagers, police dispositions cohere around the view that girls are in some way or other implicated in the troublesome antics of boys:

> The number of fights you go to where there's a couple of guys fighting and there's women there egging them on. It's because of these women that these guys are fighting. And that's the worst, because you get there and the women turn on you. And the two poor guys knocking lumps out of each other because of this woman are the ones who are going to get arrested because they're fighting in the street. Yet it's the women who have caused it. (*Male beat officer*)

These constructions change markedly in the light of young mens' transitions. Here, all of a sudden, young women are transformed from *agent provocateurs* into 'civilising' influences; their role now pivotal in hastening the path of disordered young men towards an inclusive transition. However, at another level of significance, these substantive shifts count for little; young women remain fixed in the police world according to their impact on the actions of young men, rather than in terms of their own experiences and concerns:

> In my experience it's amazing the calming effect, especially for guys, young lads that have been involved in crime; it's amazing the transformation when they get a woman and get involved and have a family. It's amazing the calming effect the woman can have. Even the big so-called hard men. (*Male area officer*)

As far as the bulk of young people are concerned, perhaps the most significant policing effect of inclusive transitions is that the routine, supervisory aspects of policing begin slowly to recede from their lives. As the unstructured use of public space is superseded by the more specific use of cultural amenities, so young people's contact with the police becomes more incident-related and less obviously to do with the moral ordering of public space. One aspect of this – as Table 5.1 above illustrates – is that young people, and young men especially, come to attract considerable police attention through the use of their newly acquired cars:

> I've been stopped, and I'm not joking, in my car at least about 25 times and told to bring my gear up to the police station. A young policeman that I ken and I got talking to kept saying to me, 'get rid of that car'. He thought I shouldnae be in that car because I was too young to drive a car like that. But I'd passed my test and paid my insurance, and I had

as much right to drive on the road as anybody else. *(20-year-old male, Bonnyrigg)*

A further consequence of inclusive transitions is that young people begin to ascribe a different set of meanings to their adversarial experiences of the police. For example, those who continue to encounter sporadic trouble with the police may – in the context of the disciplines of employment – come to view the experience as both chastening and not to be repeated:

> I was coming out the pub we used to drink in and I was walking down the road and we were singing and that and I was shouting 'Pigs'. And they got out the car and started chasing me. (. . .) They took me to the cells and I spent the night in the cells. Never again, Jesus! There was this boy sitting greeting [crying] all night, I was going spare. I had my work in the morning. Three o'clock in the morning they let me out. *(21-year-old male, Gorebridge)*

The focussing of police–youth contact on discrete incidents, and the removal of (now incorporated) young people from the police's moralising gaze, contributes much to this changing attribution of meaning. As older teenagers are reconstituted as sporadic 'offenders' rather than routinely 'offensive' (Ericson, 1982), police–youth encounters are less often characterised by the 'paradox of face', and more likely to generate something approaching mutual recognition and respect, however grudgingly acknowledged.

Consider, for example, the two accounts narrated below by an eighteen-year-old from Craigmillar. Both concern incidents in which the young male concerned was taken to the police station; the first for alleged trouble outside a football match when he was fifteen, the other for retaliating having been attacked in Edinburgh city centre by a 'casual' at the age of eighteen. The sense of an unjust and capricious imposition of authority which resonates through the first account, contrasts starkly with the legitimacy accorded to police actions in the second:

> I was coming from a football game, I dinnae support football, I'd just been to this one game, this was years and years ago. I was ready to cross the road, they said, 'you're going in the back of the van'. I said, 'what have I done?'. 'Nothing, but you're going in the back of the van.' And he started hitting my elbows against the parked car – bang! bang! – kept hitting them. I was fifteen at the time. They put me in the back. Took me up to the High Street and they kept trying to charge me. But they wouldnae touch my mum, and she came up and proved it and I got let away.

A: They were good. They werenae good at first, but that's to be expected. They were expecting trouble from us. Cos we got in a taxi and drove away, got stopped up the road by the police. We got taken to the police station and they were all right. They were a wee bit ignorant at first. But we got talking to them. They never done anything violent or that. We were let out in the morning and that was it. I've not heard nothing since.

IL: Do you think the police should be involved in something like that in the city centre?

A: Of course. Like I'd want them to be there, ken if I was getting battered, I'd want them to split it up. I'd want them to stop it. Some of them are all right, some are them aren't. (*18-year-old male, Craigmillar*)

Inclusive transitions may also have some significant consequences for young people's understanding and use of police services. Among younger teenagers, as we have seen, conceiving of the police as service providers appears fanciful when set against their routine experiences of policing. But as collective social practices and their associated loyalties fragment, and the control dimensions of policing become less prevalent in young people's everyday lives, the police may be more readily be construed as offering a service.[6] Young people may thus become minded to mobilise 'abstract systems' of protection such as the police on a more frequent basis (Giddens, 1990). One irony of this is that these new consumers of police services may start to demand routine control of the very social practices that were once so central to their lives and identities:

A: I mean there's young guys playing football, playing till one in the morning outside the house, and I'm in my bed trying to sleep. I'll shout at them and sometimes I phone the cops, cos they wouldnae move ken, they'll just stay and give you abuse. They won't give me abuse, but they'll give other folk abuse, young women and that. And the cops come and they do get moved, but they're always there the next night.

IL: What should the police do in that situation?

A: Just talk to them, cos they've got a wee bit of authority, so they move. Or if they're not moving, they get done with loitering; loitering with intent, or breach of the peace. (*21-year-old male, Craigmillar*)

The overarching criminological effect, then, of inclusive transitions is to reconstitute the force and service aspects of policing that older, incorporated teenagers experience. As young people acquire the material trappings of consumer capitalism, as well as the burdens that both facilitate and accompany them, their place within prevailing social hierarchies is transformed. In short, young people secure membership of those 'respectable' social groups who the police do things for rather than to (Shearing, 1981). They are on the way to becoming part of the (supposedly) silent majority who currently figure so prominently in the legitimation of the police in Britain.

THE POLICE AND MARGINALISING TRANSITIONS: BECOMING A 'REGULAR CUSTOMER'

What though of those young people denied access to the world of work and consumption, those whose future has little constructive to offer? How are their relationships with the police transformed in the immediate post-sixteen years? Let us note here, first of all, that it is among marginalised youth that the limits of police pedagogy are to be found. In respect of this population, the attempt to proffer young people with sound advice seems rarely to bring positive results. And at some point officers simply give up; forced by experience to accept that a minority of economically excluded teenagers are destined to become 'regular customers' of the criminal justice system:

> I give kids a lot of advice regarding their future but there's some of them you'll find that their future is bleak and they will continue to commit crime and in another few years they will definitely be in some form of penal institute whether it's Polmont or Saughton. (*Male area officer*)

Among some officers, an appreciation of the problems faced by marginalised teenagers is readily apparent. As one put it: 'There's not a lot, especially for the fifteen to eighteen age group where they've just left school. They've still got all their friends around, but they haven't got jobs. That's a very difficult time for them. There's that gap of a few years where they get a wee bit lost.' Such empathy can even amount to an understanding of the relationship between youth and crime which moves beyond a prevailing 'law and order' paradigm. The following is typical and worth quoting at length:

> A: These Newcastle riots the other day, there's this whole Government thing saying, 'they're just hooligans, that's the end of it, full

stop'. That defeats the purpose of actually trying to find out why it happens, because it's just putting it into black and white. Yes, maybe they're young hooligans, but why are they young hooligans, why were they chucking bricks? I don't want to sound like I maybe should go and work in the social work department, cos I don't. But I'd say 90 per cent of the people that I arrest and detain, are okay. I understand quite a lot of them steal stuff. It doesn't excuse it but you can see it, understand why they do it.

IL: Why do you think it is then?

A: Theft? Social problems, there's no doubt about it. And because they live in a shitty place like Craigmillar where, because of a lack of investment, lack of resources, they live in this shitty place and that's what they get into because everybody else is doing it. So it's no good saying they steal because they're drug addicts so they're bad people. We know a lot of drug addicts are bad people. But there's a lot of MPs that are bad people; places like Niddrie or Craigmillar don't have a monopoly on bad people. (. . .) You've got to address the root cause. There's no point in just saying, 'they're just all buggers and they should be locked up'. As I say, they are little buggers, but why are they little buggers? You've got to ask yourself why they're doing it. (*Male beat officer*)

Outlooks such as this, while clearly evident, tend not to predominate among officers. The police more commonly view the criminological consequences of marginalising youth transitions in an occupationally specific, classicist manner. They see the increasingly serious offending of (some) unemployed youths in terms of individual choice and personal failing (understandings that undoubtedly render the police's ever more coercive tasks more palatable). Those young people who come to assume a prominent place within routine police workloads are constructed as a small 'hardcore' increasingly set in their lawbreaking ways:

You're wasting your time, you're never ever going to convert them. I can't think of one person who I've spoken to who has done an about turn and gone the right way. Once they're in, they're in deep. They'll not change their ways. That's young folk as well as older people. It's quite disheartening. (*Male beat officer*)

In setting apart this small 'hard core' from the majority of (unemployed) youth, officers foreground dispositions that are kept largely in abeyance while young people are 'growing up'. As petty delinquency and antisocial behaviour are superseded by more serious modes of offending, such matters are no longer conceived of as the 'natural exuberance' of (especially male) adolescence. Rather, two different registers of understanding come into play. First, the small 'hard-core' of repeat offenders are repositioned as the only to be expected products of local criminal families:

> With certain families you can see it happening. You can see where the big brother's seventeen, the younger child's three. The older one's been committing crime and you can see the younger one coming up, by the time he's ten he's been charged with a couple of offences. I've seen it in one family, every one of them has come to the notice of the police year after year. It starts off with running away from home, then minor crime, then more serious crime. (*Male beat officer*)

Second, and more encompassingly, the social practices of teenage youth are seen as fragmenting into a class culture characterised by hostility and anti-police sentiment:

> We're the bad people in the world. It's just the way the kids have been brought up, if you like. They don't like the police in this area. You get the occasional ones who are for the police, but a large percentage don't want to have anything to do with the police. (*Female beat officer*)

These new registers of understanding are not without their effects. As police officers come to view their 'regular customers' as serious, persistent offenders, some of their long harboured suspicions about teenage troublemakers are vindicated. The themes which dominate the routine policing of younger teenagers are thus stripped of their paternalism, and marginalised youth are reconstituted as 'police property' in a more unqualified fashion. Here, the demise of children's panels is of particular significance. Where juvenile 'offenders' have notched up an 'informal' record in the eyes of the police during their early teens, a sixteenth birthday can be an event of no little import. The force of the moment is appreciated by both the police and young people alike:

> You've got to realise that you get some people at fifteen who are hardened criminals. Nobody will admit this, but people in the system are marking time waiting for them to reach sixteen. (*Male juvenile liaison officer*)

A: Ken what they done? They ringed his sixteenth birthday on the calendar so they could get him in and leather him, I'm telling you it's the truth.

IL: How did you find that out?

A: Because they told him, 'wait till you're sixteen you wee bastard, we're going to kill you'. (*16-year-old females, Craigmillar*)

Marginalising transitions can also have consequences for young people's experiences of, and dispositions towards, the police. Of course, this is not the case, or at least not to any significant degree, among all unemployed youth. Those whose lives are increasingly centred around the home can, for example, largely insulate themselves from routine police attention. As one jobless eighteen-year-old male put it: 'I still like to have a laugh and that. I like a smoke of the hash, but as long as the police dinnae find out it dinnae bother me.' Such insulation is possible, not only because young people carry on their activities in the private realm (Stinchcombe, 1969), but also because their somewhat resigned accommodations present little (instrumental or symbolic) threat to social order. The police have neither reason nor opportunity to 'remind' such jobless teenagers of their plight.

The same cannot be said, however, of those who persist in hanging around public locations beyond sixteen. In the context of marginalising transitions, prevailing conceptions of hanging around as 'out of place' are reinforced among the police, shop owners, and local residents alike. Not only are older, unemployed teenagers expected to have 'grown out' of such practices, but their lack of incorporation within the disciplines of work signals, at best, idleness, at worst, trouble. Such perceptions can clearly rankle among the youths involved:

A: They shouldnae be doing the things they are doing. You could be standing at the corner right, not bothering anybody and they come along and it's 'fuck off away from here'. But you're not doing nothing. They're treating you like shite.

B: But we are shite to them. (*21/22-year-old males, Wester Hailes*)

This account suggests that marginalising transitions can place police–youth relations under some considerable strain, making conflict and hostility the order of the day. In these circumstances, policing can be a difficult business. Where trust has atrophied and mutual dialogue is rendered all but impossible, a whole series of routine police practices come to assume new, negative meanings. Thus, to take but one example, what police officers understand to be appropriate and occupationally sensible precautionary measures may – in this tension-ridden atmosphere – be viewed by the youths concerned as undue harassment propelled by spurious, class-based assumptions:

I was down Milton Road last week, Duddingston Road, outside the big houses. I stopped in my van to check a noise out, what happens? Police

stopped right behind me, never said what's wrong with your van, just
'what are you doing stopping in a neighbourhood like this?' . . . They
asked me where I come from first and I told them I stayed at Niddrie
Marischall: 'Oh aye, what are you doing stopping at this particular
house?' I said, 'if you think the house has been broken into, go and
check it'. And they did! That was as soon as I mentioned I was from
Niddrie. (*23-year-old male, Niddrie*)

Perhaps the most serious policing consequences of marginalising transitions are felt by those who use, or are suspected of using, various forms
of lawbreaking as a means of dealing with unemployment. Those among
marginalised youth who become police 'regulars' must learn to cope with
experiences and problems that the vast majority of young people have
barely to think about. The contrast with their former contemporaries could
not be more stark. As police stations, courts and penal institutions become
part and parcel of everyday life, these young people encounter new forms
of isolation and powerlessness, and have to find new ways of surviving
them. The following account illustrates this well:

There was four of them all questioning me at the same time all related
to one another. It was like they'd put all these questions into a hat and
they'd all pulled them out. Four of them firing questions, it was like
fucking *Mastermind*. Very intimidating. We were in this wee square
officey thing in the station right. You were the only one on that side
of the desk and these other four were on the other side, like an audi-
ence. All sitting in front of you all firing questions at you. Very, very
intimidating. (. . .)
    They can be bastards if they want to. Like when they've got you
in that police station, you're powerless, there is nothing you can do.
Nothing, zilcho. They can do away with you like that and nobody
would know. They could cover it up no bother. You're in there on
you're own. (. . .)
    You get the good cop and the bad cop, the one that's giving you the
fags and the one that's shouting at you. Every time. No matter if you
go in 25 times in a day it's always the same, always, always, always.
And you just sit there and laff cos you're so used to it: 'So you're the
good cop and you're the bad one, so can I have a cigarette now then
please.' They just laff at you and they just stop their wee act. But
you've got to let them know that you know or they'll just continue it.
Sometimes you just play along with it, sometimes it's good. You do
get a laff when you play along. (*19-year-old male, Broughton*)

Once embroiled in a complex of experience such as this, an understanding of policing as force comes, not surprisingly, to assert itself among marginalised youth. They thus have scant motivation to call upon the police for assistance; this concept forming little or no part of what, for them, policing is about. Constituted as 'police property', and as far from meeting the criteria of the 'ideal' victim as it is possible to imagine (Christie, 1986), the experiences and demands of marginalised teenagers as victims are less and less likely either to come to the attention of, or be taken seriously by, the police. Among some, a practical cognisance of this is reinforced by fleeting experiences of the police as victims of crime:

> See I was in a fight . . . on Thursday right, it was like three Glaswegian boys and they said, 'how you doing big man', and they started going on and a fight broke out, but when the police came in right, I was the one with all the cuts on my faces, but I was drunk, and I was told to, 'fuck off, before we charge you with breach of the peace and that'. And my girlfriend was there and I had other witnesses, cos I was just sitting there with my girlfriend, and they came in a started mouthing off. But when the police came in they told me to fuck off or I was getting lifted. But if I go and punch somebody, they're going to believe that person before they believe me cos I got previous. But on Thursday, I should have got them charged. I dinnae like the police. (*22-year-old male, Wester Hailes*)

Marginalising transitions, then, create circumstances in which young people and the police are likely to become increasingly and mutually Other. On the one hand, a small 'hard core' of offenders are constructed within the police world almost solely in terms of regulation. While for economically and socially excluded youth, the police come to be viewed as merely one among a multitude of problems that have to be confronted on a daily basis. The prospects for democratic communication could hardly be more remote. Yet these circumstances – desperate though they are – offer some valuable lessons, not only about the effects of social divisions on the quality of police–youth relations, but also about the limits of democratic communication. They serve, in particular, to remind us that what marginalised young people require most, is not mutual dialogue with the police (however beneficial that might turn out to be), but the creation of economic and social conditions which might enable the prominent place that crime and policing currently occupy in their lives to be eclipsed.

6 Talking Blues: Youth, the Police and Prospects for Communication

In coming to terms with young people's understandings of the police, we must move beyond the received idea that young people are – for reasons of age and immaturity alone – 'anti-police'. This view is seriously flawed. It is insufficiently alive to the substantive discrepancies that occur in young people's experiences of the police, as well as to the contrasting dispositions towards police authority they occasion. And it rests upon the complacent and politically paralysing assumption that because young people are undergoing a 'passing phase', their current experiences and demands *vis-à-vis* crime, safety and policing need not be taken too seriously.

Instead, we need to pay attention to the ambivalent and contradictory manner in which young people make sense of the police as a social institution. The following account is paradigmatic in this respect:

> Anybody who says we dinnae need the police is a fool. Because you need the police, you need the fire brigade, you need the ambulance, because if there wasnae people would be kicking in doors and raping people. Murders, stabbings, rapes, pillaging, gang bangs and everything. You need the police, there's no question about it. As much as you hate them, you need them. (*23-year-old male, Niddrie*)

My aim is this chapter is to explore the various ways in which this ambivalence manifests itself, focusing, in particular, on young people's philosophy of the police function and their perceptions of good and bad policing, and good and bad officers. The interpretation is informed, however, by a broader set of concerns. In analysing the accounts of young people and police officers, my overriding purpose is to examine the prospects for, and obstacles to, mutual dialogue that obtain within the present, as well as to consider the consequences of its absence for prevailing police–youth relations.

My contention shall be that sufficient reciprocal ground exists between young people and the police to make democratic communication more than a mere utopian pipedream, but that such possibilities are blocked by current institutional arrangements, and the patterns of experience and negative stereotypes they engender. The absence of democratic communication produces police–youth relations that render such communication more difficult to accomplish; the more it has to offer, the more difficult it is to achieve. But with these paradoxes we run ahead of ourselves. Let us begin with young people's grasp of the police function.

AN AGENCY OF LAST RESORT: YOUNG PEOPLE'S PRACTICAL PHILOSOPHIES OF THE POLICE FUNCTION

Perhaps the clearest refutation of the view that young people are blanketly 'anti-authority' is that they overwhelmingly recognise a legitimate role for the police. Despite often routine adversary encounters with the police, and a practical aspiration to minimise their contact with them, young people clearly believe the police to be necessary. Among some, this is part and parcel of a Hobbesian worldview which sees the police as holding the social together. As one seventeen-year-old put it: 'If there's no police force man, all the shops would be getting panned and people would be stabbing each other to death.' In a similar vein, the police are deemed necessary either to save young people from themselves, or to protect offenders from the vengeance of an impassioned public:

A: If there was no police, we wouldnae be sitting here, we'd be away breaking into shops and that.
B: Aye, getting money.
A: I wouldnae be sitting here, I'd be off. The [youth] club wouldnae be open because everybody would steal everything out of it, and smash it up and that. (*16-year-old females, Leith*)

IL: Do you think we need a police force then?
A: Oh aye, definitely. Cos if I got into a shop and stole a bike if there wasnae a police you could just chop my head off . . . Oh aye we definitely need the police. Just to control the public if anything else. (*20-year-old male, Niddrie*)

In general, however, the question of the police function evokes a certain ambivalence among young people, the seemingly arcane nature of the issue jarring with the logic they employ to make sense of everyday experience. Young people understand the police in terms of the concrete and particular, and their perceptions are filtered through this interpretive frame.

Questions concerning the police role thus surrender to the contradictions and ambiguities of a very practical consciousness:

IL: Do the police ever do any good?

A: Maybe if they went on strike?

IL: You think it would be a better place if we had no police at all?

A: Yeah, well maybe no. There would be a lot more killings and what have you. But there's far too many of them. There's more in Leith than what there is in Drylaw and Gayfield put together.

IL: How do you know that?

A: Well, put it this way, you walk down Leith Walk during the day and see at least twelve plain clothes walking about.

IL: Do you know their faces?

A: Aye.

IL: Do you think we need a police force then?

A: We need a police force, but not as many as what there is.

IL: What do you think they should be doing then?

A: I don't know, I just think there's far too many in Leith. (*17-year-old male, Leith*)

The divergence between the nonconcrete problem of the police function and a residual or, in some instances, ongoing experience of adversary contact generates among young people a number of tensions. The perceived necessity of the police is, for example, often grudgingly acknowledged, with young people drawing a sharp distinction between a generalised acceptance accorded to the institution, and the unacceptability of many of its practices. Abstract recognition sits uneasily alongside a practical sense of the police as enforcers of an unnegotiated public order:

I think we need the police, it disnae matter what they're like, if they're bent or crooks or whatever, you need them. Bairns [children] get raped, people get stabbed. You need the police for that. But for how they treat the working-class people, man, it's bad. There's no getting away from it. We're just dirt to them, that's what we are. (*23-year-old male, Niddrie*)

IL: Do you think we need a police force then?

A: If there was no police this place would be running wild.

B: You can say you can have a police force, but there's some things they shouldn't be able to do, like hit people with truncheons and stuff. (*17/18-year-old males, Mayfield*)

Young people most readily associate the police role with disruptions to social life that require some kind of external, authoritative force – incidents that rarely form part of their everyday experience. As one nineteen-year-old female put it: 'You need them to catch people, murderers, those who abduct kids, break into houses, things like that?' In this respect, young people believe the police's principal task to be regulating the behaviour of others; they are not an institution thought capable of impacting positively on young people's lives:

IL: If you could meet the police and tell them what you thought of them, what sort of things would you say?

A: I'd have a field day. It would be all cursing and swearing, definitely.

IL: But if the police said to you, 'what exactly do you want us to be doing?'.

B: I'd just say nothing. I dinnae want anything from you.

IL: But you said you need a police force.

B: Aye, only for stuff like murder, house break-ins, shop break-ins, rapes and what not. (*16-year-old females, Leith*)

For further illustration of this 'agency of last resort' interpretation of the police function, we might usefully recall the question of reporting crime. We saw in Chapter 3 how young people are for the most part reluctant to involve the police in their lives, either as victims or witnesses, fearing the amplificatory effects of such involvement. However, there exist thresholds beyond which this reticence is suspended, two of which stand out. First, the police are deemed necessary to deal with offences of acute seriousness, such as murder or child abuse: 'Child murders or abuse, I'd phone for that, I think everybody would phone for that . . . that's what I'd phone the police for, nothing else.' Here, concerns about the police amplifying the situation are neutralised by the fact that the predictability of the future has already been violently undermined. Indeed, formal police intervention may be seen as crucial step on the road to repairing the damage.

Police involvement is also considered necessary in respect of incidents whose evident injustice is such that an authoritative external force is required to make things good. In such cases (assaults on old people were the most often cited example), the role of the police is to intervene on behalf of the injured party and generate an equitable resolution:

IL: What if you saw someone being raped or murdered?

A: If it was anything to do with rape or that aye, I think I would. But just kids breaking in and that . . . if I seen a guy getting assaulted I wouldn't. If I seen a lassie getting hassled with guys,

ken what I mean, I would say something then. (*16-year-old
female, Craigmillar*)

If one of my family got done in by somebody I'd report that, but if
it's something like if a guy was beaten up by another guy, that's fair
enough, one to one, but say it was a group jumping somebody, one of
your pals, I would report it. (*16-year-old male, Gorebridge*)

The police role, then, is constructed by young people as pertaining to
events that do not impinge upon their everyday lives. Two aspects of this
are noteworthy. It seems, first of all, that the notion of the police as service
providers falls largely beyond young people's very practical grasp of policing, and that youth understandings are as a consequence thinly imbued
with the rhetorics of crime control so central to police legitimation among
'respectable' social groups. Secondly, and in a prefigurative context, these
accounts suggest that democratic reform oriented to increasing face-to-
face dialogue between young people and the police may not – in isolation at least – be either feasible, or effective in eliciting young people's
various concerns *vis-à-vis* policing.[1] Where trust is thin, and where young
people seek to minimise their contact with the police irrespective of its
nature, the advantages of direct, democratic communication are far from
immediately apparent.

INVISIBLE DISCOURSES: GOOD POLICING, GOOD OFFICERS

It has been evident throughout the last three chapters that young people
make sense of the police principally by telling stories about them. Story-
telling, as Agnes Heller (1982, ch. 3) among others has pointed out, is a
prominent feature of everyday life. Stories help people to orientate themselves in the world and thereby make their way in it. As such, the tales
people narrate to one another are judged, not so much in terms of their
truth or falsity, but according to how authentic or plausible they are; good
stories are those which 'fit' people's lives, helping them to order and make
sense of prevailing experience and expectation.
    Paramount among the stories young people tell about the police are
those which help them distinguish between good and bad policing, and
good and bad officers. Stories of this kind surfaced frequently during the
interviews, though they have, as will shortly become apparent, a markedly
different status, mode of construction and persuasive force. Let us consider good policing and good officers first.[2]
    At their most concrete, accounts of good policing pertain to how the

police control young people's collective use of public space. We saw in Chapter 3 that the policing of hanging around generates considerable bewilderment and even resentment among young people. This does not mean, however, that they believe such policing to be always in principle illegitimate. Rather, practical distinctions are made regarding how the police should and should not deal with congregating youths. Thus, young people causing trouble for others are seen as justifying police intervention, something most often voiced in respect of 'casuals', or by young women bothered about the actions of their male peers:

> I think they should be able to move them on if there is a really big group hanging about one shop, or not even a really big group. If there's three or four people hanging about in a quiet place, or not letting people past, then they should be able to move them on. And like if there is big groups of 'casuals' at the end of Princes Street shouting and bawling, I think they should be moved on as well. (*18-year-old female, Craigmillar*)

> IL: If you speak to the boys they say, 'we just get hassle from the police when we're not doing anything'. Do you think they're right to say that?
>
> A: No, because usually if they're hanging about in a group and you walk past them you get hassled and shouted at and that. (*18-year-old female, North Berwick*)

However, even in circumstances where young people feel police intervention to be warranted, they still wish to place limits on precisely what courses of action are open to the police. Good policing of young people hanging around requires that officers talk to those involved and appraise themselves of the situation. And it means making some effort to investigate the substance of the complaint, rather than unthinkingly dispersing the youths concerned:

> IL: What do you think the police should do if they get complaints like that?
>
> A: Just go and have a look and see if there's anything really wrong, because there's folk who phone the police just because there's a group, not because they're doing anything. They see there's somebody smoking a cigarette, 'oh, it must be drugs' or a guy with a can of juice, 'oh, alcoholics'. There's folk like that. (*16-year-old male, Gorebridge*)

Young people also evince a number of more generalised claims about the content of good policing. These amount, for the most part, to a wish to see more police officers patrolling the beat. As one nineteen-year-old female remarked: 'I'd like to see more policemen around the streets, not so much here but in the town. Around pubs and discos, and especially at night where there's trouble.' Among some, this is buttressed by a grounded understanding of the limits of car patrols:

> A: I think they should concentrate a lot more on the streets, instead of zooming about in their cars. I think we should have them back walking the streets. There should be a lot more than just the one or two.
>
> IL: Why would that make things better?
>
> A: Because you hear things on the streets that you dinnae hear stuck in a car driving past. If you walk on the streets you dinnae get a chance to miss much, you're seeing everything that passes you, everything that goes on. People hanging about on corners. In cars you dinnae do that. (*18-year-old female, Craigmillar*)

In a prefigurative vein, these accounts suggest that seeking to elicit from young people their concerns about the police will not always merely generate a succession of atrocity tales, but might actually furnish some positive suggestions about forms of acceptable policing. In the right circumstances, where some level of trust between the respective parties can be generated and sustained, defensive dispositions can be overcome and constructive dialogue is able to proceed. The conditions however must be right.[3]

In the absence of such conditions, the stories young people tell about good policing are rendered an invisible discourse, lacking any vehicle for institutional expression. Young people's sense of what legitimate policing might be is unable to contribute in any meaningful way to public deliberation about police policy and practice. And young people are accorded little opportunity either to demonstrate that they are not destructively 'anti-police', or to break down the mutually negative stereotypes engendered by prevailing patterns of police–youth contact.

Against this backdrop, accounts of good policing appear set to remain a subterranean influence among young people, a weakly persuasive contributor to their overall 'picture' of policing. They also seem likely to remain both hypothetical accounts of what good policing might look like, rather than recollections of its occurrence; and constructions of an interview context that rarely if ever circulate among young people outside of this setting. In short, these accounts are anticipations of good policing that rest uneasily alongside prevailing experience and expectation. They presently have little chance of becoming anything else.

What though of good police officers? What characteristics ought such officers to exhibit? Two aspects are apparent here. Negatively, a good officer is one who refrains from acts of physical violence. In more positive terms, he or she is someone young people can talk to. As one sixteen-year-old put it, a good officer is: 'Just somebody that's fair with you. Somebody that listens to reason. Just somebody that listens to you and disnae try and give you a slap.' The possibility of striking up a dialogue is thus central to what makes an officer acceptable, such dialogue being important in enabling police actions to be based upon a local knowledge of young people, rather than on sweeping generalisations about contemporary youth:

> A sergeant that I ken, he's brilliant with us, ken. He disnae pick anyone up in the streets for any reason at all. He's a really good guy. But the majority of the folk they bring them in from places in the town and they dinnae really ken anybody, they see somebody that looks like a trouble-maker and pick them up. But like the policeman Joe Smith, he kens everybody, and everybody kens what he's like. You can talk to him. (*16-year-old male, Gorebridge*)

In sharp contrast to those concerning good policing, stories of the good police officer tend to be constructed around officers young people have themselves known at some time or other. Against a backdrop of tense police–youth relations and predominantly adversary contact, good officers are often powerfully inscribed on young people's collective memory. Precisely because they stand out from the mass of their colleagues, such officers make a lasting impression on young people. In both senses of the term, they are exceptional:[4]

> A: A couple of police, they talk to you man, but not the bums who go about in the cars, but you get some good ones. That Jim man on the beat in Craigmillar, he used to talk to you.
>
> IL: What made him so different from the rest of them.
>
> B: Cos he used to talk to us, ken he never treated us like a piece of shit like the rest of them . . . He's just like one of the boys, but you get police who come up to you, 'right see you up the street right you're getting lifted'. (*17/18-year-old males, Craigmillar*)

Notwithstanding their 'exceptional' status, good officers continue to be connected by young people to the institution they embody and represent, something which can have important and paradoxical consequences. The decision to move a popular constable is, for example, often interpreted by young people as some Machievellian plot to deprive them of officers who become overly affable. As one eighteen-year-old female reflected: 'When

we first moved into Greendykes we had a friendly policeman, but he became too involved and too friendly with some of the people in Greendykes
so he was shifted.' In this respect, good officers can serve by default to
indict further 'the system' within which they operate:

> A: There was this policeman used to be in Broomhouse, like he got
> taken away from Broomhouse cos he was too good.
> B: Who was that?
> A: Barry. He was a really good policeman, like he used to sit and
> speak to you, like 'got any problems and all that'. So he used to
> give you time, like he's come to the door to collect your fines and
> he says, 'aye next week but dinnae let me down and that'. But he
> got moved from Wester Hailes to a desk job.
> C: Aye and Tony he was a brilliant old cunt.
> B: And Stevie he's good.
> A: But they've shipped them all out. (*20/22-year-old males, Wester
> Hailes*)

This conflation of individual and institution can have further effects. Principal among these is that officers who attempt to empathise with young
people are often understood to be 'after something'. As one sixteen-year-
old female commented: 'The only one I like is Tom Smith. He's in the
drug squad. But what he does is get on the good side of you and then he'll
say, "have you heard of anybody been selling tablets an that?" He gets in
your good books and then tries to find out information. Apart from that,
he's an all right guy.' Once apprehended in this way, good officers tend
to engender among young people a mixture of amused tolerance, suspicion
and outright cynicism:

> IL: Do you ever get good and bad police officers?
> A: No, some try to keep in with you for a wee bit.
> IL: How do they do that?
> A: Stand round for about an hour having a laugh.
> IL: Do you put up with them?
> B: Some of them you can put up with, some of them are just trying
> to pick your brain. They're fishing for information.
> IL: Don't they realise you know what they're up to?
> A: Some of them realise, but some keep coming back. (*16/17-year-
> old males, Leith*)

Officers who strive single handedly to improve police–youth relations face
an uphill struggle. In all sorts of ways, they are constrained and undermined by the institutional conditions they currently operate within, liable

to have their work undone at a stroke. Good officers set out to neutralise asymmetrical power relations between young people and the police by personalising them; in Weberian terms, they try to forge a charismatic authority around the attributes of an individual officer. Herein lie the reasons for failure. Against the backdrop of a system of accountability which provides few institutional opportunities for good relations between young people and the police to be generated and sustained, good officers compensate for, without ever overcoming, the resulting structural mistrust: they are 'good apples' in a 'bad barrel'.

INVESTMENTS IN BITTERNESS: BAD OFFICERS, BAD POLICING

In addition to furnishing various accounts of good policing, young people narrated during the interviews a whole range of stories concerning bad officers and bad policing. These tales, which were often recounted with both ease and relish, appear to be far more rooted in many young people's shared experience than those pertaining to acceptable police practice. And they seem to play a prominent part in constituting young people's overall sense of what policing is about. It is therefore crucial to come to terms with both their meanings and effects.

Unlike their positively apprehended colleagues, bad police officers are taken by young people to be emblematic of their routine experience of the police. Indeed, it often seems that all the capricious police behaviour that young people encounter gets embodied in the person of the bad officer, one whose abiding characteristic is to 'act smart' merely because he or she wears a uniform:

IL: How should things be different from how they are at the moment?
A: Not so cheeky, not so nosey.
B: And not so wide, because they're a bit wide for my liking. They think they're it because they've got uniforms on. (*16-year-old females, Leith*)

IL: What bothers you most about them?
A: The way they think they're the law. They think they can do whatever they want, because they've got a uniform on. (*16-year-old male, Leith*)

Bad officers are also those who base their actions upon what young people view as unwarranted stereotypes about local youth and the areas in which they live. As a twenty-year-old from one of Edinburgh's peripheral

housing schemes put it: 'They treat everybody the same, cos of where you
stay . . . they think "oh you're just a vandal and a thief". And nine times
out of ten they're wrong. But you just get tarred with the same brush.
That's what wrong with them.' Among some, a marked police reluctance
to communicate with local residents is seen as one predictable correlate
of this:

> They dinnae bother about the scheme. What happens when a car comes
> down Niddrie? Do they come out the car? If there's a gang of people
> standing there, what happens to the police, what do they do? Stop and
> pull down their windows, that's it. They'll not come out and talk to you.
> (*23-year-old male, Niddrie*)

Much of the raw material for young people's stories of bad policing
derives from the regulation of their use of public space. At the level of
priorities, many young people clearly feel that the police devote an undue
and disproportionate amount of attention to groups of youths hanging
around, and that it ought properly to be accorded less weight. Against this
backdrop, the justifications offered for police intervention often cut little
ice. As one eighteen-year-old male incredulously exclaimed: 'Calls off
neighbours because of a load of kids hanging about the streets? Why can
they not go and catch real criminals, ken what I mean?'

These misgivings about the way in which public space is controlled
focus, more specifically, on how officers handle discrete police–youth
encounters. Here two concerns stand out. Young people appear, first of
all, to resent the language officers employ and the attitude towards them
that it bespeaks:

> The way they talk to you and that ken. You get stopped and that and
> they tell you, 'you've got an attitude problem'. It's the way they speak
> to you ken. It's not as if they cannae say 'can I question you just now
> would you mind stepping in the car'. Down here it's 'get in the car or
> you'll get nicked'. That's what's it's like down here, that's what it's like.
> Police think just cos they're police officers they can do anything they
> want . . . but they cannae. (*18-year-old male, Niddrie*)

Secondly, there is evident frustration at the differential and seemingly
arbitrary outcomes which result from what young people regard as the
similar actions of each party:

> A: I dinna think it's right we get charged for hitting police and that
>   but they dinna get anything done to them if they batter us.
> IL: Has that happened to you?

A: I was doing something wrong and the police come. They were being cheeky and I was being cheeky back. This police wifey started to be wide, so I just hit her because she was being smart. So she started hitting me back and the police guy started on me too, so I got taken away and charged with assault for hitting the police wifey and the guy. But nothing happened to them for battering me. (*16-year-old female, Leith*)

Unlike young people's accounts of acceptable policing, those concerning bad policing are assembled from fragments of experience; they take the form, that is, of stories recounting incidents that happened either to young people themselves or to their peers. This, together with the ease with which they are recounted, suggests that tales of police malpractice circulate widely among young people (beyond the interview setting), and occupy a prominent place in their overall 'picture' of policing. The impact of bad policing can, it seems, be both widespread and lasting; with young people depositing accounts of such policing in a 'memory bank' to be drawn upon whenever the occasion demands:

A: They just victimise young people, that's what they do?
IL: But the police would say this group of young people was hanging about and we had a complaint?
B: I used to stay at Craigmillar, and there was about four of us at the bottom of the stair just talking to each other and nobody complained and the police car comes up and says right you go that way, you go that way, you go that way. They can't go about telling you what to do.
IL: What if the police are dealing with complaints from local residents?
A: Oh that's pish man.
IL: Do you really think it is?
A: They just say it, cos we're just standing like and they come up and tell you to shift and they come and sit somewhere else, and they come back and tell you to shift again. Eventually you get done and you ask them what you're getting done for and they dinnae say. (*17/18-year-old males, Niddrie*)

The resonance that narratives of bad policing have among many young people is largely a product of existing institutional arrangements and the patterns of police–youth contact they generate. Telling, receiving and transmitting these stories enables young people to make some sense of a routine experience of the police which all too often appears arbitrary and unfair. Here, the absence of opportunities for democratic communication can be especially marked in its effects. Not only does this absence generate among young people a feeling that police behaviour is almost entirely beyond their control, but it also enables the stories that emerge to make sense of this to persist unchallenged, thereby sustaining outlooks which render mutual dialogue more difficult to accomplish.

It is in these conditions that young people acquire an investment in bitterness. Bad policing – and the stories which radiate around it – becomes the grid through which young people's powerlessness *vis-à-vis* the police is registered and understood. For many, it is more important to come to terms with this powerlessness than to bother with remote abstractions about what good policing might look like:[5]

> If there was five houses broken into, I'd get charged for it, even though I didnae do it. It's just that you're from here and you get charged from the police, if anything's gone wrong, you can get charged for anything. They call it the powers, they just want to clear their books up so they just charge you for it. They've got that stop and search, they can pull up anybody at random. You could have a haversack walking along the road and they could stop you: 'I want to have a look in your haversack.' They've got the authority to do anything they want man. (*23-year-old male, Niddrie*)

This sense of powerlessness is symbolised most starkly by the police station, and it is here that the 'horror' stories about such locations which circulate among young people must be situated. Two themes predominate in these narratives. They are, first of all, largely third-hand accounts; representations by young people of what they think has happened to others, whether they be friends, family or peers. Secondly, they almost always concern incidents in which police officers are alleged to have meted out serious violence to young suspects. The following two accounts are typical in these respects:

> IL: How do you think the police treat young people round here?
> A: Bad. Very bad.
> IL: In what ways?
> B: You get knocked about and that at the police station.
> A: Especially when you're on your own, they just kick the shit out of you if you give them any cheek, they leather you.
> B: Aye. If you've been caught doing something they take you up and shove you in a cell and if you start being lippy they just come in and start on you, the bastards. (*16/18-year-old males, Craigmillar*)

They just take you into the cell and if they know they've not got enough evidence to charge you they give you six hours anyway, so they'll just give you a licking into the bargain. (*17-year-old male, Leith*)

I have no sure way of knowing whether, and if so to what extent, accounts such as these are 'true'. What does seem clear, however, especially given the frequency with which such tales arose during the research, is that police station 'horror' stories circulate widely among – and are taken to be authentic by – many young people, including those who have never set foot inside a police station. Young people's informal culture appears to provide an environment within which such stories can flourish:

A: Bracton station is getting a right reputation, I dinnae ken if you've heard about that. There's three people died since it opened. Johnny was one of them, a boy from Muirhouse. A boy from Tranent, what was his name?, Tam's brother, he died in the police station. He was a junkie. (. . .) There's a case going on about that the now, trying to sue the police. There's another one, what's his name. He died in Bracton police station. It's just since that Bracton opened, cos the High Street and that was okay. Fair enough, you'd get a wee bit of a skelp. But Bracton station, every fucking young laddie round about says you get battered. I've seen people with black eyes when they come out the station.

IL: How do you hear about these things?

A: The word on the street's never wrong. If there's word on the street something's happened, everybody adds his piece to every story, they all add their own wee bit. But you say to yourself, well, the guy did get a kicking but maybe he's exaggerating what happened. Bracton police station is getting a really bad reputation and it's not been opened that long. (*23-year-old male, Niddrie*)

Police officers are themselves acutely aware of the fact that tales of police violence are fairly common currency among young people. And they know too of the damage this state of affairs can exact upon police–youth relations. As one officer lamented: 'Even now, you get a young person in the police box and they think they're going to get a doing. They look around as if to say, "when's it start then". It's sad, very sad.' The police also have to hand an array of explanations for the apparent resonance of police station 'horror' stories. A few officers sense that these narratives may have a kernel in actual events; as one put it: 'I'm sure a few of them have had a thick ear from time to time.' Even so, the police believe these tales to have been greatly exaggerated by the time they solidify into local folklore:

It's like a popular myth and I think it spreads so fast because everybody's always heard a story of somebody who knew somebody, who knew somebody else, who was taken into a police station and had a bad time, and he went into complain about something and was told to piss off. It's like Chinese whispers, it just gets bigger and bigger. (*Male beat officer*)

In a slightly different vein, some officers feel that these narratives allow young people (and we are talking here mostly of young men) to use their detention as a way of augmenting their reputation among peers; something that requires the construction of a heroic story in which the young suspect endures – and survives – police violence. As one beat officer put it: 'They'll go back to their mates and say they've been knocked about by the police, just for the image to their cronies. Ninety-nine times out of a hundred it isn't the case at all, but it's the macho thing to say, "the police gave me a doing". It doesn't happen.'

More commonly, police officers point to the acute difficulties of assaulting a suspect given the circumstances in which the alleged incidents are supposed to have happened. As one officer observed: 'The thing is, you come into this place, there's video cameras everywhere, you've got everyone and their brother looking over their shoulder and you daren't raise your hands to somebody.' In this context, one officer commented specifically on the ill-fated police station mentioned above:

There was a thing in the paper recently, somebody writing in and complaining about Bracton, saying that everybody who was brought in there was beaten up and all the rest of it, and this friend had told him that this happened. I think the bosses fall down here because they never seem to challenge these things, they just let them go. Bracton has got cameras everywhere, anyone they've brought in there there's no way anyone's going to do anything to them, and yet the bosses never kill these rumours straight away, they just sort of ignore them. (*Male beat officer*)

These various explanations cohere around the firmly held belief that young people's assertions concerning police violence are mistaken, either wilfully or because they have been misled. In this respect, officers evince an overwhelming desire to challenge these allegations and put the record straight:

I had a lad speaking to me the other night, he hated the police and I asked him to explain why and it was things he had been told third-hand. And I went through every incident he was talking about and nothing

was a personal experience, it was a case of what he had heard about
and I was able to refute everything he said. He was a wee bit stunned.
(*Male beat officer*)

These police accounts are not without plausibility – telling a 'good' story
may well provide some young people with a means to enhance both peer
and self-esteem. But they fail – for good occupational reasons no doubt –
to address a number of important questions. Why, for example, do these
tales and not others resonate so widely and influentually among young
people? Why is it that narratives of police violence encounter a cultural
context only too willing to receive, believe and reproduce them? By neglecting these issues, current police explanations largely miss the point.

'Horror' stories about police stations take hold among young people,
not because they have been led astray by malign and dominant peers, nor,
at the other extreme, because they reflect young people's experience in
any direct, unmediated fashion. Rather, these stories resonate because they
speak to shared concerns and anxieties about routine policing; concerns
about what the police can do if they so choose. They remind young people
that the police are the thinly accountable bearers of coercive authority.
In this respect, strategies aimed at convincing young people that police
station 'horror' stories are inaccurate, and that their belief in them is mis-
placed, are both ill-judged and unlikely to succeed. If these stories are
symbolic of a more generalised distrust of the police, their persuasive
force will only diminish when police practice as a whole acquires some
greater legitimacy in the eyes of young people.

'GETTING THE MESSAGE ACROSS': POLICE PERSPECTIVES ON COMMUNICATION

Is it possible to locate in the present the seeds of a different, more communicative future for police–youth relations? The answer, I believe, is a
qualified yes. Among young people and police officers alike one finds,
expressed in highly contextualised and often inchoate forms, aspirations
for some kind of enhanced mutual dialogue. Yet in both cases, this hope
is tempered, sometimes even extinguished, by the prevailing realities of
police–youth experience. Let us consider this further, starting with the
police.

Police officers are under few illusions as to the negative effects adversarial
street encounters have on the quality of police–youth relations. In particular, many believe that such encounters generate among young people a

partial, inaccurate perception of the police as agents only of coercive control:

> The trouble is that most of the kids that we come into contact with are doing something wrong, like the kids who are hanging about street corners causing a nuisance to local residents. You come into contact with them not because you're stopping for a friendly chat, but usually because you're asking them to keep the noise down or go away and find somewhere else to stand. (*Male beat officer*)

> The only perception the kids have of the police in general is when they see police cars whizzing about with a blue light, stopping on a street corner, picking on – as far as they can see – kids for no apparent reason, without appreciating the full scenario. And they look upon us as the enemy, shall we say, or the aggressors. (*Male beat officer*)

Talking to young people is considered valuable in so far as it gives officers the chance to challenge and correct these received impressions. Communication holds out the possibility of change; the chance that entrenched hostile dispositions and negative stereotypes may be transcended. As one beat officer put it: 'If they've got gripes, fair enough. They're bound to have. It's a case of talking to the kids in these groups, they've got a mistrust of us and we've got to earn their trust, and the only way we can do that is to go and speak to them.' Among some officers, this feeling is very much a product of their experience of trying to break down barriers with young people:

> What I would say is talking does help, there's no doubt about that. If you get up a dialogue, it's better than seeing some guy in a black uniform, he's pissed off, he's walking along with a big glum face. That doesn't do any good to anybody. And that's what a lot of people actually see. Or they get somebody winding down the window and saying, 'come on, stop hanging about street corners, away you go'. So maybe if you started to talk to people it would help. (*Male beat officer*)

For some, however, significant change needs more than mere communication between young people and the police. It also requires a willingness among both 'sides' to open themselves up to criticism. As one officer remarked: 'The youngsters must see our side of it as well and not just their side of it. They must do that. In order for you to criticise somebody you must look at, and know about, the other side.' In this vein, some officers recognise that attitudes conducive to mutual dialogue are unlikely to be generated and sustained in the current climate of encounter and

experience. Rather, they need settings where asymmetrical power relations
are neutralised, and where the 'paradox of face' that pervades fleeting
police–youth contact on the street stands some chance of being dissolved:

> You couldn't stand on a street corner with a group of fourteen-year-olds
> and get stuck in, that looks terrible, they're questioning your authority.
> But if you go into a controlled environment like a school, and just sit
> there, have a forum of ten, fifteen, twenty of them and just let them have
> a go at you and try and answer that way, that might be a good start.
> Because they're getting the opportunity without the fear of getting
> themselves arrested or a foot up the backside to have a go at the police,
> and then maybe you will find out what the problems are. If there are any
> great problems you'll have a better chance of finding out what they are,
> and it gives us a chance to answer them . . . If you want to try and foster
> proper links with that age group I think you should be prepared to go
> into their environment but not to preach. (*Male beat officer*)

This is an excellent example of what is required – on the police side – if
democratic communication between the police and young people is to be
accomplished. But dispositions of this sort find themselves up against a
whole range of organisational and ideological obstacles. As an institution, the police are not presently organised in ways that facilitate ongoing
dialogue with the various 'publics' they serve. The police have tended
to operate with a 'we know best' approach to matters of 'law and order',
one reinforced by the received traditions of constabulary independence.
Officers, as a result, are rarely trained, encouraged or motivated to think
about developing genuine discursive relationships with the social groups
they police. It is simply not a central part of their work.

One consequence of this is that the day-to-day demands confronting
officers currently preclude any communication with young people beyond
that which occurs during sporadic encounters. Where officers are, or feel
themselves to be, under pressure, taking time to talk to young people,
or to reflect on the various issues at stake, is consigned to the realm of
indulgence:

> I work in a busy area. I don't have the time to actually think about these
> things in depth. All I do is do what I've got to do. I get the necessary
> details, I go through the necessary procedures, submit the reports and
> that's it finished. Because I can be doing two or three a week. So there's
> no time to actually consider what's happening, consider what they've
> done or think about it. Maybe it's not the right way, but it's not my
> problem. (*Male area officer*)

The prevailing organisational ethos also tends to generate among officers insular and defensive dispositions towards their work. These attitudes – most prominently those which imagine the police as a 'thin blue line' besieged from all sides – are clearly inimical to the possibility of genuine police–public dialogue, whether with young people or anyone else. A crucial component of this insularity is the prevalent belief that the police are under threat, understaffed and in ever-present danger of 'losing the place':

> The bosses haven't got a clue what we do, of the problems we have down here. Morale's rock bottom in this service. We've been 'losing the place' for a while now. People know it but there too scared to tell anyone. (*Male beat officer*)

> One Thursday night, during the Festival I may add, so it was more densely packed than it normally is. There were five police officers to cover that area. Now there's only so much the police can do. (. . .) We had five police officers on that night; there was an acting inspector, there was myself as acting sergeant, and there were three constables. So what do you do? What can you do? (*Male beat officer*)

This is not to say that organised communication between young people and the police does not currently take place. Indeed, during the past couple of decades, the police have made immense efforts to improve such communication, creating jobs and units – such as area constables and community involvement departments – devoted precisely to this task. But these developments have generated some paradoxical and unintended outcomes, one of which has been to minimise the importance so-called 'frontline' officers attach to this aspect of their work. Many patrol officers clearly believe that communicating with young people has been hived-off to community involvement, and need not really concern them:

> I'm not really a community type policeman. We basically get a call, we go and attend to it and deal with it as best we can. Where as you get the other type cops who you'll be speaking to, Bob McDonald for one, who are area constables and they go round the schools and try and develop a better relationship between the kids and the police. (*Male beat officer*)

Attitudes such as these are problematic because they ignore the extent to which young people's perceptions of the police are shaped, not by an occasional chat with a 'community' constable, but by their everyday experiences of policing (Anderson *et al.*, 1994, ch. 5). 'Frontline' officers unconcerned with how they talk to the young people they come across, merely undermine the work of those – 'good officers' – whose principal task is to generate and sustain dialogue. Until building trust with young people is seen as the routine responsibility of every officer, the job of 'community' constables will remain that of repairing the damage.

The obstacles to improving police–youth communication are not merely organisational, however. A number of ideological barriers also currently stands in its way. The most prominent of these has been touched upon in various contexts already and concerns the binary distinction officers make between those teenagers it is possible to talk to and those it is not. Firmly located on the wrong side of this divide are the 'trouble-makers' officers construct as almost entirely Other – beyond the pale of any rational discussion:

> These kids, if you go up to them and say 'get lost', they don't take any offence, that's the language they get at home. So you can go up to them and say, 'you lot, fuck off'. That may sound dreadful, but that's the language they use and understand, they don't think that's bad language. If you're speaking to a French person you wouldn't speak to them in another language, likewise English. They don't understand us sitting here speaking, that doesn't make sense to them, maybe in here they would, but not out on the street, that's not their language. They don't understand 'please', they just understand 'get lost'. (*Male area officer*)

On the whole, officers believe that police efforts to communicate with young people should be directed at those teetering on the brink of crime – 'The ones out there who are saveable.' One officer couched this strategy in the following terms: 'You've got to target a section of them. What's the point of targeting people that like the police or accept the need for a police service? And what's the point of targeting jail bait?' Among this carefully chosen group of youths, the objective of police 'communication' is to dis-suade them from going the way of their lawbreaking peers:

> Some of them are quite receptive to speaking once you sit down. A lot of these kids who roam Princes Street are not by any manner of means bad kids or criminals. They have just maybe never had any contact with the police whatsoever and they learn street habits from other kids they meet up town who're maybe more inclined to be criminal than they are. (*Male beat officer*)

The bifurcation of young people does not only revolve around the per-ceived depth of their involvement in crime. It is also fashioned more generally along lines of age. Many officers, for example, feel that by the time young people reach sixteen, they are set in their ways and unamenable to any positive police influence. As one officer put it: 'I'm afraid by the time they get to the teenage level, their ideas are already painted in their heads and I don't think you'll change them.' This view is prevalent among officers and it generates an aspiration to focus the police's communicative efforts on a younger age group. This is preferred for two reasons. In the first place, it enables officers to catch the next – currently pre-delinquent – generation and instil in them the right complex of attitudes before they 'start to turn'. In a more pragmatic vein, children present officers with what appears to be a less daunting task than engaging in dialogue with 'difficult' teenagers. The following account captures both these aspects well:

> By the time you reach third or fourth year at school, they're not going to listen to you. It doesn't matter what you say to them, if they're on the right track they're on the right track. What you have to do is catch them before they go on to the wrong track, at primary school. If you can catch them then and get some ideas into their heads, they'll know you are there and you're not this nasty person who goes around locking people up all the time. Then it's obviously going to catch a few of them. There are still going to be one or two who are going to go astray no matter what you say to them. But you need to catch them before they get into the bad attitudes and mixing with older ones where it's all show and bravado. (*Female area officer*)

For some officers, however, the challenge presented by older teenagers is what matters. They believe that only once young people are confronted by the imminent burdens of 'adulthood' are the police able to talk to them profitably. As one beat officer put it: 'It's not until they hit sixteen and think, "oh, I've got my exams to sit". Maybe then you'd be able to talk to them again. When they're starting to get responsible, because they're having to think about what they're going to do with their lives.' This view is accompanied, among some, by often stringent criticism of the priority the organisation currently accords to 'singing songs' with young children:

> What's the point of going along and talking to a group of five-year-olds? Anyone can go along and talk to a group of five-year-olds and they'll listen to you. I think it's just the easy option, to be honest with you. Which is maybe understandable, because why knock your head off a brick wall if you think that's what you're going to do. I think if they targeted the early teens a lot more, perhaps you would be able to foster a greater understanding. The problems we've got on a Friday or

Saturday night dealing with folk on the streets, they never understand how we feel. (*Male beat officer*)

Buried within these accounts of communication are two significant and connected themes which need to be made explicit. It seems, first of all, that the police primarily perceive communication as a process of addressing teenagers as individuals, something which renders officers largely ignorant of young people's shared experiences and concerns *vis-à-vis* crime and policing. Secondly, and perhaps more importantly, police officers tend to think of communication as a one-way process of 'getting the message across' to young people, something one officer described as: 'Trying to give them some guidance in the rights and wrongs from our point of view.' On this view, dialogue with young people is constructed as a monological encounter in which there is but one voice – that of the police:

If you're getting through to a few of them, that's a few more people on your side. That's what it's all about, trying to get them on your side, trying to get them to report things. It is difficult, but if you can catch them young enough where there's not all this bravado. (. . .) But it has to start at a young enough age where they're not already blinkered or their opinions haven't been formed by older people, because you do get that. (*Female area officer*)

I think it's a case of every little helps, if you maybe keep pounding away the message may get through to some of the people, or most of the people. But if they just take one or two points on board, it helps. (*Male beat officer*)

These conceptions of 'dialogue' have some serious shortcomings, especially when viewed from the vantage point of democratic communication. They suggest that police dialogue with young people amounts merely to the mobilisation of a paternalistic and proselytising power, whereby officers endeavour to bring about – for young people's own good – a conversion from one form of life to another. This mobilisation is largely concerned with enlisting the support of social groups perceived to have troubled relations with the police, rather than with seeking to engage young people in mutual deliberation about matters of crime and policing. As such, it posits policing as a given, already determined practice and assumes that communication can proceed apace without it threatening anything the police currently believe or do.

'YOU CAN'T BEAT THE SYSTEM': YOUTH PERSPECTIVES ON COMMUNICATION

Young people's aspirations for enhanced dialogue with the police are both less pronounced and rather more inchoate than those existing among police officers. This in many ways should come as no surprise. The police are but one of the institutions that impinge upon young people's lives, and for most, they are no nowhere near being the most important. The possibility of engaging in dialogue about matters of policing does not currently loom large in the outlooks of young people.

Nevertheless, it is possible to identify some dispositions of this kind. In most instances, these amount to young people wanting to find ways of ensuring that the police, 'take more notice of what teenagers say'. As one sixteen-year-old male requested: 'Ask them to understand us more instead of jumping to conclusions that we're all violent alcoholics.' In other words, young people conceive of communication as a way of breaking down police stereotypes of 'youth', and of enhancing mutual understanding more generally:

> I think they should try and talk to the kids, at least. If they try and talk to them, they may get some sort of a response. (. . .) You know if there was some kind of liaison or communication between the police and them. If they were there a bit more often the police could see their problems and there'd be a better understanding of them, they wouldn't just think, 'well that's pigs for you'. (*19-year-old male, Broughton*)

These aspirations have, however, to be placed in the context of young people's routine experiences of the police. In some respects, young people's dispositions bespeak a desire to find a way out of current patterns of perception and experience. But for the most part, it is this experience that wins out, serving to extinguish any discursive possibilities young people might imagine to exist. The reason for this lies in the fleeting and adversarial form of prevailing police–youth encounters. These encounters, as we have seen, provide young people with precious little opportunity to persuade police officers of the legitimacy of their actions, let alone have them act accordingly. As a result, the police are seen as having an unimpeachable capacity to determine situational reality; officers are able to bring into existence that which they utter (Bourdieu, 1991, p. 42):

> If there was a group of ten folk in the main street and a policeman came and says, 'he done such and such'. But if he never done such and such, they'd rather take the policeman's word. I dinnae think that's right, ken.

The policeman's always right and the teenagers round the streets tell
lies and everything all the time. They never believe what a teenager
says. (*16-year-old male, Penicuik*)

The power of officers to determine the direction and outcome of police–
youth encounters has a number of significant consequences. It creates,
most immediately, circumstances in which the most readily available and
seemingly effective form of 'communication' open to young people is
some kind of situational defiance:

A: I got kicked out of the place, searching my bag and everything in
     front of god knows how many people. Because I was sitting in the
     cafe, she accused me of loitering . . . You're trying to explain to
     them, 'what else am I supposed to do, I'm just sitting somewhere
     warm'. I mean I did have money and I was buying tea and chips
     and that from the cafe. I sat there for ages fair enough, but I was
     still buying things. I could understand if I wasnae. No, I couldnae
     understand it if I wasnae either. I told them that I didnae have
     nowhere to go, nowhere at all and she said, 'I'm sorry but you just
     cannae stay here'. I said, 'but why?' and the policewoman was
     getting really cheeky . . . she told me to empty my bags and I said,
     'no empty it yourself' and she said, 'empty it or I'll drag you
     along to the station by your hair'.
IL: What did you do?
A: I just emptied it, I opened the bag and tipped the whole lot on the
     floor. Right at her feet. She wasnae happy with that either and I got
     a mouthful of abuse for that as well. (*18-year-old female, Niddrie*)

This incident concerned a young women who was homeless and 'living'
in Edinburgh Waverley railway station. But it illustrates at a more general
level how – in circumstances marked by manifestly asymmetrical power
relations – the main response open to young people is that most likely to
reinforce negative police perceptions of youth. Denied an opportunity to
communicate their side of the story, and believing that the police are not
going to take them seriously, young people resort to actions which further
jeopardise already tense police–youth relations. The vicious circle that can
so easily ensue is not difficult to detect.

   These encounters – and the limited opportunities for mutual dialogue
they permit – serve, secondly, to atrophy any residual sympathy young
people have for the police and their actions. Here, once again, a chain of
action and reaction is sparked, the end result of which is that mutually
hostile stereotypes are amplified and reinforced. As one sixteen-year-old

male put it: 'A lot of them [the police] do get hassle but they provoke us, ken. They come up and make smart comments and we're just sticking up for ourselves.' The plight of the young woman 'living' in Edinburgh's railway station illustrates further this spiral of decline:

A: We used to just run about the place. We werenae doing it to begin with we were just sitting about. But when they started threatening us, taking us in to get strip-searched and all the rest of it, we didnae have to sit there and take that off of them. We werenae doing anything. We had nowhere else to go.

IL: Did you ever explain that?

A: Aye. They just said, 'it's not our fault. Basically it's nothing to do with us. We cannae help it, we're just doing our job.' Cheers! What can you say?

IL: Why do you think the police bothered you so much?

A: I think there is a lot of trouble down at the train station anyway. With people stealing. Like you get your wee paper shop, people do steal out of there, fair enough, and I can see their point that they're wanting us out the way. But I didnae think they had to do it the way they did it and use the attitudes they did use. We were troublemakers after a while, we caused trouble for them. (*18-year-old female, Niddrie*)

Police–youth encounters also create among many young people a practical sense that their utterances have, at best, a weakly persuasive force in determining the outcome of any situation. Young people know both that police language is backed up by external force, and that their own – meaningful though it is to them – is woefully inadequate to deal with the situation at hand (Bourdieu, 1991). As one twenty-one-year-old female exclaimed: 'You cannae tell them that they're in the wrong. They dinnae like it when you tell them that they're wrong.' These grounded dispositions substantially negate any belief young people may have in the prospect of genuine communication with the police, confining it to the realm of the unthinkable:

IL: If you could meet the police and talk to them about what they should be doing, what would you tell them?

A: I'd tell them to stop harassing people, telling them to move on. You're just standing there talking to your mate and you get told to shift and all that shit man. But there's nothing you can really say to the police. There's not much you can do about them is there? (*17-year-old male, Niddrie*)

IL: Do you think the police ever listen to what you say?
A: No. To them we're undesirables.
IL: Do you think they should listen?
A: Aye, everybody's got a matter of opinion. (*17-year-old male, Leith*)

Acts of situational defiance aside, young people, it seems, develop overall
a resigned acceptance of the police's capacity to define and control their
use of public space. Buffeted by experience, they come, in Giddens (1991,
p. 110) terms, to repudiate 'a controlling orientation to the future in favour
of an attitude that lets events come as they will'. In short, many young
people become fatalistic about the police; such fatalism providing them
with a way of making practical sense of an institution that to all intents
and purposes appears beyond their control. This is most often encapsulated in the refrain 'you can't beat the system':

IL: Have you ever had a bad time off the police?
A: Well, when I was younger I got a right kicking, that's when I was
    fourteen or fifteen. I was what you call a tearaway. I was trying
    to beat the system. The dog patrols used to come up here, eh . . .
    You'd get dog handlers, they used to come up here to have a
    square go with the young guys, when we were young. They used
    to just come up to have a square go. Some of it's hard to believe
    but it happened.
IL: You say you used to try to beat the system, do you still do that?
A: Oh no, you cannae beat the system. It's impossible, there's too
    many of them.
IL: What do you mean by them?
A: The police. It's like fighting an army. You cannae beat them. And
    if you complain against one they just get their pals to harass you.
    (*23-year-old male, Niddrie*)

Perhaps the most concrete illustration of this fatalism is to be found in
young people's accounts of police complaints. A meaningful chance to
complain about police malpractice is taken by most young people to be
the *sine qua non* of accountability. For them, an accountable police force
is one that 'sticks to the rules'. At the same time, however, young people
display a marked reluctance to complain about instances of perceived
police malpractice. Among some, such reticence is of a generic kind. In
so far as it disturbs further already disrupted routines, complaining about
the police is deemed simply 'not worth it':

IL: Have you ever thought of complaining [about being regularly
    stopped in his car]?

A: I did think about complaining. I've thought of going in and say-
      ing, 'this is the twenty-fifth time, police harassment and all that
      sort of thing'. It's more bother than it's worth.

IL: Would it do any good if you did?

A: It's just the system, if you can't beat them, join them. (*21-year-old
      male, Bonnyrigg*)

This reluctance to complain about police malpractice is, more specifically,
the product of young people's overwhelming belief that their complaints
will not be listened to, let alone taken seriously. As one seventeen-year-
old male put it: 'Complain to who? Who'd believe you? It's my word
against theirs in it. They're gonnae believe them before they believe me.'
Here, young people's understandings focus upon the difficulties encountered in charging an institution perceived as governing its own affairs:

You imagine six policemen coming to your house battering the shit out
of you or in the station. You try to charge six police, whose word are
they going to take, theirs or ours? You've no chance. You're up against
the system, you've just no chance. It's the cops against the cops. It's
like brickies and labourers and scaffolders, they all stick together eh,
they're all relying on each other's safety. It's the same with the police.
They're relying on each other. You cannae beat the system. (*23-year-
old male, Niddrie*)

In most cases, young people's perceptions of this issue rest on this plaint-
ive note. On occasions, however, different possibilities are glimpsed, as in
the belief that an external and independent body might provide a more
adequate means of bringing police practice to account:

IL: Would you ever complain, like about that time at the station [she
      had been required, as we saw earlier, to empty her bag in the rail-
      way station cafe]?

A: Aye, I was very annoyed about that. I didnae think about complain-
      ing. There's no point in complaining cos there's been too much
      trouble down in the train station for anybody to listen. But there
      should be somebody there who will listen, not a police officer,
      but maybe some other sort of person down there to listen to com-
      plaints like that, a councillor or something. Cos you cannae really
      go to a policeman and say this other policeman battered you, ken
      what I mean. When you work with them, they're just not going to
      listen to you. (*18-year-old female, Niddrie*)

Seyla Benhabib (1986, ch. 8) has recently made the important point that any demand for, or movement towards, greater institutionalised dialogue is always already rooted in social contexts permeated by patterns of collective learning, experience and memory. The patterns of 'learning, experience and memory' currently available to young people *vis-à-vis* the police are typified largely by encounters in public space – encounters all too often marked by the 'paradox of face'. In the odd case, these experiences create a hankering for enhanced dialogue. But for the most part, they generate the kind of mutual suspicion and hostility that confines such dialogue to the realm of the unthinkable. It seems – and this I take to be the abiding lesson of this research – that the absence of democratic communication between young people and the police creates conditions in which such communication is ever more difficult to achieve. As one nineteen-year-old male astutely put it: 'They've got an image to present to us, so we'll be bastards back to them. So it's really a no win situation I think. We'll never solve it.'

7 Towards Discursive Policing

> Pure and indirect critique can of course be forces for change. But critique that intimates no feasible or attainable alternative fails in its practical task. For defenders of the status quo, warts and all, can argue that really 'there is no alternative'. And if there is no alternative, then ultimately there is no critique. (Dryzek, 1990, p. 31)

I have in the last four chapters identified some of the tensions that currently bedevil police–youth relations and suggested how they may be a consequence of an absence of democratic communication. But can this situation be rectified? Is it possible to construct institutional arrangements capable of making good the democratic shortcomings of managerialism and improving relations between the police and young people?

My aim in this final chapter is to suggest one such possibility. Drawing upon some recent political theory, I want to outline and defend a principle of *discursive policing* and indicate how it might enhance the democratic accountability of the police in general, and police–youth relations in particular.[1] By discursive policing I mean police policies and practices that are formulated, implemented and evaluated on the basis of public deliberation among all affected parties; such deliberation proceeding by reference to the common good and requiring participants to justify their claims in the light of that good. Discursive policing is, in this respect, a principle of organisation; a way of structuring the relationship between the police and the 'publics' they serve.[2] Its aim is to create a police force responsive to all citizens; one with the organisational capacity to encourage dialogue, take account of new ideas, recognise the public good, and respect the claims and entitlements of even the least powerful social groups. Discursive policing demands, in other words, that the police act as a moral institution; one concerned not only with achieving its crime control, order maintenance and associated goals, but also with protecting and enhancing democratic rights and values (cf. Selznick, 1992).

Thus conceived, discursive policing does not specify the exact shape that institutional arrangements for governing the police must take. But this does not allow us to abdicate from the task of institution-building entirely. For not only does the idea of discursive policing need embedding in some kind of institutional form, but its worth can only properly be assessed once it has been elaborated in these terms. This chapter therefore sets out what these institutional mechanisms might look like. Dealing, in turn, with the limits, settings, boundaries and practices of discursive policing, my aim is to outline the contours of a regulatory body capable of ensuring that policing proceeds in accordance with the principles set out above. This proposed body I shall call a police commission.

In developing these ideas, it is not my intention to come up with a utopian blueprint to be accepted or rejected *en bloc*. My aim rather is to establish an 'enlarged way of thinking' (Arendt, 1961, p. 220) about the question of police governance; one that seeks to challenge, relativise and transcend the narrow, administrative preoccupations of the present. In this sense, the ensuing proposals are unapologetically utopian, however. They remind us that the developments currently taking place under the sign of managerialism are but one of the available options for policing in Britain. Other more democratic and socially just futures are possible.

DECENTRING THE POLICE: THE LIMITS OF DISCURSIVE POLICING

I want to begin outlining the case for discursive policing by establishing the limits of its potential. Though this may seem a rather curious starting point, it is in the present context a vital one. For the research suggests that many of the troubles which presently bedevil police–youth relations are not amenable to a specifically policing solution, whether of a discursive or any other kind. Three examples will suffice to illustrate this.

We need to recognise, first of all, the deleterious effects of unemployment and poverty on police–youth relations. The accounts discussed in Chapter 5 suggest that one all too likely consequence of youth joblessness is to intensify adversary contact between young people (especially young men) and the police, and reinforce what are often already negative stereotypes and dispositions. Under these circumstances, police–youth relations are placed under immense strain and democratic communication is constructed by both young people and police officers alike as a remote, not to say irrelevant, prospect. The enhancement of these relations requires not so much discursive policing, as the creation of economic and social conditions that enable the police to recede from the currently prominent place they occupy in the lives of many unemployed and disaffected young people.

There are, secondly, lessons to be learnt from young people's experience of being moved on by the police while hanging around in public places. This – in some cases routine – contact presently generates among the teenagers involved a combination of often lasting bewilderment, cynicism and fatalism, and contributes much to their overall sense of what policing is about. The accounts discussed in Chapter 4 also suggest that police officers consider such policing to be a waste of time and resources. Yet officers feel compelled to respond to public complaints about noisy teenagers, the result being that disputes about the legitimate use of public space get 'resolved' by the police in ways that do untold damage to their relations with young people. The difficulty here is not so much how this policing is currently carried out (though aspects of this are of concern), but the fact that congregating youths are thought of and acted upon as a policing problem at all. Lasting, effective and just solutions require the depolicing of young people's collective use of public space; the issue needs reconstituting outside of a 'law and order' paradigm and subjecting to processes of democratic communication and mediation. Only then will the various disputants have any chance of reaching a settlement that does not constantly threaten to criminalise one of the parties involved.

The third example addresses a slightly different point – the limits of police responsiveness. An important theme of both this and other recent research has been that young people individually and collectively develop ways of managing the risks of public space, such as hanging around in groups or telling 'cautionary tales' about people and places perceived as dangerous (Anderson *et al.*, 1994). Insofar as these informal routines rest on a practical knowledge of both the limits of formal policing and the amplificatory consequences of reporting crime, the police, in responding to young people's victimisation, must be careful not to colonise and undermine them. The police, in short, need to be decentred. Rather than unthinkingly seeking to encourage crime reporting, and taking for granted the propriety of police intervention, we need to acknowledge the limits of what the police can do to ensure young people's safety. This is not to let the police off the hook as regards youth victimisation. Nor does it mean failing to challenge those aspects of young people's informal practices that brutalise others. But it does require the police to recognise, respect and build upon the skills and knowledge young people employ to manage their own safety.

These examples illustrate very well the hard-won criminological lesson about the secondary role of criminal justice institutions in reducing crime, protecting the public, and sustaining social order. They also attest to the importance of approaching the question of police accountability in a manner which recognises what police reform may or may not be able to accomplish. For while prevailing economic and social inequalities continue to generate problems with which the police are called upon to deal, such problems permit of no policing resolution, something we would be wise not to forget.

Discursive policing, then, offers no panacea for the tensions that currently mark police–youth relations because, couched in terms of policing alone, no such panacea exists. These relations are currently determined by such things as the construction of young people (and especially teenage boys) as Other; a climate of official and popular opinion which thinks of teenagers in terms of crime, and youth crime in terms only of offending; and economic and social policies which opt to banish and exclude rather than reconcile and integrate. Against the backdrop of all this, policing becomes a tense and difficult business, and democratic communication will struggle to make it otherwise.

None of this is meant, however, as a counsel of despair. Recognising the limits of policing does not entail the kind of structure fetishism which views police reform as parasitic upon some wholesale transformation of the social fabric.[3] Even in the midst of marked inequality, policing retains the capacity to impact for better or worse on the quality of (young) people's lives, and police reform is therefore capable of generating a difference that makes a difference. Thus, to return to the examples propounded above, there are many more responsive ways of policing young people's collective use of public space than those which currently obtain. Similarly, the reluctance of young people to relay their experiences of crime to the police is in part a product of a specific police failure to take youth victimisation seriously; something that effectively denies young people the option of a formal police service, and places immense strain on their informal routines for managing safety. And the limited opportunities available to young people to communicate their concerns *vis-à-vis* crime and policing contribute a great deal to the over-control and under-protection they encounter as users of public space. In each of these cases, discursive policing might go some considerable way to improving the situation.

In the light of all this, two things need to be said about the possibilities and limits of discursive policing. Such policing aims, first of all, to realise the democratic ideals that are embodied in the legitimation claims of the police, but so thinly inscribed in present arrangements for accountability. This entails creating institutions capable of providing the doctrine of policing by consent with some meaningful substance; something which requires, in turn, the establishment of reflexive and ongoing public deliberation about specific matters of police policy and practice. This, following Seyla Benhabib (1986, ch. 8), we may term the 'politics of fulfilment'.

But discursive policing must also be coupled with what Benhabib calls the 'politics of transfiguration'. This means, in practical terms, designing institutions for governing the police that can remain alive to the ever-present connections between 'policing' problems and economic and social policy more generally. And it means these institutions attending to the 'impossible mandate' with which the police are currently saddled (Manning, 1977), as well as striving to create social relations in which the police have a minimal instrumental and symbolic presence.

BEYOND LOCALISM AND CENTRALISM: THE INSTITUTIONS OF DISCURSIVE POLICING

How though are these objectives to be embedded in institutional settings? What might the institutions of discursive policing look like? I want to address these questions by setting out the contours of a new body for rendering the police democratically accountable. Following Jefferson and Grimshaw (1984), I propose to call this body a police commission. Operating independently of the established structures of local government, it is intended to make good the democratic shortcomings of the current institutional arrangements for governing the police.

The police commission would have vested in it many of the capacities and duties presently bestowed upon the central government, chief constables and local police authorities. The commission would have a legal responsibility to enforce the law, as well as an obligation to interpret the general legal duty of the police. And it would take responsibility for policing policy and practice in all areas of police competence beyond which the law ceases to provide officers with guidance. The police commission would thus 'be a body of a new type that bestrides the conventional division of non-elected judicial offices and elected offices of the executive' (Jefferson and Grimshaw, 1984, p. 174). It would, in particular, engage in the proactive task of generating and sustaining public deliberation about matters of policing. This it would undertake with a view to formulating, implementing and evaluating public policies for law enforcement – policies that particular police forces would be required to operate within. The commission would, in short, serve as a *continuous public enquiry* into policing.

But at what institutional sites should this police commission be located? This question brings to mind a dispute which has long figured prominently in the public conversation about British policing: that concerning central as against local forms of police organisation and control. This debate has – as we saw in Chapter 1 – recently found something of a *de facto* resolution in the increasing influence of central government over police policy and finance, and the almost total eclipse of local police authorities. However, far from eliding the questions of principle raised by the localism-centralism debate, current managerialist developments merely make a consideration of that debate a more pressing task.

Advocates of localism *vis-à-vis* policing and its regulation may cite in their favour a litany of substantive claims. These include an enhanced opportunity to facilitate public participation in decision-making, as well as the chance to 'tap the experientially-grounded knowledge of people in their everyday lives and utilise their energies' (Doyal and Gough, 1991, p. 307). Local forms of decision-making are also able to deliver services sensitive to the needs of diverse public audiences, and can take account of the experiences and concerns of hitherto excluded groups, such as young people. Moreover, localised practice is able to respond promptly and with minimal constraint to changing circumstances, thereby enabling poor decisions to be rectified before extensive damage accrues (Doyal and Gough, 1991, pp. 306-9).

By contrast, centralised service delivery and control is alone possessed of the scope and resources needed to ensure the provision of properly coordinated services (Lustgarten, 1986, pp. 177-9; Doyal and Gough, 1991, pp. 300-5). Central provision is able to take advantage of greater economies of scale, as well as securing basic entitlements that can compensate for asymmetries of power and wealth between localities, and mediate uneven service delivery. Through the articulation of universal rights and minimum national standards of service, central regulation can safeguard a conception of the public good and secure protection for groups who might otherwise constitute vulnerable local minorities. Again, young people spring readily to mind.

One is confronted, in other words, with a zero-sum game. Local and central modes of regulation offer distinct possibilities for service delivery and accountability, each compensating for the dangers and shortcomings of the other. On its own, for example, local participation and service delivery may serve to mask the continued marginalisation of young people, and even exacerbate their powerlessness. It can also help to perpetuate 'local tyrannies' and encourage insular dispositions towards the issues at hand. Conversely, centrally delivered services may all too easily become aloof from their users, lack the capacity for creativity and change, and as a consequence, generate institutional environments in which 'the rational evaluation and subsequent improvement of services becomes impossible' (Doyal and Gough, 1991, p. 306).

This all suggests that the long-standing debate about localism and centralism in British policing is unlikely to find satisfactory resolution in the triumph of any one pole. Policing is constituted with local, national and increasingly global dimensions, and the institutional arrangements for democratic accountability must be cognisant of these dispersed sites of operation. The pertinent questions concern the relationship between various levels of control, and the appropriate division of responsibility between them; something which requires us to stop thinking of institutions as sovereign bodies exercising exclusive lawful authority over specific fields of decision-making.

One way forward here is to reconceptualise the question of police accountability in *federal* terms; the significance of federal arrangements being that they situate sovereignty, not within particular institutions, but in the rules that coordinate the relationship between overlapping institutional sites. Drawing upon David Held's (1992) recent reflections on democracy and globalisation, it is possible to envisage a series of institutional mechanisms consisting of 'multiple systems of authority bound by fundamental ordering principles and rules' and enacted through 'a common structure of rules for action to which assent has been given' (Held, 1992, p. 226). In the realm of policing, this federal approach has a number of virtues, not the least of which is the prospect of building productive conflict into processes of accountability:

> It is dangerous to concentrate all power over a particular service at any one level of government. Permanent, institutionalised tension between different levels of the political process is as firm a guarantee against the abuse of power as democracy can devise. (Lustgarten, 1986, p. 178)

I propose therefore a police commission operating at a number of semi-autonomous yet overlapping sites; that is, in institutional locations which correspond to distinct levels of policing practice, and maximise the 'access points' through which the commission may enact its deliberative functions (cf. Giddens, 1990, ch. 5). I have neither the space, competence nor desire to provide a detailed elaboration of these federal designs. It is possible, however, to illustrate the principles involved by sketching in broad terms the division of responsibility within a police commission functioning at three levels – national, regional and local.

A national police commission might exercise its executive and judicial functions in relation to two specific aspects of policing and its regulation. It would, first of all, have responsibility for spheres of police operation with national and increasingly international dimensions (Den Boer and Walker, 1993). For example, it might initiate public debate, formulate police policy and monitor policing practice in respect of issues such as the control of drugs and organised crime. It may also undertake, where appropriate, more sporadic enquiries into matters of policing whose significance or implications reverberate nationally, such as police use of firearms, or public order policing. Secondly, it might assume responsibility for overseeing policing on a national basis and ensuring minimum universal forms of provision. It would, in particular, take on the task of establishing national standards of service within which regional and local police commissions would be required to operate (so as to prevent the development of 'local tyrannies'). The national police commission would report on an annual basis both to Parliament and to regional commissions.

Regional police commissions would mirror geographically the scope of the police forces for whom they are responsible. Given the importance of taking decisions in forums that permit maximum public representation, it is vital that the bulk of decision-making (about, for example, styles of policing and police priorities) be conducted at this level. In respect of 'their' police forces, regional commissions would be responsible for the formulation and evaluation of policing policy, and for issuing guidance (both proactively, and on request) to chief constables on questions of law enforcement. Such commissions might also be charged with the task of facilitating public enquiries into matters of policing both in general terms, and, when they arise, on specific issues. Annual conferences of regional commissioners may also be held to discuss and disseminate 'best practice' guidelines. Regional commissions would report annually both to Parliament, as well as to the national commission and their appropriate local commissions.

Local police commissions would have responsibility for those local crime and policing issues that escape the attention of their regional counterparts. Within the confines of regional policing policy, these commissions might be empowered to take decisions (at, for example, sub-divisional or basic command unit level) on local policing matters, and would thus be accorded a sphere of autonomy within which new ideas could be tried out. They might also prepare submissions to regional commissions regarding policing policy and practice, thereby enabling them to act as a vehicle for generating and articulating local concerns and opinion. More specifically, local commissions might serve as forums within which public deliberation on local crime and policing problems could take place. Such forums could have as their remit crime prevention in the broadest sense, thus enabling them to discuss a whole range of social policy matters as they affect the locality. Local commissions would submit annual reports both to the relevant regional commission and to appropriate local agencies.

These proposals have as their aim the creation of a strong democratic structure of police accountability, one spanning both central and local levels. As such, they draw much of their inspiration from the attempts recently made by political theorists to rethink the relationship between the state and civil society (Held, 1987, ch. 9; Keane, 1988). For the idea of a police commission seeks to secure, in one particular sphere of public provision, a democratic overhaul of existing institutions of central regulation, and a radical decentralisation of power that creates in a thriving civil society institutions capable of facilitating ongoing democratic communication about matters of crime and policing.

PUBLIC JUSTICE AND MAJORITY RULE: THE BOUNDARIES OF DISCURSIVE POLICING

Democratic communication is about the expression of difference. It is concerned to enable all voices contained within a political community to articulate their experiences, claims and aspirations, and to have them heard and taken seriously. But left to its own devices, democratic communication has no way of protecting such difference. It lacks the means of preventing some of those voices being silenced by more powerful others, or of precluding a majority from bringing the entire conversation to an abrupt halt.

These issues are raised in particularly acute ways in the realm of policing. In a democratic society, the police, in seeking the consent of a majority, run the ever-present risk of pandering to prevailing prejudice and undermining the legitimate entitlements and expectations of unpopular minorities. None of this of course is meant to happen. Constabulary independence, the 'professional' judgement of officers, and a whole panoply of legal protections are all in place to prevent such abuse. The present research, however, offers little support for this rosy official picture. We have seen how the relationship between legal, work and democratic 'structures of control' (Grimshaw and Jefferson, 1987) currently allows certain influential groups (such as the informal democratic structure of local residents) to mobilise the police as a means of controlling young people's use of public space, irrespective of whether the complaints of that group are justified or not. Present arrangements for rendering the police accountable permit the very 'tyranny of the majority' that the language of formal equality claims to preclude.

But the spectre of the 'tyranny of the majority' also haunts democratic – and by extension, discursive – policing. A number of commentators have seen in the prospect of greater democratic control of the police the distinct possibility that these local tyrannies will be reproduced, even exacerbated (Lea and Young, 1984, p. 270). This fear has, for example, long underpinned Robert Reiner's (1992a) contention that – whatever its principled worth – democratic accountability is of limited prudential value in ensuring forms of policing that respect the rights of marginalised social groups. For Reiner (1992a, p. 216), the overarching problem of policing in a liberal democratic society is how to protect vulnerable minorities from police oppression sanctioned by 'communal morality', something, he argues, that 'limits the potential of "democratic accountability" as a panacea against abuse'.

So will discursive policing, far from improving the situation of young people, actually worsen their plight? Might democratic communication be 'captured' by powerful majorities and used to direct policing against unpopular local minorities, such a black youth? Not I think if discursive policing is coupled with some conception of justice. For if democracy is about the expression of difference, then justice is about its protection. A conception of justice might therefore allow democratic communication to proceed in a way that protects both vulnerable minorities and the process of communication itself.

One recent attempt to inject into policing debates a concern with justice is to be found in the work of Jefferson and Grimshaw (1984). In *Controlling the Constable*, they articulate an understanding of justice in terms of that which 'guards the rights and common interests of all' (1984, p. 157), and go on to propose – rightly in my view – a conception of public justice concerned with the question of:

> How *all* citizens within a democracy can have their interests in the legal operations of the police recognised; [and] how all individuals as democratic citizens may gain a 'fair' share of the limited police attention available. (1984, p. 157; emphasis in original)

In setting out proposals for police reform, Jefferson and Grimshaw outline a further distinction between individualist and socialist conceptions of public justice. Individualist justice, they suggest, is concerned to enact forms of policing which engender 'equal protection by law and equal subjection to law' (1984, p. 161); the equalisation, that is, of both the offender and victimisation rates of different social groups. Socialist justice, by contrast, takes heed of broader economic and social inequalities, and endeavours to (re)distribute the 'public good' of policing in such a way as to compensate for these inequalities. It thereby takes account of both the social impact of victimisation and the social conditioning of offenders, and gears police practice towards a disproportionate reduction in the offender and victimisation rates of powerless social groups *vis-à-vis* more advantaged groups.

Jefferson and Grimshaw evince a clear preference for a police commission whose decision-making is informed by a socialist conception of public justice. Though I am sympathetic towards this formulation, it manifests a host of conceptual and practical problems. It remains unclear, for example, exactly how, and to what extent, a principle of compensation might operate. What economic and social disadvantages are to be accommodated? Does this principle warrant the complete non-policing of certain social groups? How are the competing claims of class, gender, race, age and sexuality to be weighed? More significantly, a conception of distributive justice tends towards a certain police-centredness, whereby the police are cast in the structurally unlikely role of a crypto-socialist institution at the forefront of efforts to bring about radical social change. The virtues of a socialist understanding of justice become something of a weakness when applied to policing.

In the light of this, I want to accept the spirit of Jefferson and Grimshaw's enterprise (that the deliberations of a police commission be informed by a conception of public justice), but to recast the issue in terms of the respective merits of procedural and substantive justice; that is, justice conceptualised as maximising the opportunities for citizens to participate in decision-making processes, and justice concerned with generating outcomes from such processes that guard the rights and common interests of all.

A procedural conception of justice has a number of principled and prudential virtues. In respect of the former, public participation can be viewed as a necessary component of a democratically legitimate decision-making process; for if any ensuing decision is to be just, 'everyone who follows it must in principle have an effective voice in its consideration and be able to agree to it without coercion' (I. M. Young, 1990, p. 34). Such participation is also a vital ingredient of a society that seeks to foster individual and collective autonomy in its citizens (Held, 1987, ch. 9; Gould, 1988). In these respects, public participation is intrinsically connected to a understanding of democracy as a collective learning process in which discursive skills can be cumulatively acquired and put to use. Such a democracy would from school onwards encourage young people to develop the civic consciousness of citizens; they would learn about and 'mature' into the institutional practices of participatory decision-making.

In a more practical vein, procedural justice is able to enhance the quality of democratic decision-making. It maximises, first of all, the amount of practical knowledge and social experience that is entered into the decision-making process. Participation also has the capacity to augment public understanding of complex political choices, reduce intolerance, and generate among citizens more accepting dispositions towards the claims of others (Manin, 1987). It may thus transform what were once pre-given and frozen positions into contingent understandings that exist in a state of constant flux.

In terms of policing, two aspects of these reflections on procedural justice are noteworthy. They indicate, first of all, some of the ways in which public participation is fundamentally connected with the possibility of policing by consent, as well as the extent to which such deliberation is a necessary part of any police policy-making process that lays claim to the mantle of legitimacy. More concretely, participative decision-making holds out the prospect of diverse social groups (young people included) being able to enter into the formulation and monitoring of policing practice in forums that enable entrenched dispositions and mutually hostile stereotypes to be challenged, maybe even transcended.

A solely procedural understanding of just decision-making has, however, a number of lacunae. Perhaps most significantly, it forgets that democracy is not merely a way of enhancing collective learning, but is also a mechanism for solving problems and reaching practical decisions. As David Beetham (1993, p. 61) notes, 'the point of participation, surely, is to have some say in, and influence upon, collective decisions; and its value is principally to be judged by how far it contributes to this end, and for whom.' Two specific shortcomings of procedural justice are apparent here. First, democratic processes on their own provide little or no indication of what decisions are required to be taken, and how they might be reached; an overarching concern with procedural rights 'cannot', in other words, 'provide content and guidance for the exercise of those rights' (Mouffe, 1992, p. 7). Secondly, a procedural focus that remains entirely agnostic with regard to substantive outcomes is unable to prevent such outcomes from undermining universal rights to take part in communicative political processes.

It is in overcoming these shortcomings that the virtues of substantive justice are to be found. In positive terms, substantive justice is able to furnish decision-making processes with a 'regulative ideal' around which they may cohere; one which acts as an incentive for social groups to participate, and as a stimulus to richer and more informed deliberation. In a more prescriptive vein, a substantive conception of justice confers upon decision-making processes a set of 'rules of the game' which, by removing certain items from the discursive agenda, protect dispossessed social groups from (for example, racist and sexist) oppression at the hands of the majority, and enable deliberative processes to survive in a democratic form.[4]

Substantive conceptions of justice must nonetheless be handled with some care. For not only is it difficult – in the context of a modernity characterised by warring 'gods and demons' (Lukes, 1982) – to arrive at a consensus on such matters prior to discourse, but substantive principles of justice also have profound anti-democratic implications. The greater the level of anterior constraint placed upon practices of democratic communication, the more the impetus towards them, and the possibilities created by them, are lost. As Benhabib (1992, p. 81) succinctly puts it: 'The attempt of a political theorist to provide citizens with a normative yardstick [is] a preemption of their right to democratic politics.'

I want to suggest, therefore, a police commission that operates according to a hybrid principle of public justice; one which couples a strong procedural element with a number of minimal substantive constraints. This principle would operate at all three levels of the commission, and a failure to abide by it would render any ensuing decision open to proceedings for judicial review.[5] This conception of justice can be formulated in the following way:

> In conducting its deliberations, the police commission shall at all times be concerned to:
> (1) elicit and take account of the views of all individuals and social groups likely to be affected by the relevant decision;
> (2) arrive at the decision that secures the broadest level of public consent without (a) prejudicing the fundamental active rights of any affected individual or social group, or (b) being disproportionately detrimental to the other interests and aspirations of these individuals and groups, in such a way as might prejudice the future operation of decision-making processes.

The first of these limbs is intended to enshrine within the workings of the police commission what Thompson (1990, p. 325) calls a 'principle of non-exclusion'. This would secure rights to participate in decision-making processes for social groups currently excluded from the formulation of policing policy and practice, such as young people. In this respect, the principle of public justice compensates for broader economic and social inequalities at the level of public participation (cf. Jefferson and Grimshaw, 1984). It would constitute part of a democratic political process that 'uniquely equalises the formal powers of individuals in society, in contrast to the greater inequality of resources which derives from the market or from the claims of technical competence' (Rustin, 1985, p. 38).

The second limb provides both a positive criteria for coming to a 'good' decision, and a set of substantive restrictions which modulate a majoritarian principle of decision-making in certain significant respects. These restrictions are designed to preclude entirely decisions that prejudice the active rights of citizens (such as those that may be constitutionally entrenched in a Bill of Rights[6]), while also requiring commissioners to be sensitive to the impact of their decisions on the interests of all those affected by them.[7] As such, they would form part of a deliberative process which endeavours to devise policing policies in accordance with the common good, while at the same time protecting – among others – young people from the potentially adverse consequences of unconstrained public discourse.

MODES OF REPRESENTATION AND PARTICIPATION: THE PRACTICE OF DISCURSIVE POLICING

But could this principle of public justice be enacted in practice? How might democratic communication about matters of crime and policing be generated and sustained on a routine basis? These questions traverse two issues that are all too often treated separately, but which are more properly considered as parts of a single whole. They raise, first of all, the issue of how different social groups and interests may be represented within institutional arrangements for rendering the police accountable. Secondly, they demand consideration of the various forms of participation that might be employed to elicit the views of different police constituencies.

The second of these issues has in fact been much neglected in discussions of police governance (cf. Jefferson *et al.*, 1988), with the result that questions concerning the formal constitution of bodies such as local police authorities have come to assume perhaps undue prominence. In a polity where participation is an all-or-nothing affair, it matters a great deal whether different social groups are directly represented on appropriate decision-making bodies. One consequence of a policy-making process understood as a set of participative and deliberative practices, may be to diminish the overarching importance that has hitherto been attributed to issues of institutional composition.

Questions of representation cannot be entirely effaced, however. Representative institutions are of pivotal importance in securing the democratic accountability of the police, and free, direct elections remain the best means of producing such institutions. The principal virtue of elections is that they accord equal weight to all those whose interests are affected by the actions of the institution concerned, thereby preventing the decisions of such bodies from being determined by the demands of the most active, articulate or merely noisy. Representative elections also help establish democratic institutions which guarantee political equality in material circumstances – such as the economy of time, and the complex character of late-modern societies – that inhibit direct democratic participation (Beetham, 1993). One necessary, if insufficient, condition of democratisation then is the extension of representative electoral processes to a greater number of the institutions of state and civil society (Bobbio, 1987).

I propose, therefore, that the police commission – notwithstanding its judicial character – be constituted at all levels through the periodic election of lay members (Jefferson and Grimshaw, 1984, pp. 170–6).[8] In and of itself however, the electoral process does not guarantee a universal articulation of interests within policy-making forums (Parliament and local government have, for example, long under-represented the interests of women, blacks, lesbians and gays, as well as young people). These exclusions are especially pertinent in relation to a prospective police commission; for the social groups who constitute 'police property' are also those most likely to be under-represented within formal democratic institutions. Young people, for example, are currently excluded from voicing their experience in such ways, first by reason of age, and later (it was suggested in Chapter 5) because of their cynicism towards, and disaffection from, established political structures. Democratisation confined to augmenting electoral mechanisms for representing the concerns of young people may serve merely to reproduce current exclusions.

These exclusions can in part be made good by devising procedures which ensure on the police commission a balanced composition of interests. Two possibilities suggest themselves here. It might, first of all, be possible to reserve places on the commission for certain presently excluded social groups. The grounds for such ring-fencing would, of course, be open to dispute, but they might include either documented disaffection from the formal political process, a history of poor group relations with the police, or disproportionately high levels of victimisation. The representation of such groups on the commission could then be ensured by means of 'elections within elections' for an apportioned number of seats. For instance, one might establish on regional and local commissions a number of 'youth seats' for which candidates could stand for election among a sub-population of sixteen to twenty-one-year-olds.

Alternatively, it might be possible to set aside a certain proportion of seats on to which representatives of particular social groups or organisations could – for a specified period – be coopted. This principle has long been recognised within local government (Gyford, 1991, pp. 55–9), and currently obtains – in respect of magistrates and 'independent members' – on police authorities in England and Wales. In terms of a police commission, the process of cooption might be organised around a principle of democratic compensation, one which operates to secure a voice for those social groups who are under-represented through the electoral process. This again might enable the cooption of individuals (or professionals such as youth workers) to represent the interests of young people; though such processes raise all sorts of difficult questions regarding the 'representativeness' of the individuals and groups concerned (Jefferson *et al.*, 1988).

However, the principle of public justice cannot be fully realised by representative means alone. Representation must be supplemented by participation. The election of police commissioners should signal the beginning, rather than the end, of a democratic process. Commissioners would not be elected merely to implement some pre-determined manifesto. They would, as we have seen, have a duty both to elicit the views of all those affected by their decisions, and, more generally, to initiate and sustain public deliberation about crime and policing matters. To this end, the commission would at all levels have to mobilise a range of institutional methodologies, something that requires it to adopt an 'open, participatory, reflexive and, above all, *experimental* approach to all practices' (Jefferson, 1990, p. 144; emphasis in original).

Given this, Marx's maxim about recipes for the cookshops of the future not being written in the present quite properly applies here. I consequently want to conclude by merely indicating some of the ways in which the police commission might practically carry out its designated tasks. For this purpose, I shall draw upon some of the problems in prevailing police–youth relations identified by the research, and explore how discursive policing might facilitate their democratic and socially just resolution. I shall limit my attention to the prospective workings of regional and local police commissions.

In formulating policy for the police in their area, regional police commissions would be required – in order to fulfil the principle of public justice – to seek the views of a whole range of affected interests; a task for which a number of general procedures may be utilised. These include the following:

1. drawing upon existing resources of criminological research, or commissioning new research (such as crime surveys) on the distribution and impact of crime and policing problems in the region;

2. inviting written submissions from local groups and organisations, and undertaking a series of open meetings in places of collective association and organisation within the area, such as schools and workplaces;[9]
3. meeting with, and seeking submissions from, the relevant police force at the level of both senior officers and police constables – through, for example, the Police Federation, or forums at local police stations;[10]
4. taking advantage of local communications media to foster public discussion about crime and policing;
5. initiating local 'notice and comment' procedures about prospective policing policies.

In respect of young people, however, regional police commissions would have a number of specific and important issues to consider. The present research suggests, for example, that young people have disproportionately high levels of contact with all dimensions of crime, perhaps most significantly in relation to victimisation in public places (see also, Anderson *et al.*, 1994; Aye Maung, 1995; Hartless *et al.*, 1995). It also intimates that young people occupy a distinct and structured place within police workloads and understandings; thought of and acted upon as 'trouble', yet largely unrecognised as victims of crime with demands to make of a police service. And it suggests that – despite being one of the social groups most likely to be affected by the outcomes of deliberation on policing policy – young people currently express little confidence in the workings of formal political institutions.

In these circumstances, regional police commissions might have to think imaginatively about how to ensure the inclusion of youth voices within decision-making processes. They might, for example, take steps to enable groups of young people to talk among themselves as a constituency before entering wider forums of public deliberation (cf. Fraser, 1992). This could be accomplished by the commission providing a range of resources (such as materials, information and advice) to local schools, colleges and youth organisations in order to facilitate the production of 'youth submissions' to the policy-making process. Such resourced enhancement has a number of likely benefits. Not only might it allow young people to develop their confidence and discursive skills, it would also enable them to reflect collectively on their experiences and concerns *vis-à-vis* crime and policing, and draw up a common agenda. Over time, this process might even help to build among young people an active trust in the police, and break down – in one small but important area of public provision – their fatalism towards established political structures. Although policy decisions might not always go their way, the policing of young people would now take place in an environment in which their claims are routinely taken into account.

It is anticipated that local police commissions would work by adopting a focused, problem-solving approach to policing issues in particular localities. In this respect, the present research has documented a host of issues that local commissions might take up. Prominent among these is the 'problem' of young people hanging around in public places. Here, it seems, local commissions would be confronted with a pattern of police–youth contact marked by the 'paradox of face', and generative of little other than bewilderment and mistrust. They would also be up against demands from local residents, and – less vocally – from some young people, for 'something to be done'. And they would face police officers who consider the routine policing of congregating youths to be a waste of time and resources. How in these circumstances might local police commissions proceed?

One possible way forward is for local commissions to act as a mediator between the disputing parties. Here, commissioners might initially seek to foster internal communication among local teenagers, residents and police officers about the issues at hand, before proceeding to bring together their respective views and draw up an agenda for discussion. On this basis, local commissions might then establish forums in which the parties – or their chosen representatives – could meet with the aim of negotiating a settlement that would secure the consent of all 'sides'.[11]

This process would of course encounter a number of difficulties. The research prefiguratively indicates, for example, that encouraging young people to participate would be no easy task. Such forums might also serve to exacerbate existing tensions by enabling teenagers, local residents and police officers to exchange 'horror' stories. But mediation also holds out the best chance of overcoming the mutual suspicion and defensiveness that characterise the present impasse. It would enable young people to convey their concerns about crime, policing and public space in settings where asymmetries of power have been neutralised. And it would provide residents and the police with the opportunity to confront young people – and especially teenage males – about their practices, in circumstances where they are unable to hide behind the bravado that 'protects' them on the street. Mediation would, in short, allow people to voice their concerns, vent their frustrations and discuss their claims in front of those who previously constituted a distant and hostile Other. And as participants become familiar with the previously unknown, what once seemed like rather entrenched and conflicting positions might be challenged, altered and recreated.[12]

These processes might also help transform some of the more reactionary, defensive and 'we know best' aspects of police culture. For instead of constructing police officers as a mere obstacle in the path of reform, mediation views them as a potential resource (cf. Goldsmith, 1990). By enabling officers to participate in local problem-solving mechanisms in which their opinions are sought and taken seriously, mediation holds out a number of possibilities. Not only might it generate agreements about local policing which command support from the officers required to implement them (something the research suggests is not entirely fanciful, especially given the ambivalence officers feel towards the policing of congregating youths); it would also enhance the role of the police officer, and furnish officers with a source of identification beyond that currently provided by the canteen. This, surely, represents a better way forward for the police than the neo-Taylorist prescriptions of managerialism.

These ideas, like all the others elaborated in this chapter under the heading of discursive policing, are not guaranteed to improve the plight of young people *vis-à-vis* the police. No such guarantees exist. But they do, I believe, hold out a greater chance of making the police more democratically accountable, and of enhancing the quality of police–youth relations, than the initiatives currently being propounded under the banner of managerialism. Discursive policing is about creating a police service that responds to the claims of all citizens, rather than just to those of its most vocal consumers. Only when this happens will it be possible to speak meaningfully of policing by consent.

Notes

1 Policing and the Youth Question

1. The regulation of policing is governed, in England and Wales, by the Police Act 1964 and, in Scotland, by the Police (Scotland) Act 1967. These have both recently been amended by the Police and Magistrates' Courts Act 1994, though the changes are more fundamental in respect of England and Wales.

2. 'Constabulary independence' has – in respect of external direction at least – commanded a less hallowed place in Scotland than it does in England and Wales; the Procurator Fiscal, for example, having the power (under s.17 of the Police [Scotland] Act 1967) to direct police forces in the conduct of criminal investigations. With regard to internal direction, constables on both sides of the border hold an independent office and cannot – in formal legal terms at least – be instructed by senior officers to carry out their duties in this way or that.

3. In this respect, the doctrine of constabulary independence rests rather uneasily alongside the potentially more democratic idea of policing by consent, a tension mediated in practice by allowing chief constables to exercise a 'professional' judgement over what kind of policing the 'public' is deemed to want.

4. Police authorities in Scotland remain unaffected by these changes. They continue to consist entirely of elected councillors and are under no obligation to draw up a local policing plan.

5. The original Police and Magistrates' Courts Bill attempted to sever entirely the link between the police and local democracy, the government's prefered model for the new police authorities being the unelected NHS trusts (Loveday, 1994). The Bill, for example, contained a proposal to allow the Home Secretary to appoint all five 'independent members', including the chairperson; something which was defeated in the House of Lords. However, despite the mauling it received at the hands of the Lords, the ensuing Act still represents a significant centralising measure.

6. It should be noted, however, that recent developments, such as the Metropolitan Police's 'Plus' programme, have gone some way to remedying this lack of managerial direction within the force.

7. The initial launching document set out the ambit and key tenets of the Charter. It has been followed subsequently by individual charters covering different fields of social policy, such as The Tenant's Charter, The Patient's Charter and The Victim's Charter (Cooper, 1993).

8. In addition to providing the Home Secretary with the power to set national police objectives and performance targets, the Police and Magistrates' Courts Act 1994 has introduced (in both England and Wales, and Scotland) short-term contracts for officers of the rank of Deputy Chief Constable and above. It also provides the government with the power to introduce such contracts for Superintendents at some future date (a concession the government made

in order to appease police opposition to the Sheehy Report which first re-
commended these changes).

9. It would be a mistake to see the current consumerist vogue as the exclusive
    preserve of the new right, as concern about unresponsive public bureaucra-
    cies now spans the political spectrum. Many on the liberal-left have even
    seen a qualified version of 'consumerism' as a means of rendering public
    services more responsive to their users (Potter, 1988). It is my view, however,
    that 'consumerism' is too marked by its private sector lineage, and too
    heavily implicated in the new right's attempt to recast citizenship in economic
    terms, to be a fruitful way of reconstructing social democratic (let alone
    democratic socialist) politics. Those engaged in the project of radical demo-
    cracy must endeavour to articulate another theoretical language with which
    to advance their concerns, rather than engaging in tortuous attempts to forge
    a 'left consumerism'.

10. At the level of representation young people are not exclusively the property
    of the police. A whole array of histories, symbols, vocabularies and 'theor-
    ies' are – at any one time – in play in the construction of public sensibilities
    towards 'youth', and the police have no monopoly over their deployment
    and circulation. Politicians, journalists, social pundits and a host of pro-
    fessional groups all in various ways profess to speak with authority about
    (and even 'own') the 'problem of youth'. The police, however, occupy a
    distinct and powerful position within this discourse. As 'knowledge work-
    ers' – producing and disseminating information about prevailing sources
    of insecurity – they are blessed with enormous symbolic power (Ericson,
    1994). They also have privileged access to national and local communica-
    tions media and exude – at all levels of the organisational hierarchy – a
    philosophy which claims that 'we know best' about matters of 'law and
    order' (Fielding and Fielding, 1991). As such, the police play a major –
    if rarely uncontested – role in establishing the contours of public debate
    about crime, ascribing social problems with particular meanings and
    'constituting populations in their respective risk categories' (Ericson, 1994,
    p. 168).

11. Imagine for a moment what the criminological field might look like if it
    were replete with thousands of studies of young people's experiences as
    victims of crime and only a handful of recent accounts of juvenile offend-
    ing. Consider also what this tells us about the kind of society in which
    criminological research is conceived, funded and undertaken.

2 Communicative Action

1. In developing these arguments, my purpose is to contribute to an emerging
    body of work which is endeavouring to find practical 'applications' in dif-
    ferent fields of social enquiry for the somewhat abstract formulations of
    critical theory (Forester, 1985a; Dryzek, 1990; R. Young, 1990).

2. Habermas (1993) has recently remarked that he wishes he had never coined
    the term 'ideal speech situation' as it conjures up a vision of a concrete form
    of life, rather than a set of critical procedures.

3. In Britain, such rights have never been formally enshrined in a Bill of

Rights, though they have been given indirect legal force by the European Convention on Human Rights to which Britain is a signatory.

4. To limit issues of legitimation to the question of protecting the individual from the state is to adopt a frightened and rather defensive posture towards democracy (Phillips, 1991). In the realm of policing, this kind of liberalism has long been paramount, the thin democratic arrangements licensed by constabulary independence and legal accountability being limited for the most part to preventing abuses of police power by means of retrospective explanation.

5. A prefigurative conception of the relationship between theory and practice must, however, remain alive to the fact that it employs what Bourdieu (1990) terms 'the scholarly gaze'. Bourdieu warns that theoretical knowledge is never generated under conditions of practice, but is the product of a 'contemplative eye' that has partially 'retired' from the social world. This observation serves here as a useful reminder that the accounts generated in interviews are a product of a research context, rather than of institutionalised relations with immediate effects. It warns also against the danger of collapsing the 'practical logic' of young people and police officers into the 'theoretical logic' of social science – a mistake Bourdieu terms the 'scholastic fallacy'. Above all, it alludes to the fact that prefigurative (or indeed any) social research must couple its role as advocate of institutional change with an explanatory account of the possibilities for – and limits to – such change.

6. When I say that meaning is 'finite', I am not suggesting that the process of interpretation has some telos at which the correct and final interpretation will be found. I mean merely to say that it is possible for texts to be *mis*read, and that at any particular historical moment some of the available readings of texts will be more plausible or adequate than others. We can of course only ever come to a valid judgment on such matters on the basis of dialogue, something which is – and should be – an ongoing process wherein existing interpretations can be revised or even discarded, and new interpretations continually forged (Bernstein, 1983).

7. It is of course impossible within a single enquiry to make adequate sense of the meanings and effects of all pertinent axes of inequality, and it is thus necessary to privilege (for the purposes of analysis) one or other dimension of social division. The account that follows is primarily concerned with thinking through the ways in which 'age' as a category of social division shapes young people's experiences and understandings of crime and policing. A concern with class and gender – though not in this case ethnicity or sexuality is also mobilised in constructing the interpretation.

3 The Uses and Meanings of Public Space

1. The following editing marks are used throughout the interview text: (1) ... pause in, or interrupted, response; (2) (...) material omitted; (3) [explanatory material inserted].

2. The names of the stations at which police officers work have been omitted in order to protect anonymity.

3. The group interviews tended in this regard to privilege identities that depend upon a shared loyalty to peer group or place; for when faced with the confident and embellished assertions of their peers, those young people for whom collective social practices are of little or no importance were often reluctant to talk about the constituents of their own identities. This process was on occasions reinforced by the gatekeepers to the research. Despite my frequent retorts that I was not concerned with juvenile delinquency, or interested only in those who had experienced contact with the police, youth workers and teachers would often try and point me in the direction of those young people who 'had good stories to tell'. My attempts to arrange interviews at the youth project at which I volunteered for the duration of the research also met with instructive failure in this regard; one member of the group with whom I requested an interview – the only one to have entered higher education and to have experienced little or no adversary contact with the police – politely turned down my request on the grounds that he 'would have nothing to say to me'.

4. The names all those refered to in the interview accounts have been changed.

4 Policing Public Space

1. One explanation for this discrepancy is that race has never featured as an issue within police politics in Scotland in quite the prominent way it has in England. In particular, Scottish cities have never generated well-publicised and disputed locations over which the police feel it necessary to establish material and symbolic control (cf. Keith, 1993).

2. It is, of course, not an offence merely to refuse to move on when requested to do so by a police officer (Christie, 1990).

3. The children's hearing system was established in Scotland in 1968 to deal with young people under sixteen who are either engaged in juvenile offending (other than serious crimes such as rape and murder), truanting from school, or considered in need of care and protection (because of parental neglect for example). The official objective of the panels is to keep young people away from the formal criminal justice system, and produce outcomes consistent with the 'needs' of the child. Aside from the legally-trained reporter who accepts and processes cases referred to the system, and decides whether a hearing is required, panels consist of lay members recruited from the local community. I had not originally proposed to ask police officers about children's panels, but they were raised by a number of officers during the initial interviews and the issue was then pursued more systematically. This perhaps in and of itself indicates the prominent place the panels hold within the culture of police officers in Scotland.

4. This is not to say that police officers do not make such referrals. The number of offence-related referrals have, however, fallen slightly over the last decade. In Lothian in 1993, 10.2 young people per 1000 of the under sixteen population were referred to the Reporter on offence grounds, compared with 12.6/1000 in 1983. For Scotland as a whole, 11.9/1000 were referred on such grounds in 1993 as against 13.2/1000 in 1983 (The Scottish Office, 1994).

5. With the important exception of child abuse, the recent upsurge of policy interest in victims of crime has largely ignored the question of youth victimisation. The recent Victim's Charter, for example, makes conspicuously little mention of young people's experiences as victims of crime (Home Office, 1990; cf. Morgan and Zedner, 1992b).
6. It is noticeable that no officers express analogous concern for victims and witnesses who have to endure a similar process inside the police station. This suggests that police officers effect a cognitive distancing of the police from other institutions of criminal justice who are construed as an 'obstacle' to a successful prosecution.

5 Transitions in Trouble

1. Giddens (1984, p. 33) defines these terms as follows: 'Allocative resources refer to capabilities – or more accurately, to forms of transformative capacity – generating command over objects, goods or material phenomena. Authoritative resources refer to types of transformative capacity generating command over persons or actors.'
2. In total, 51 per cent of male victims of these offences were under 25, compared to 32 per cent of women. A significant proportion of men were victimised in the street (25 per cent for men, as against 9 per cent for women) or in places of public entertainment (18 per cent, compared with 9 per cent).
3. The victims of personal crime were most commonly found to be men between the ages of sixteen to 30; though it should be noted that 66 per cent of young women had encountered harassment by men while out in the city centre (experiences that were far more evenly distributed throughout the day).
4. This pattern of experience does not hold so much for young women. For example, the British crime survey (Scotland) found that in 80 per cent of cases, women victims of assault and threatening behaviour were attacked by men, and that the majority of female victims knew all (71 per cent) or some (7 per cent) of their assailants. 24 per cent of these incidents took place inside the home.
5. The data for sixteen to 30-year-olds is taken from the Edinburgh crime survey and covers contact occuring during the previous twelve months (Kinsey, 1992, ch. 2). That for contact between 11- to 16-year-olds and the police comes from a separate survey conducted among schoolchildren in Edinburgh and covers a nine-month period (Anderson *et al.*, 1994, ch. 5). No comparative data are available for three of the categories.
6. Though it is true to say, as reporting levels among older populations attest, that many of the generic reasons for not reporting crime to the police remain in force (Anderson *et al.*, 1990; Kinsey and Anderson, 1992).

6 Talking Blues

1. My only attempt to arrange such a meeting during the research met with instructive failure when none of the young people turned up. The local

youth worker informed me that an 'acid house' party had been organised for the same evening. This should not, I believe, be interpreted to mean that young people do not have things to say to the police; merely that they are unwilling to give up their free time to say them, especially in a forum (such as that generated by the presence of a researcher) which offers no immediate prospect of influencing police practice.

2. 'Good' and 'bad' are used here merely to describe the evaluations used by young people, and imply no judgement on my behalf.

3. One condition I regularly had to meet was to assure young people I was not a police officer, or associated with the police in any way. During the introductory exchanges, I therefore endeavoured to reassure respondents that the purpose of the interviews was to elicit and discuss their experiences and opinions on matters of crime and policing, and nothing else. For the most part, I believe they were convinced. In this respect, the research suggests that any institutionalised dialogue between the police, young people and other social groups would best be mediated through an external and autonomous agency, so as to avoid reproducing the 'paradox of face' within communicative forums.

4. Recent research on police–schools liaison schemes supports this interpretation, finding that officers who go into schools are not perceived by young people as typical of their colleagues (Hewstone and Hopkins, 1991).

5. It is of course possible, given the police's role as bearers of the state's monopoly of coercive force, that stories of malpractice would remain predominant in shaping young people's understandings of even the most legitimate and responsive police force.

7 Towards Discursive Policing

1. I draw particular inspiration here from recent attempts to develop the idea of discursive or deliberative democracy (Cohen, 1989; Dryzek, 1990; Miller, 1993). On the related notion of associative democracy, see Cohen and Rogers (1992) and Hirst (1994).

2. As such, this principle is equally capable of governing commercial and citizen-based forms of social ordering.

3. According to Unger (1987, p. 205), structure fetishism 'denies that we can change the quality as well as the content of our formative contexts' and holds that these contexts 'impose on our practical, passionate and cognitive relations a script that we cannot easily rewrite'. In the realm of policing, as in other areas of social policy, this position is liable to postpone forever the prospect of institutional change and dissipate imaginative possibilities. In contrast, Unger (1987, p. 4) offers a more fecund conception of institutional change committed to the view that, 'the components of an institutional and imaginative order are only unevenly and loosely related. They can be replaced piece by piece rather than only as an inseparable whole.' From this perspective policing is as suitable a site as any in which to undertake radical democratic reform.

4. Some such restrictions are necessary on these grounds because: 'If there are no substantive constraints on what can be introduced into a practical

discourse, what is to prevent the outcome from conflicting with some of our most deeply held moral convictions? What is to prevent the participants from agreeing anything or, more plausibly perhaps, never reaching any general agreement at all?' (Baynes, 1988, p. 304). In other words, and the paradox here is only apparent, constraints on pluralism are required if the integrity and plurality of the public sphere is itself to be protected (Hirst, 1994).

5. Subjecting the commission's decisions to judicial review secures an added level of protection for vulnerable minorities, by removing the ultimate decision in cases of conflict from forums that operate a majoritarian principle of decision-making.

6. Golding (1984, pp. 122–3) defines this class of rights as those that 'correspond to a sphere of sovereignty in which the individual is morally free to act on the basis of his [sic] own choice'. Though in other spheres of public provision a broader formulation encompassing welfare rights (or what Golding calls 'claims of entitlement to goods') may be preferable, in the present context, a substantive constraint on decision-making limited to active rights best accords with the structurally limited competences of policing.

7. In particular, it is intended to prompt reflection upon decisions that may undermine the confidence of affected parties in the integrity of the commission's decision-making processes. The now infamous 'Swamp 81' operation conducted prior to the Brixton riots springs to mind as a pertinent case in point.

8. The commission would though be supplemented by a secretariat who might, among other things, conduct research and provide lay members with support, information and legal advice.

9. An analogous process to that envisaged here has recently taken place in Northern Ireland. The independent Opsahl commission – named after the Norwegian lawyer who chaired it – conducted nineteen full days of oral hearings on Northern Ireland's futures, in addition to taking written testimonies. The commission spent the first two months of 1993 travelling around the province eliciting opinion from all sides of the political and religious divide, finishing – interestingly enough for present purposes – with two 'school assemblies' in Derry and Belfast (Pollak, 1993).

10. The police could in this way be included in deliberations about policing policy in a context in which their 'expertise' is subject to democratic debate, and thus not privileged.

11. Precedents for this can be found in the various community mediation schemes that have sprung up across England and Wales in recent years (Marshall, 1992).

12. A compelling description of this process at work is to be found in Braithwaite and Mugford's (1994) account of the community conference approach to dealing with juvenile offenders currently operating in Australia and New Zealand.

Bibliography

Anderson, S., Grove-Smith, C., Kinsey, R. and Wood, J. (1990) *The Edinburgh Crime Survey* (Edinburgh: The Scottish Office).
—— Kinsey, R., Loader, I. and Smith, C. (1994) *Cautionary Tales: Young People, Crime and Policing in Edinburgh* (Aldershot: Avebury).
Arendt, H. (1961) *Between Past and Future: Six Exercises in Political Thought* (London: Faber).
Audit Commission (1984) *Economy, Efficiency and Effectiveness: The Audit Commission Handbook on Improving Economy, Efficiency and Effectiveness in Local Government* (London: HMSO).
Aye Maung, N. (1995) *Young People, Victimisation and the Police: British Crime Survey Findings on Experiences and Attitudes of 12 to 15 Year Olds* (London: HMSO).
Banks, M., Bates, I., Brakewell, G., Bynner, J., Emler, N., Jamieson, L. and Roberts, K. (1991) *Careers and Identities* (Buckingham: Open University Press).
Barber, B. (1984) *Strong Democracy: Participatory Politics for a New Age* (San Francisco: University of California Press).
Barron, A. and Scott, C. (1992) 'The Citizen's Charter Programme', *Modern Law Review*, vol. 55, no. 5, pp. 526–46.
Bauman, Z. (1987) *Legislators and Interpreters: On Modernity, Post-modernity and Intellectuals* (Cambridge: Polity Press).
Baynes, K. (1988) 'The Liberal/Communitarian Controversy and Communicative Ethics', *Philosophy and Social Criticism*, vol. 13, no. 3.4, pp. 293–313.
Beetham, D. (1991) *The Legitimation of Power* (London: Macmillan).
—— (1993) 'Liberal Democracy and the Limits of Democratization'; in D. Held (ed.) *Prospects for Democracy: North, South, East, West* (Cambridge: Polity Press).
Benhabib, S. (1986) *Critique, Norm and Utopia: A Study of the Foundations of Critical Theory* (New York: University of Columbia Press).
—— (1992) *Situating the Self: Gender, Community and Postmodernism in Contemporary Ethics* (Cambridge: Polity Press).
Bernstein, R. J. (1983) *Beyond Objectivism and Relativism: Science, Hermeneutics and Praxis* (Philadelphia: University of Pennsylvania Press).
Bhavnani, K. K. (1991) *Talking Politics: A Psychological Framing for Views from Youth in Britain* (Cambridge: Cambridge University Press).
Bittner, E. (1990) *Aspects of Police Work* (Boston: Northeastern University Press).
Black, D. (1980) *The Manners and Customs of the Police* (New York: Academic Press).
Bobbio, N. (1987) *The Future of Democracy* (London: Verso).
Bohman, J. (1990) 'Communication, Ideology and Democratic Theory', *American Political Science Review*, vol. 84, no. 1, pp. 93–109.
Bottomley, A. K. and Pease, K. (1986) *Crime and Punishment: Interpreting the Data* (Milton Keynes: Open University Press).
Bottoms, A. E. (1987) 'Reflections on the Criminological Enterprise', *The Cambridge Law Journal*, vol. 46, no. 2, pp. 240–63.

Bourdieu, P. (1977) *Outline of a Theory of Practice* (Cambridge: Cambridge University Press).

—— (1986) 'Forms of Capital', in J. G. Richardson (ed.) *Handbook of Theory and Research for the Sociology of Education* (Westport Conn.: Greenwood Press).

—— (1990) *The Logic of Practice* (Cambridge: Polity Press).

—— (1991) *Language and Symbolic Power* (Cambridge: Polity Press).

Box, S. (1987) *Recession, Crime and Punishment* (London: Macmillan).

Braithwaite, J. and Mugford, S. (1994) 'Conditions of Successful Reintegration Ceremonies: Dealing with Juvenile Offenders', *British Journal of Criminology*, vol. 34, no. 2, pp. 139–71.

Brogden, M., Jefferson, T. and Walklate, S. (1988) *Introducing Policework* (London: Unwin Hyman).

Butler, T. (1992) 'Police and the Citizen's Charter', *Policing*, vol. 8, no. 1, pp. 40–50.

Campbell, B. (1993) *Goliath: Britain's Dangerous Places* (London: Methuen).

Christie, M. (1990) *Breach of the Peace* (Edinburgh: Butterworth).

Christie, N. (1986) 'The Ideal Victim', in E. Fattah (ed.) *From Crime Policy to Victim Policy* (Basingstoke: Macmillan).

Clarke, J. (1976) 'Style', in S. Hall and T. Jefferson (eds) *Resistance Through Rituals: Youth Subcultures in Post-war Britain* (London: Hutchinson).

—— Cochrane, A. and McLaughlin, E. (1994) (eds) *Managing Social Policy* (London: Sage).

Clifford, J. and Marcus, G. (1986) (eds) *Writing Culture: The Poetics and Politics of Ethnography* (Berkeley: University of California Press).

Coffield, F., Borril, C. and Marshall, S. (1986) *Growing Up at the Margins* (Milton Keynes: Open University Press).

Cohen, J. (1985) 'Why More Political Theory?', *Telos*, vol. 40, pp. 70–94.

—— and Arato, A. (1992) *Civil Society and Political Theory* (Cambridge, Mass.: MIT Press).

Cohen, J. (1989) 'Deliberation and Democratic Legitimacy' in A. Hamlin and P. Pettit (eds) *The Good Polity: Normative Analysis of the State* (Oxford: Blackwell).

—— and Rogers, J. (1992) 'Secondary Associations and Democratic Governance', *Politics and Society*, vol. 4, pp. 393–472.

Cohen, P. (1979) 'Policing the Working Class City', in B. Fine, R. Kinsey, J. Lea, S. Piciotto and J. Young (eds) *Capitalism and the Rule of Law: From Deviancy Theory to Marxism* (London: Hutchinson).

Cooper, D. (1993) 'The Citizen's Charter and Radical Democracy: Empowerment and Exclusion Within Citizenship Discourse', *Social and Legal Studies*, vol. 2, no. 2, pp. 149–71.

Corrigan, P. (1976) 'Doing Nothing', in S. Hall and T. Jefferson (eds) *Resistance Through Rituals: Youth Subcultures in Post-war Britain* (London: Hutchinson).

Crawford, A., Lea, J., Woodhouse, T. and Young, J. (1990) *The Second Islington Crime Survey* (Middlesex: Centre for Criminology).

Davis, J. (1990) *Youth and the Condition of Britain: Images of Adolescent Conflict* (London: Athlone).

Den Boer, M. and Walker, N. (1993) 'European Policing After 1992', *Journal of Common Market Studies*, vol. 31, no. 1, pp. 3–28.

Dixon, D. (1992) 'Legal Regulation and Policing Practice', *Social and Legal Studies*, vol. 1, no. 4, pp. 515–42.

Doyal, L. and Gough, I. (1991) *A Theory of Human Need* (London: Macmillan).

Dryzek, J. (1990) *Discursive Democracy: Politics, Policy and Political Science* (Cambridge: Cambridge University Press).

Ericson, R. (1982) *Reproducing Order: A Study of Police Patrol Work* (Toronto: University of Toronto Press).

—— (1994) 'The Division of Expert Knowledge in Policing and Security', *British Journal of Sociology*, vol. 45, no. 2, pp. 149–75.

—— and Shearing, C. (1986) 'The Scientification of Police Work', in G. Bohme and N. Stehr (eds) *The Knowledge Society* (Amsterdam: Reidel).

Farrington, D. P., Gallagher, B., Morley, L., St. Ledger, R. J. and West, D. J. (1986) 'Unemployment, School Leaving and Crime',. *British Journal of Criminology*, vol. 26, no. 4, pp. 335–56.

Fielding, N. and Fielding, J. (1991) 'Police Attitudes to Crime and Punishment: Certainties and Dilemmas', *British Journal of Criminology*, vol. 31, no. 1, pp. 39–53.

Fischer, F. (1990) *Technocracy and the Politics of Expertise* (London: Sage).

Forester J. (1985a) (ed.) *Critical Theory and Public Life* (Cambridge, Mass.: MIT Press).

—— (1985b) 'Introduction', in J. Forester (ed.) *Critical Theory and Public Life* (Cambridge, Mass.: MIT Press).

—— (1992) 'Critical Ethnography: On Fieldwork in a Habermasian Way' in M. Alvesson and H. Willmott (eds) *Critical Management Studies* (London: Sage).

Fraser, N. (1992) 'Rethinking the Public Sphere: A Contribution to the Critique of Actually Existing Democracy', in C. Calhoun (ed.) *Habermas and the Public Sphere* (Cambridge, Mass.: MIT Press).

Furnham, A. and Gunter, B. (1989) *The Anatomy of Adolescence: Young People's Social Attitudes in Britain* (London: Routledge).

Galbraith, J. K. (1992) *The Culture of Contentment* (Harmondsworth: Penguin).

Geertz, C. (1975) *The Interpretation of Cultures* (London: Hutchinson).

Gelsthorpe, L. (1986) 'Towards a Sceptical Look at Sexism', *International Journal of the Sociology of Law*, vol. 14, pp. 125–52.

Giddens, A. (1984) *The Constitution of Society* (Cambridge: Polity Press).

—— (1987) *Social Theory and Modern Sociology* (Cambridge: Polity Press).

—— (1990) *The Consequences of Modernity* (Cambridge: Polity Press).

—— (1991) *Modernity and Self-Identity* (Cambridge: Polity Press).

—— (1993) *New Rules of Sociological Method*, 2nd edn (Cambridge: Polity Press).

Golding, M. (1984) 'The Primacy of Welfare Rights', *Social Philosophy and Policy*, vol. 1, no. 2, pp. 119–36.

Goldsmith, A. (1990) 'Taking Police Culture Seriously: Police Discretion and the Limits of Law', *Policing and Society*, vol. 1, no. 2, pp. 91–114.

Gould, C. (1988) *Rethinking Democracy: Freedom and Social Cooperation in Politics, Economy and Society* (Cambridge: Cambridge University Press).

Griffin, C. (1985) *Typical Girls?: Young Women from School to the Job Market* (London: RKP).

Grimshaw, R. and Jefferson, T. (1987) *Interpreting Policework: Policy and Practice in Forms of Beat Policing* (London: Allen and Unwin).

Gyford, J. (1991) *Citizens, Consumers and Councils: Local Government and the Public* (Basingstoke: Macmillan).

Habermas, J. (1969) *Toward a Rational Society* (Boston: Beacon Press).

—— (1974) 'The Public Sphere: An Encyclopedia Article', *New German Critique*, vol. 3, (Fall), pp. 49–55.

—— (1975) *Legitimation Crisis* (London: Heinemann Educational Books).

—— (1979) *Communication and the Evolution of Society* (Boston: Beacon Press).

—— (1984) *The Theory of Communicative Action: vol. 1, Reason and the Rationalisation of Society* (London: Heinemann Educational Books).

—— (1987) *The Theory of Communicative Action: vol. 2, System and Lifeworld: A Critique of Functionalist Reason* (Cambridge: Polity Press).

—— (1989) *The Structural Transformation of the Public Sphere* (Cambridge, Mass.: MIT Press).

—— (1990) *Moral Consciousness and Communicative Action* (Cambridge: Polity Press).

—— (1993) *The New Conservatism* (Cambridge: Polity Press).

Hagan, J. (1993) 'The Social Embeddedness of Crime and Unemployment', *Criminology*, vol. 31, no. 4, pp. 465–91.

Hall, S., Critcher, C., Jefferson, T., Clarke, J. and Roberts, B. (1978) *Policing the Crisis: Mugging, the State and Law and Order* (London: Macmillan).

Hartless, J., Ditton, J., Nair, G. and Phillips, S. (1995) 'More Sinned Against than Sinning: A Study of Young Teenagers' Experiences of Crime', *British Journal of Criminology*, vol. 35, no. 1, pp. 114–33.

Hebdige, D. (1979) *Subculture: The Meaning of Style* (London: Methuen).

Held, D. (1980) *Introduction to Critical Theory: Horkheimer to Habermas* (Berkeley: University of California Press).

—— (1987) *Models of Democracy* (Cambridge: Polity Press).

—— (1992) 'Democracy, the Nation-State and the Global System' in D. Held (ed.) *Political Theory Today* (Cambridge: Polity Press).

Heller, A. (1982) *A Theory of History* (London: RKP).

Hewstone, M. and Hopkins, N. (1991) 'Police–Schools Liaison', *Policing*, vol. 7, no. 2, pp. 110–16.

Hirst, M. (1991) 'What Do We Mean by Quality?', *Policing*, vol. 7, no. 3, pp. 183–93.

Hirst, P. Q. (1994) *Associative Democracy: New Forms of Economic and Social Governance* (Cambridge: Polity Press).

Holdaway, S. (1983) *Inside the British Police* (Oxford: Blackwell).

Hollands, R. G. (1990) *The Long Transition: Class, Culture and Youth Training* (Basingstoke: Macmillan).

Home Office (1990) *The Victim's Charter* (London: HMSO).

—— (1991) *The Citizen's Charter* (London: HMSO).

Ianni, E. R. and Ianni, F. (1983) 'Street Cops and Management Cops: The Two Cultures of Policing', in M. Punch (ed.) *Control in the Police Organisation* (Cambridge, Mass.: MIT Press).

Jefferson, T. (1990) *The Case Against Paramilitary Policing* (Milton Keynes: Open University Press).

—— and Grimshaw, R. (1984) *Controlling the Constable: Police Accountability in England and Wales* (London: Muller).

—— McLaughlin, E. and Robertson, L. (1988) 'Monitoring the Monitors: Accountability, Democracy and Policewatching in Britain', *Contemporary Crises*, vol. 12, pp. 91–106.

—— Sim, J. and Walklate, S. (1992) 'Europe, the Left and Criminology in the 1990s', in D. Farrington and S. Walklate (eds) *Offenders and Victims: Theory and Practice* (London: British Society of Criminology).

Johnston, L. (1988) 'Controlling Police Work: Problems of Organisational Reform in Large Public Bureaucracies', *Work, Employment and Society*, vol. 2, no. 1, pp. 51–70.

Jones, C. (1993) 'Auditing Criminal Justice', *British Journal of Criminology*, vol. 33, no. 3, pp. 187–202.

Jones, T., Newburn, T. and Smith, D. (1994) *Democracy and Policing* (London: Policy Studies Institute).

Keane, J. (1984) *Public Life and Late Capitalism* (Cambridge: Cambridge University Press).

—— (1988) *Democracy and Civil Society* (London: Verso).

Keith, M. (1993) *Race, Riots and Policing: Lore and Disorder in a Multi-racist Society* (London: University College London Press).

Kinsey, R. (1992) *Policing the City* (Edinburgh: The Scottish Office).

—— and Anderson, S. (1992) *Crime and the Quality of Life: Public Perceptions and Experiences of Crime in Scotland* (Edinburgh: The Scottish Office).

—— Lea, J. and Young, J. (1986) *Losing the Fight Against Crime* (Oxford: Blackwell).

Lea, J. and Young, J. (1984) *What is to be Done About Law and Order?* (Harmondsworth: Penguin).

Lee, J. (1981) 'Some Structural Aspects of Police Deviance in Relations with Minority Groups', in C. Shearing (ed.) *Organisational Police Deviance* (Toronto: Butterworth).

Loveday, B. (1994) 'The Police and Magistrates' Courts Act', *Policing*, vol. 10, no. 4, pp. 221–33.

Lukes, S. (1982) 'Of Gods and Demons: Habermas and Practical Reason', in J. B. Thompson and D. Held (eds) *Habermas: Critical Debates* (Cambridge, Mass.: MIT Press).

Lustgarten, L. (1986) *The Governance of the Police* (London: Sweet and Maxwell).

Lyotard, J.-F. (1984) *The Postmodern Condition: A Report on Knowledge* (Minneapolis: University of Minnesota Press).

McCarthy, T. (1994) 'Rejoinder to David Hoy' in T. McCarthy and D. Couzens Hoy *Critical Theory* (Oxford: Blackwell).

McLaughlin, E. (1994) *Community, Policing and Accountability: The Politics of Policing in Manchester in the 1980s* (Aldershot: Avebury).

—— and J. Muncie (1994) 'Managing the Criminal Justice System' in J. Clarke, A. Cochrane and E. McLaughlin (eds) *Managing Social Policy* (London: Sage).

Manin, B. (1987) 'On Legitimacy and Political Deliberation', *Political Theory*, vol. 15, no. 3, pp. 338–68.

Manning, P. (1977) *Police Work* (Cambridge, Mass.: MIT Press).

Marenin, O. (1982) 'Parking Tickets and Class Repression: The Concept of Policing in Critical Theories of Criminal Justice', *Contemporary Crises*, vol. 6, pp. 241–66.

Mark, R. (1977) *Policing a Perplexed Society* (London: Allen and Unwin).

Marsh, P., Rosser, E. and Harre, R. (1978) *The Rules of Disorder* (London: RKP).

Marshall, G. (1978) 'Police Accountability Revisited', in D. Butler and A. H. Halsey (eds) *Policy and Politics* (London: Macmillan).

Marshall, T. F. (1992) (ed.) *Community Disorders and Policing: Conflict Management in Action* (London: Whiting and Birch).

Matza, D. (1964) *Delinquency and Drift* (New York: Wiley).

—— (1969) *Becoming Deviant* (New York: Prentice-Hall).

Meehan, A. J. (1993) 'Internal Police Records and the Control of Juveniles: Politics and Policing in a Suburban Town', *British Journal of Criminology*, vol. 33, no. 4, pp. 504–24.

Miller, D. (1993) 'Deliberative Democracy and Social Choice', in D. Held (ed.) *Prospects for Democracy: North, South, East, West* (Cambridge: Polity Press).

Morgan, J. and Zedner, L. (1992a) *Child Victims: Crime, Impact and Criminal Justice* (Oxford: Clarendon).

—— and —— (1992b) 'The Victim's Charter: A New Deal for Child Victims?', *The Howard Journal*, vol. 31, no. 4, pp. 294–307.

Morgan, R. (1989) 'Policing by Consent: Legitimating the Doctrine', in R. Morgan and D. Smith (eds) *Coming to Terms with Policing* (London: Routledge).

—— (1992) 'Talking About Policing', in D. Downes (ed.) *Unravelling Criminal Justice* (London: Macmillan).

Mouffe, C. (1992) 'Democratic Politics Today', in C. Mouffe (ed.) *Dimensions of Radical Democracy* (London: Verso).

Muir, K. W. (1977) *Police: Street Corner Politicians* (Chicago: Chicago University Press).

Oliver, I. (1987) *Police, Government and Accountability* (London: Macmillan).

Payne, D. (1991) *Police and Public in Scotland* (Edinburgh: The Scottish Office).

Pearson, G. (1983) *Hooligan: A History of Respectable Fears* (London: Macmillan).

—— (1994) 'Youth, Crime and Society' in M. Maguire, R. Morgan and R. Reiner (eds) *The Oxford Handbook of Criminology* (Oxford: Oxford University Press).

Phillips, A. (1991) *Engendering Democracy* (Cambridge: Polity Press).

Pile, S. (1990) 'Depth Hermeneutics and Critical Human Geography', *Environment and Planning D: Society and Space*, vol. 8, no. 2, pp. 211–32.

Pollak, A. (1993) (ed.) *A Citizen's Enquiry: The Opsahl Report on Northern Ireland* (Dublin: Lilliput Press/Initiative 92).

Pollitt, C. (1988) 'Bringing Consumers into Performance Measurement: Concepts, Consequences and Constraints', *Policy and Politics*, vol. 16, no. 2, pp. 77–87.

—— (1990) *Managerialism and the Public Services: The Anglo-American Experience* (Oxford: Blackwell).

Potter, J. (1988) 'Consumerism and the Public Sector: How Well Does the Coat Fit?', *Public Administration*, vol. 66, pp. 149–64.

Prison Reform Trust (1993) *Trends in Juvenile Crime and Punishment* (London: Prison Reform Trust).

Punch, M. (1979) *Policing the Inner City* (London: Macmillan).

Reiner, R. (1991) *Chief Constables* (Oxford: Oxford University Press).

—— (1992a) *The Politics of the Police*, 2nd edn (Brighton: Harvester).

—— (1992b) 'Fin de Siècle Blues: The Police Face the Millennium', *Political Quarterly*, vol. 63, no. 1, pp. 37–49.

—— and Spencer, S. (1993) 'Conclusions and Recommendations' in R. Reiner and S. Spencer (eds) *Accountable Policing: Effectiveness, Empowerment and Equity* (London: Institute for Public Policy Research).

Ricoeur, P. (1976) 'Hermeneutics: Restoration of Meaning or Reduction of Illusion?', in P. Connerton (ed.) *Critical Sociology* (Harmondsworth: Penguin).

—— (1981) *Hermeneutics and the Human Sciences* (Cambridge: Cambridge University Press).

Rustin, M. (1985) *For a Pluralist Socialism* (London: Verso).

Rutherford, A. (1992) *Growing Out of Crime*, 2nd edn (Harmondsworth: Penguin).

Sacks, H. (1972) 'Notes on Police Assessment of Moral Character', in D. Sudnow (ed.) *Studies in Social Interaction* (New York: Free Press).

Said, E. (1978) *Orientalism* (Harmondsworth: Penguin).

—— (1994) *Culture and Imperialism* (London: Vintage).

Scarman, L. (1982) *The Scarman Report: The Brixton Disorders* (Harmondsworth: Penguin).

Schutz, A. (1967) *The Phenomenology of the Social World* (Evanston, Ill.: Northwestern).

Selznick, P. (1992) *The Moral Commonwealth* (Berkeley: University of California Press).

Sennett, R. (1970) *The Uses of Disorder* (Harmondsworth: Penguin).

Shearing, C. (1981) 'Subterranean Processes in the Maintenance of Power', *Canadian Review of Sociology and Anthropology*, vol. 18, no. 3, pp. 283–98.

—— and Ericson, R. (1991) 'Culture as Figurative Action', *British Journal of Sociology*, vol. 42, no. 4, pp. 481–506.

Sheehy, P. (1993) *Report of the Inquiry into Police Responsibilities and Rewards* (London: HMSO).

Skolnick, J. (1975) *Justice Without Trial*, 2nd edn (New York: Wiley).

Smith, D. and Gray, J. (1983) *Police and People in London* (Aldershot: Gower).

Smith, S. (1986) *Crime, Space and Society* (Cambridge: Cambridge University Press).

Stanko, E. (1990) *Everyday Violence: How Men and Women Experience Sexual and Physical Danger* (London: Pandora).

Stephens, M. and Becker, S. (1994) (eds) *Police Force, Police Service: Care and Control in Britain* (London: Macmillan).

Stewart, J. (1992) 'The Rebuilding of Public Accountability', in J. Stewart, N. Lewis and D. Longley *Accountability to the Public* (London: European Policy Forum).

Stinchcombe, A. (1969) 'Institutions of Privacy in the Determination of Police Administrative Practice', *American Journal of Sociology*, vol. 63, pp. 150–60.

Suttles, G. (1967) *The Social Construction of Communities* (Chicago: Chicago University Press).

The Scottish Office (1994) *Statistical Bulletin: Social Work Series*, no. 18 (Edinburgh: The Scottish Office).

Thompson, J. B. (1990) *Ideology and Modern Culture* (Cambridge: Polity Press).

Unger, R. M. (1987) *Social Theory: Its Situation and Tasks* (Cambridge: Cambridge University Press).

Walklate, S. (1989) *Victimology: The Victim and the Criminal Justice Process* (London: Unwin Hyman).

Wallace, C. (1987) *For Richer, For Poorer: Growing Up In and Out of Work* (London: Tavistock).

Weatheritt, M. (1993) 'Measuring Police Performance: Accounting or Account-ability?' in R. Reiner and S. Spencer (eds) *Accountable Policing: Effectiveness, Empowerment and Equity* (London: Institute for Public Policy Research).

Willis, P. (1984a) 'Youth Unemployment 1. A New Social State' *New Society*, 29th March, pp. 475–77.

—— (1984b) 'Youth Unemployment 2. Ways of Living' *New Society*, 5 April, pp. 13–15.

—— (1990) *Common Culture: Symbolic Work at Play in the Everyday Cultures of the Young* (Milton Keynes: Open University Press).

Woodcock, J. (1991) 'Overturning Police Culture', *Policing*, vol. 7, no. 3, pp. 172–82.

Worpole, K. (1992) *Towns for People: Transforming Urban Life* (Buckingham: Open University Press).

Young, I. M. (1990) *Justice and the Politics of Difference* (Princeton: Princeton University Press).

Young, R. (1990) *The Critical Theory of Education: Habermas and Our Children's Future* (New York: Teacher's College Press).

Index

Controlling the Constable, 167
 see also Jefferson, T. and
  Grimshaw, R.
Corrigan, P., 28, 52
Crawford, A., 20, 26
crime, *see* juvenile crime, reporting
 crime
crime surveys, 173
'criminal families', 126
Criminal Justice and Public Order Act
 1994, 36
Criminal Justice (Scotland) Act 1981,
 16
critical theory, 31–6, 41, 44–6, 49,
 178n
cultural anthropology, 45, 47
cultural capital, 12, 27, 29
customer satisfaction surveys, 6, 8,
 21, 39–40

Davis, J., 24
deconstruction, 44
delinquency, *see* juvenile crime
democracy
 associative, 182n
 as collective learning, 168
 discursive/deliberative, 182n
 late modernity and, 30
 liberal, 8, 30, 36–7, 39–40, 48,
  167, 179n
 managerialism and, 2, 22, 38–9
 participation and, 168–71, 173–6
 policing and, 2–3, 35–41,
  158–76
 radical, 178n
 representation and, 171–3
 'thin', 21, 110–11, 179n
democratic accountability, 10–12, 14,
 162, 164, 167
democratic communication
 civil society and, 166
 consequences of absence, 2, 60,
  101, 142
 difference and, 166–7
 difficulties of, 75, 134
 fatalism and, 111
 limits of, 159–62
 policing and, 39–42
 prospects for, ix, 145–57

restrictions on, 32
 as unthinkable, 154–5, 157
democratic structure
 formal, 7, 10–12
 informal, 10, 12, 82, 166
 see also 'structures of control'
Den Boer, M. and Walker, N., 164
depth hermeneutics, 41, 44–9, 179n
 see also research
discourse ethics
 main themes of, 34–6
 democracy and, 35–7
 policing and, 35–41
discursive policing
 boundaries of, 166–71
 defined, 158
 institutions of, 162–6
 limits of, 159–62
 practice of, 171–6
Dixon, D., 9, 14
Doyal, L. and Gough, I., 163
drugs, 115–16
Dryzek, J., 158, 178n, 182n

'economy, efficiency and
  effectiveness', 2, 16, 18, 22
Edinburgh, x, 42–3
Edinburgh crime survey, 42, 108,
 181n
Edmund-Davies, Lord, 16
education, further/higher, 106
elections, 171–2
 see also police commission
Ericson, R., 85, 122, 178n
 and Shearing, C., 18
European Convention on Human
 Rights, 179n

Farrington, D., 114
fatalism
 of police officers, 91
 about the police, 155–7
 about politics, 109–11, 174
 see also young people
fear of crime, young people and,
 60–9
federalism, 164–5
 see also police commission
Fielding, N. and Fielding, J., 91, 178n